Portraits of Conflict

JAMES J. PETTIGREW
sixth-plate tintype
*Photo courtesy of University of
North Carolina, Chapel Hill*

Portraits of Conflict

A PHOTOGRAPHIC HISTORY

OF SOUTH CAROLINA

IN THE CIVIL WAR

Richard B. McCaslin

With a Foreword by the General Editors,

Carl Moneyhon and *Bobby Roberts*

Portraits of Conflict Series

The University of Arkansas Press

Fayetteville   1994

Library of Congress Cataloging-in-Publication Data

McCaslin, Richard B.
    A photographic history of South Carolina in the Civil War /
Richard B. McCaslin : with a foreword by Carl Moneyhon and
Bobby Roberts.
        p.   cm. — (portraits of conflict)
    Includes bibliographical references (p.) and index.
    ISBN 1-55728-363-X (cloth : alk. paper)
    1. South Carolina—History—Civil War, 1861–1865—Pictorial
works.   I. Title.   II. Series.
E577.9.M38   1994
973.7'457—dc20   94-5238
                                       CIP

To the dedicated businessmen
who photographed the Civil War
in South Carolina

Preface and Acknowledgments

Some members of cultures that are unacquainted with technology allegedly do not allow photographs to be made of them because they believe that portraits somehow entrap all or part of their souls. While those who live in more technological societies obviously do not believe that photographs snare their souls, they do realize that the camera has the almost magical power to record the character of a human subject. This is especially true of men and women who are taking part in a momentous event at the time that a photograph is taken of them, such as those who had their portrait made during the Civil War period. Literary descriptions cannot convey the sparkle shown in the tilt of a head or the lift of an eyebrow as easily as a photograph. At the same time, the vague misgivings of a recruit can be revealed by a camera despite his best effort to maintain a brave facade.

This collection of portraits, supplemented with a few outdoor scenes of South Carolina during the war, is intended to enhance previously published narratives of wartime experiences by taking a look at the period through the revealing lens of a camera. It does not offer a new interpretation of the war or a substantial new synthesis of existing analyses. Instead, it combines images with narrative in an attempt to provide a human perspective on events that are probably already familiar to many scholars. By bringing the reader face-to-face with participants in the war and focusing on events as they were experienced by each individual, this work seeks to promote an understanding of the war's impact beyond the almost incomprehensibly large aggregate statistics on casualties and property losses.

This volume is the first in this series to be written by a person other than the principal editors. I appreciate the trust that editors Carl Moneyhon and Bobby Roberts have in me, and I appreciate their support for my efforts while this project was underway. Without their assistance at every step of the way, this work would have become a nightmare without end; as it was, it became an enjoyable task as well as an educational experience. The general editors and the staff of the University of Arkansas Press have been remarkably patient. I look forward to continuing my working relationships and enjoying my newfound friendships.

This collection is by no means exhaustive, but it would not exist at all without the patient assistance of many archivists in South Carolina, for which I am grateful. The staff, especially Eleanor M. Richardson, of the South Caroliniana Room at the University of South Carolina in Columbia provided the greatest number of images for this volume and were more than gracious with their support. John M. Bigham of the nearby South Carolina Confederate Relic Room and Museum generously provided excellent copies of some portraits in his tremendous collection and practical answers to my bumbling questions as I began this project. Jane Yates of the Citadel Archives and Museum surprised me with dozens of portraits of alumni who served the Confederacy. The Special Collections of Cooper Library at Clemson University had to be visited twice due to a camera malfunction, but the staff was gracious each time. Finally, local museums are underutilized troves of historical material, and the Darlington County Historical Society proved to be no exception to this rule. Director Horace Rudisill and his assistant, Doris Gandy, dug through their treasures to provide a handful of real jewels.

Of the archives located outside of South Carolina that allowed me to reproduce their photographs, the United States Army Military History Institute at Carlisle Barracks in Pennsylvania had the largest number of useful images, this source is indicated by the abbreviation *U.S.A.M.H.I.* appears frequently throughout this volume; *MOLLUS, Mass.*, designates the photographs located in the Military Order of the Loyal Legion of the United States—Massachusetts Commandery Collection. Michael Winey and his staff have a fantastic archive of military images as well as an impressive reserve of valuable information. Both Mary Ison of the Library of Congress and Corinne Hudgins of the Eleanor S. Brockenbrough Library at the Museum of the Confederacy provided guidance and several handfuls of photographs; excellent copies of those found at the latter institution were made by Katherine Wetzel. Too, the staff of the National Archives helped fill some last-minute gaps in this volume. In North Carolina, near my academic home of High Point University, the staffs of the Perkins Library of Duke University and the Southern Historical Collection of the University of North Carolina at Chapel Hill provided photographs that gave me a good starting point for this work. In addition, a number of generous individuals permitted me to reproduce images from their private collections; I hope that the finished product pleases them as well as the professionals.

This work contains a substantial amount of biographical material to complement the images. Researching this information often resembled the proverbial search for the needle in the haystack, and certainly I must express my gratitude to those who helped in this endeavor. The archivists and individuals mentioned earlier provided valuable information about the people and places in the images they allowed me to reproduce, but this volume would have been impossible without the assistance of the staff of the South Carolina State Archives in Columbia. To them, and to all those who trustingly gave me information, I apologize for any errors in this text, and I assume full responsibility for any butchery that I may have unwittingly committed on the material they gave to me.

My colleagues at High Point University play a large part in my literary productions. The members of the Department of History, Political Science, and Geography patiently endure my absences on research trips and proctor the class assignments I leave behind to compensate for my absence. Student assistant Rita Hunt has patiently assisted in the compilation of the index for this work and has trudged across campus with armloads of interlibrary loans provided by librarians Lauren Ingold and David Bryden. I thank all of them for their assistance, though I suspect some of them would rather read that all of this will not happen again.

My wife, Jana, firmly believes that she is married to an eternal adolescent. The sight of me sitting cross-legged on the floor happily sorting photographs for the past year has only confirmed her belief. She remains supportive of my indulgences, however, and I appreciate that. My daughter, Christy, like most teenagers, is convinced that history is boring. I offer this volume as a counterargument, if only for the intriguing fact that her oddly misguided father could write it. I must admit that I could not do any of this without the two of them.

Key to Photographic Locations

U.S.A.M.H.I.: The United States Army Military History Institute, Carlisle Barracks, Pennsylvania. MOLLUS, Mass., refers to the Military Order of the Loyal Legion of the United States—Massachusetts Commandery Collection.

Contents

Foreword

Photography's impact on historical perception of the American Civil War has been enormous and Americans have long remained interested in the war's photographic legacy. Mathew Brady and other wartime photographers received popular acclaim during the war and toured the nation afterward with magic lantern shows of their best wartime material. Beginning in 1911, with the publication of the first volume of Francis T. Miller's *Photographic History of the Civil War,* numerous efforts have been made to use these photographs more systematically to create a history of the war that would be more accurate than one told in words.

The photographic technology that existed during the 1860s, which required a lengthy exposure time, always limited the story that the photograph itself could tell. No clearly genuine action scenes exist. There are few pictures of battle scenes, except for some taken afterward showing the human carnage and material destruction. Most Civil War pictures are of individuals, groups of soldiers posing for the camera, or inanimate objects. Of these, photographic histories have largely ignored the individual portraits, except for famous persons, and focused on such things as buildings, bridges, fortifications, ships, and weapons. Unfortu-

nately, this emphasis has minimized the place of the individual soldier in the war's story.

Portraits of Conflict, as originally conceived, tried to recapture the experience of the common soldier, which too often disappeared in the larger view, by using that largely ignored component of the massive photographic legacy of the war—the individual portrait. By merging the photographs of soldiers, their particular stories, and the broader narrative of the war, the *Portraits* series has attempted to show and explore, perhaps even to emphasize, the human aspects of this great national conflict. The editors have appreciated the reception their work has received. We have valued the support and encouragement offered by both the general public and scholars in this effort.

Portraits of Conflict: A Photographic History of South Carolina in the Civil War is the first volume in the series not produced by the editors themselves. The reader will find that it remains true to the original intent of the series. We hope that it meets the same approval.

CARL MONEYHON
BOBBY ROBERTS
General Editors

Portraits of Conflict

Chapter 1

Dedicated Businessmen: Photography in South Carolina during the Civil War

The Civil War provided a unique business opportunity for those who made the art of photography their vocation in South Carolina. The United States Census Bureau reported in 1860 that there were more than three thousand photographers, of all varieties, in the United States. Interestingly, very few South Carolinians told a census taker that photography was their primary occupation; in fact, only twenty-six were listed as ambrotypists, daguerrotypists, or photographers, though some of the three dozen who said they were artists may have been one of the former. Because the 1860 census listed 81,631 employed white persons in South Carolina, photographers appear to have been a very select group. These dedicated businessmen in 1861 were suddenly presented with an unprecedented chance to record a historical event of tremendous magnitude, and they responded in exemplary fashion, producing a body of work, all of which was offered for sale, that is remarkable in its scope and content.

Among this tiny group, three—George S. Cook, Charles J. Quinby, and Richard Wearn—stand out both for the quality and quantity of their work.

Cook has been compared favorably to Mathew B. Brady for the work he did during the Civil War. His studio portraits reflect his belief that "There is beauty in every face," while his outdoor pictures of South Carolina units and installations belie the assertion that "Confederate field photography almost ceased to exist after 1861."[1] Quinby, a fellow Charlestonian, rivaled Cook with his studio work, while Wearn's photographs of the ruin of Columbia in 1865 are perhaps more eloquent than his own portraits. Together with small-town photographers such as John R. Schorb and more famous Union army cameramen, this small cadre created a compelling photographic record of South Carolina in the Civil War.

Cook was born in Stratford, Connecticut, in 1819 and was raised by his maternal grandmother in Newark, New Jersey, after both of his parents died. At the tender age of fourteen, he left home and made his way after several years to New Orleans. He studied to be a portrait painter, but he became intrigued with the newly imported photographic process. He subsequently neglected the art of painting and began to study the daguerrotype, taking charge of one of the best-known and subsequently most successful portrait galleries in the city.

Cook left New Orleans in the summer of 1845 and toured the South for several years while taking photographs and teaching others the art of photography. He married Elizabeth Smith Francisco in Newark, New Jersey, in 1846 and then settled in Charleston three years later with two children and a well-established reputation as a mentor to many portrait makers throughout the South. He won prizes in state competitions during 1850 and 1851 with his daguerrotypes, attracting the attention of Mathew B. Brady, who chose him to manage his Broadway Gallery in New York while he was on a trip to Europe in 1851. Cook opened his own gallery in Manhattan, but he closed it in 1852 and returned to Charleston, which would be his home for the next twenty-eight years.

Prior to the outbreak of the Civil War, Cook became a pioneer in paper photography, scorning the use of the more economical tintype, which he believed to be inferior. He carefully maintained his business connections with the North, selling a number of images to Northern newspapers and publishing houses. At the same time, he formed several partnerships, opening a photography studio in Chicago and two in Philadelphia. His home remained Charleston, though, and he sold his interests in the other galleries when the war began.

Cook was quick to capitalize on the business opportunity that the outbreak of the Civil War presented. He made many portraits of prominent South Carolinians involved in the secession movement as well as of the Federal officers trapped in Fort Sumter. He went to Fort Sumter on February 8, 1861. There he took a photograph of Maj. Robert Anderson and his officers, despite the hostile suspicions of Capt. Abner Doubleday that Cook was in fact a spy. Surgeon Samuel W. Crawford also convinced a reluctant Anderson to sit for an individual portrait. Both images proved to be quite popular and were among those that Cook sold to the New York firm of E. and H. T. Anthony. An engraving from the group picture was published in *Harper's Weekly*, uncredited, on March 23, 1861, while Major Anderson's portrait quickly became a bestseller at twenty-five cents apiece. Many other images sold by Cook to Anthony appeared in *Frank Leslie's Illustrated Weekly* during the spring of 1861.

Cook remained active even after events following the fall of Fort Sumter reduced his national market by half. He was not the first photographer to enter Fort Sumter after its surrender—that honor went to F. K. Houston of Charleston—but he visited the post on April 15 and took a number of pictures. He also toured Castle Pinckney during August 1861 and photographed Federal prisoners captured at First Bull Run shortly after they arrived. At the same time, he stayed quite busy making studio portraits of the many young men who had joined the Confederate army as well as of their older but no less vain officers.

Sometimes Cook's zeal led him to expose himself to great danger. On September 8, 1863, during a bombardment by Federal fleet and shore batteries, Cook climbed on the parapet of battered Fort Sumter to photograph some of the Union vessels that were engaged. He captured a remarkable image of the monitors *Montauk, Passaic,* and *Weehawken* firing on Fort Moultrie before he was ordered to leave the walls because Union gunners were training on him; in fact, a shell carried away some of his equipment before he could take cover. This image—the negative for which has been lost—was printed for the first time in Francis T. Miller's landmark compilation, *The Photographic History of the Civil War,* in 1911.[2] He recorded the bursting of another round in the parade ground, along with revealing images of the damage done by Union artillery to the post.

Supplies became a problem for Cook by 1864. He initially got his photographic chemicals from blockade runners, some of which came from the

New York firm of E. and H. T. Anthony in crates deceptively marked "quinine," but the Federal campaign against Charleston in the summer and fall of 1863 virtually stopped all trade.[3] Cook remained a shrewd businessman, investing in blockade runners and in land with specie he earned from working as a photographer and from selling a large stock of scarce staples that had been brought through the blockade earlier.

Clever bargaining could not overcome a sharp decline in supplies, however, and a fire that destroyed much of his inventory in 1864 must have been the last straw. Cook left Charleston for Richmond and did not return until after the war ended. He resumed his work with portraits and stereographs to support his family, now expanded to four children, but sadly reduced by the death of his wife. He opened a New York City studio in 1874, but it folded quickly and he focused once more on his Charleston business. In 1880 he left his Charleston studio in charge of his son, George L. Cook, and moved to Richmond, where he prospered as a portrait maker until his death in 1902 at the age of eighty-three.

Cook's principal rival in Charleston for many years was Quinby and Company. Charles J. Quinby made daguerreotypes in New York City from 1855 to 1860, then moved that year to Charleston, where he became partners in a dry-goods store on King Street and reopened his gallery in the second story of the same building, which was in the same block as Cook's studio. Quinby began making *cartes de visite* and stereographs and, during the spring of 1861, sent a dozen images to New York, all of which appeared as engravings in *Frank Leslie's Illustrated Newspaper* that season. He made no photographs after 1863, but after the war ended he reopened with the help of several partners, the most noted of which was George N. Barnard. In 1870 they advertised "A large and fine collection of Chromos and Stereoscopic Views of Charleston and Fort Sumter for sale,"[4] but the next year Quinby sold his studio and went out of business for good.

Columbia photographer Richard Wearn came with his family from the Isle of Man, his birthplace, to the United States prior to the Civil War. He lived in Charlotte, North Carolina, and Newberry, South Carolina, before settling in Columbia, South Carolina, in 1859. A "very energetic man during the business of his entire life," Wearn produced both studio portraits and outdoor pictures during and after the war. A fire destroyed his business in 1869, but he reopened with a partner, William P. Hix. In 1870 the census taker found the two men prosperous and living next door to each other on Main Street; both had three children and were able to employ black servants. Many residents of Columbia were shocked when Wearn committed suicide at the age of forty-five on January 9, 1874; the Columbia *Phoenix* reported that he succumbed to "temporary insanity."[5]

There were a number of photographers working in the small towns of South Carolina at the time of the Civil War. One of the most industrious was John R. Schorb, a native of Neiderwald, Germany, who came to the United States in 1834 with his family, settling in New York City. He studied at Hamilton College in Clinton, New York, where he encountered a chemistry professor who taught him to make daguerreotypes. After graduating in 1842, he launched an itinerant career as a photographer that took him through much of the United States before he settled in Yorkville, South Carolina, in the 1850s. His primary occupation was as a professor; he taught in a number of schools and was president of the Yorkville Female Academy. He remained active as a photographer, however, making images that included people connected with the King's Mountain Military Academy. In 1870 he told the census taker that he was a "photographic artist," and he continued to make photographs until his death in 1908 at the age of ninety.

When Federal troops occupied Port Royal in November 1861, they provided an opportunity for Northern photographers to make their own record of the war in South Carolina. One of the first to arrive was Timothy H. O'Sullivan, who joined the staff of Brig. Gen. Egbert Viele to photograph Union operations at Beaufort and Port Royal from December 1861 to May 1862. O'Sullivan was born either in Ireland or New York City about 1840. By his mid-teens, he was working in Brady's New York gallery and was with Brady at the outset of the war. After O'Sullivan was discharged at Hilton Head, he went to Virginia, where he made a number of well-known photographs, but he returned to the Charleston area in 1863 to record the Union summer campaign. His camera was knocked over twice by Confederate artillery, but he accomplished his task. After the war, he became one of the most noted photographers of the American West before he died of tuberculosis in 1882.

Henry P. Moore of Concord, New Hampshire, came to Hilton Head with the 3rd New Hampshire Infantry in 1862 and returned home the next year after taking photographs of that unit and numerous other subjects. He operated a portable gallery in a small tent, recording scores of remarkable images that included soldiers and slaves, buildings, vessels, and even scenery. After he returned to Concord, he prepared these as five-and-one-half-by-eight-inch albumen prints. Many of these were published in contemporary photographic journals and, before Moore died in 1911 at the age of seventy-eight, they periodically reappeared in local history publications.

The full names of Union photographers Haas and Peale are not remembered; perhaps, as a later author wrote, they were content to "let the war speak for itself" through their vivid and semi-anonymous photographs.[6] Haas and Peale chronicled the futile efforts of Gen. Quincy A. Gillmore to take Charleston in the summer of 1863. The images they recorded on Morris and Hilton Head islands represent almost the entire catalog of their work during the Civil War. Their use of five-by-seven-inch prints for outdoor scenes, rather than

of stereographs or oversized "imperial" prints, was too much ahead of its time; prints such as they made became more popular after, not during, the Civil War.

After Haas and Peale came Samuel A. Cooley, who had operated a gallery in Springfield, Massachusetts, before the war. Cooley had a series of military contracts, but many of the photographs that he made, especially portraits of individuals, he did on his own, using the titles "Photographer Tenth Army Corps" and "U.S. Photographer, Department of the South" to add a bit of legitimacy to his private business deals.[7] In 1864 he had three permanent shops in South Carolina—at Folly Island, Hilton Head, and Beaufort—where he prepared and sold his stereographs of outdoor views.

When Gen. William T. Sherman marched into Georgia during the summer of 1864, George N. Barnard accompanied his troops as the official photographer for the Department of Engineers. Barnard was already well known for his work. Born in Connecticut in 1819 (like George S. Cook), he began his career in Oswego, New York, about 1843. He soon moved to Syracuse, where in 1853 he served as secretary of the New York State Daguerran Association. During 1857 he went to work for Brady at his Washington gallery, earning notice four years later for his photographs of Abraham Lincoln's inauguration and his *cartes de visite* of prominent persons in the national capital.

Barnard recorded a unique series of images of war-torn Georgia, including some haunting images of the captured city of Atlanta, but he did not accompany Sherman into the Carolinas. He did finally come to Charleston during March 1865 and quickly took pictures of the ruins of Fort Sumter and the burned district of the port city. He recorded other images in Columbia during a brief stay in late March or early April 1865 and then moved on to North Carolina. A folio of his wartime photographs published in 1866 included several of his South Carolina pictures.

Barnard returned to Charleston in 1868 to become partners with Charles J. Quinby in his photographic gallery on King Street. The pair made numerous *cartes de visite* and cabinet prints, as well as stereographs of Charleston and Fort Sumter. *Harper's Weekly* published some of their work, and they won a prize as the best photographers at the South Carolina Institute Fair in 1870. Diversifying their increasingly popular operation, they began to produce and sell chromolithographs. In the spring of 1871 they sold their business, including all of the negatives in stock, to Stephen T. Souder, who then operated under his own name.

Barnard moved to Chicago, where he lost much in the great fire of 1871. He continued to pay taxes on property in Charleston and in 1873 returned to the city, buying the old Quinby establishment from Souder. Barnard resumed the production of portraits and took hundreds of stereographs of both outdoor scenes and posed artistic shots, several of which were published. His entire stock was destroyed by a fire in 1875, but he reopened once more at his King Street address. He remained in business there until 1880, when he sold out for good and returned to Rochester and began experimenting with the dry-plate process.

By the time the Civil War ended, an impressive number of photographs had been recorded of South Carolinians involved in conflict and of outdoor scenes within the war-torn state. The fact that most of these images were made in response to the capitalistic needs of the photographers, and not from an artistic urge, does not reduce their value. The portraits were treasured by family members and friends, some of whom had little more by which to remember a deceased soldier. The outdoor scenes sold well to the curious and to veterans who served in the state during the war. Together, these images provide a compelling record for scholars interested in the human impact of the Civil War.

JAMES H. TRAPIER
carte de visite
George S. Cook

Charleston photographer George S. Cook photographed a number of prominent Confederates from South Carolina; his portraits can always be recognized by the distinctive vase of flowers in the background. Cook usually made three exposures per sitting and boasted that he rarely had to reshoot a subject. If a customer did not agree that the image was the best he ever had, he was entitled to another sitting, which rarely happened according to Cook. The subject of this picture is James H. Trapier, who graduated in 1838 from West Point with Pierre G. T. Beauregard.

During a ten-year career with the army, Trapier supervised river and harbor improvements, including the construction of Fort Sumter. After leaving the army, he returned to South Carolina, his native state, and became a planter. He also served South Carolina as chief of ordnance for the militia and as captain of the state engineers. He built batteries for the bombardment of Fort Sumter in 1861 and initially directed the construction of defenses at Port Royal. He then became a brigadier general in charge of the Department of Eastern and Middle Florida and was given command of a division in Mississippi during 1862. He returned to South Carolina in November, where he commanded the 4th District for the rest of the war, except for a stint as commander of Sullivan's Island. *Photo courtesy of the University of South Carolina, Columbia.*

PALMETTO BATTERY
albumen prints
George S. Cook

George S. Cook also made a number of photographs of entire units, including this intriguing series of three images of an artillery organization that he identified only as the "Palmetto Battery." Notes indicate that the picture was taken at Charleston in 1861, but scholars disagree about the identification of the company. Historian Rowena Reed asserts that it is Company I (Palmetto Battery) of the Charleston Light Artillery, but no such unit designation appears in official service records.[8] This may be Company A (Palmetto Guards) of the 18th Battalion, South Carolina Artillery, also known as Manigault's Battalion or the South Carolina Siege Train, or it could well be a company from the 3rd (Palmetto) Battalion, South Carolina Artillery, which mustered at Charleston in 1861.[9] Only one artillery company was commonly known as the Palmetto Battery, and that was the unit organized in the South Carolina town of that name. It was commanded by Capt. H. Garden and served for the duration of the war with the Army of Northern Virginia.[10] Note the black servant working with the gun crew. *Photos courtesy of Library of Congress, no. B8184-10358 [at rest], no. B8184–10674 [in battery], and no. B8184-4390 [camp scene]*

PALMETTO BATTERY
albumen prints
George S. Cook

FORT SUMTER, APRIL 1861
albumen print

All of these photographs of Fort Sumter have been attributed to George S. Cook, who visited the post on April 15, 1861, and took a number of pictures, but these may be only his prints of images taken by other photographers. The picture of a seven-star Confederate flag flying over the interior of the fort, in which can be seen the burned barracks and the derrick by which the Federal garrison lifted the guns to the barbette level, was probably made by F. K. Houston. His shop was located near Cook's on King Street in Charleston. James M. Osborn and F. E. Durbec of King Street allegedly made both the photograph of the battered exterior of Sumter, which is actually a composite of three images taken with a stereograph camera, and the picture of Wade Hampton III (tall figure in hat) and others inspecting a ten-inch Columbiad. This large gun was emplaced as a mortar and trained on Charleston; a tragedy almost occurred when a test-firing of this weapon by Federal officers nearly landed a shell in the city.[11] *Photos courtesy of National Archives [seven-star flag], University of South Carolina, Columbia [facade], and Library of Congress [Hampton and others]*

FORT SUMTER, APRIL 1861
albumen prints

In these photographs of the interior of Castle Pinckney taken in August 1861 by George S. Cook, the Zouave Cadets stand guard on the parapets while Union prisoners taken at the First Battle of Bull Run watch from the parade ground that they used as an exercise yard. The Cadets were recruited during the summer of 1860 from some of the most prominent families of Charleston and were assigned to the 1st Regiment of Rifles in the 4th Brigade of South Carolina militia. In January 1861 they assisted the Citadel Cadets in the building of emplacements on Morris Island for three 24-pounders, which fired on the *Star of the West* when it tried to reach Fort Sumter. The Zouave Cadets served on Sullivan's Island during the bombardment of Sumter in April 1861, then were posted at Castle Pinckney as prison guards. Many of the Zouaves later joined other units after the reorganization of the 4th Brigade.

Among the men in the yard are members of the 79th New York Infantry, known as the Highlanders. Ironically, after their exchange they fought on James Island during June 1862 against a Confederate force that included a Charleston unit known as the Highland Company, who wore tartan kilts with white horsehair sporrans and black bonnets trimmed with a red-and-white checked band. Both units wore trousers in combat. *Photos courtesy of Library of Congress, nos. B8184-5139 and B8184-4375A*

CASTLE PINCKNEY, AUGUST 1861
albumen prints
George S. Cook

13

CASTLE PINCKNEY, AUGUST 1861
albumen prints
George S. Cook

Castle Pinckney was almost useless for harbor defense, but as George S. Cook recorded with his camera during August 1861, it served admirably as a prison after doors and partitions were installed across the arched openings of the casemates and bunks were built inside to create snug, if not comfortable, quarters.

The prisoners standing outside Casemate Number Seven are members of the 69th New York Infantry who were captured at the First Battle of Bull Run. One of them had performed with Christy's Minstrels, hence the sardonic sign, "Musical Hall, 444 Broadway." These men, most of whom were of Irish ancestry, bickered with their guards and confidently predicted they would soon be exchanged.

Casemate Number One held men from the 11th New York Infantry captured at First Bull Run. They were referred to as the "Fire Zouaves" because most of them were recruited from the New York Fire Department, as their silver badges and the "N.Y.F.D." sign over the door attest. They were also known as the "Ellsworth Zouaves" in honor of their first colonel, E. Elmer Ellsworth, who was killed by a Virginia hotel owner who resented the removal of a Confederate flag from the roof of his establishment. Like the 69th New York, they were exchanged in October 1861.
Photos courtesy of Library of Congress, no. B8184-4374 [Casemate Number Seven] and no. B8184-4376 [Casemate Number One]

FORT SUMTER, SEPTEMBER 1863
albumen print
George S. Cook

George S. Cook visited the beleaguered post of Fort
Sumter on September 8, during the Federal bombardment that began in the summer of 1863. Having
already photographed three of the Union monitors
that were shelling Sumter and losing some equipment
to several near misses, Cook returned to the parade
ground to make an image of the battered walls. While
exposing a wet plate, a shell from the USS *Weehawken*
burst over the central parade ground of the installation, providing Cook with a rare picture of a round
actually exploding. Cook himself later admitted that
the "extraordinary conditions" under which this
photograph was taken made some retouching necessary. *Photo courtesy of Library of Congress, no. B8184-
10082*

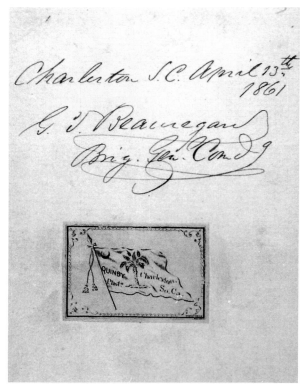

Pierre G. T. Beauregard
carte de visite
Quinby and Company

Charles J. Quinby, George S. Cook's primary rival in Charleston, also photographed many prominent Confederates. The subject of this portrait, Pierre G. T. Beauregard, triumphantly endorsed it on April 13, 1861, the day that his former teacher, Maj. Robert Anderson, surrendered Fort Sumter to him.

A native of Louisiana who had graduated second in his class from West Point, Beauregard was wounded twice in the Mexican War. He later supervised Federal engineering projects at New Orleans and, in January 1861, served five days as superintendent of West Point. He was dismissed from the latter position for telling a Louisiana cadet that he would join his state if it seceded. He then resigned and became a brigadier general in Confederate service.

Sent to Virginia after the fall of Sumter, he was promoted to general for his victory at First Bull Run. He quarreled with Pres. Jefferson Davis after the defeat at Shiloh, where he was second-in-command, and was relieved of his duties in the West and returned to Charleston in 1862. Early in 1864 he again went to Virginia, where he blocked a Federal advance toward Richmond at Drewry's Bluff in May and defended Petersburg against the Army of the Potomac in June. Returning once more to the Carolinas, he was Joseph E. Johnston's second-in-command at the war's end.
Photo courtesy of Clemson University

In a self-portrait, Columbia photographer Richard Wearn poses with his portable darkroom in front of the ruins of the State Armory on Arsenal Hill, which was destroyed during the fire that swept through Columbia after it was occupied by Gen. William T. Sherman's troops in February 1865. This wagon is allegedly a duplicate of Mathew B. Brady's darkroom buggy. Such vehicles were essential because taking a photograph during the Civil War was a cumbersome process. The most advanced technique of the day was the wet-plate method, in which a plain glass plate was coated with a chemical solution and exposed to the light projected by the camera lens. The glass plates had to be kept unbroken and as clean as possible, often during muddy or dusty travel over almost nonexistent roads, while the coating, exposing, and developing processes all had to be done in a little more than ten minutes, the latter two stages in almost complete darkness. A stray breath or puff of wind across the glass plate during coating or development could ruin the image, so the photographer had to be sheltered. *Photo courtesy of MOLLUS, Mass., U.S.A.M.H.I.*

Richard Wearn
albumen print
Richard Wearn

MARY BOYKIN CHESNUT
carte de visite
Richard Wearn

South Carolina's female Confederates did not escape the camera's lens. Mary Boykin Chesnut was an ambitious supporter of James Chesnut, her husband, throughout his life. She then won a measure of posthumous fame for her observations of the Confederacy, which she recorded during the war and laboriously edited and expanded afterward.

Born in 1823 at Statesville, she was the daughter of Stephen D. Miller, a slaveholder who served as a congressman, legislator, and governor of South Carolina. She attended a boarding school in Charleston, then at the age of seventeen married Chesnut, who was nine years her senior. The couple, who had no children, settled with his family near Camden, where she read avidly to cope with the enforced idleness of her life on the plantation.

She enjoyed politics and reveled in the antebellum social life of Washington, where her husband served in Congress, and she reveled in the social life of Richmond during the war, when her husband was an aide to Jefferson Davis. Interestingly, although she was considered attractive by many of those around her, she never cared to have her own image recorded. Richard Wearn may have copied this one from a photograph made by Quinby and Company in April 1861, about which she remarked that she appeared "uglier than ever." *Photo courtesy of University of South Carolina, Columbia*

Many small-town photographers in South Carolina made photographs of Confederates as they prepared for war. One such entrepreneur was John R. Schorb of Yorkville, South Carolina, who made this image of Asbury Coward. A diminutive (five and one-half feet in height) native of Charleston, Coward had graduated from the Citadel in 1854 with Micah Jenkins and opened the King's Mountain Military Academy with Jenkins in Yorkville.

Coward served on David R. Jones' staff at First Bull Run then became a captain in Jenkins' 5th South Carolina Infantry and took command of that regiment during August 1862. They fought at Antietam, where Coward was knocked from his horse by a shell fragment, and at Fredericksburg. They then served in southern Virginia and North Carolina until they were transferred as part of James Longstreet's corps to Tennessee. They arrived too late to fight at Chickamauga, but the regiment suffered greater casualties at Wauhatchie (a total of 102) than in any previous engagement.

After the debacle at Knoxville, Coward's troops returned to Virginia, where they suffered heavy casualties in the Wilderness. Coward was shot through the arm shortly after a visit with his dying friend, Jenkins. The regiment served at Petersburg, where Coward was stunned by a shell, and surrendered at Appomattox.
Photo courtesy of University of South Carolina, Columbia

ASBURY COWARD
carte de visite
John R. Schorb

19

Union troops invaded South Carolina for the first time in the fall of 1861 at Port Royal, bringing with them several military photographers of note. One of the first to arrive was Timothy H. O'Sullivan, an Irishman who later became one of America's best-known photographers of the western frontier. O'Sullivan, who worked for Mathew B. Brady at the outset of the war, arrived at Port Royal as a member of Brig. Gen. Egbert Veile's staff and stayed until May 1862, when O'Sullivan returned to Virginia.

In "Our Mess," O'Sullivan poses with some of his comrades at Beaufort in April 1862. The photographer himself is second from the right. He photographed the 50th Pennsylvania Infantry on parade the previous month at Beaufort, which they had been the first to occupy in December 1861. Assigned to Gen. Isaac I. Stevens' brigade, they skirmished along the coast for several months before leaving South Carolina in the summer of 1862. *Photos courtesy of MOLLUS, Mass., U.S.A.M.H.I. [Our Mess] and Library of Congress, no. B8171-156 [50th Pennsylvania Infantry]*

"Our Mess" and 50th Pennsylvania Infantry
albumen prints
Timothy H. O'Sullivan

OFFICERS, 3RD NEW HAMPSHIRE INFANTRY
albumen print
Henry P. Moore

Henry P. Moore's portable gallery at Hilton Head during 1862 is marked "DAGTYPS," although he did not work with the virtually obsolete daguerrotypes. Posing here (*left to right*) are thirteen officers of the 3rd New Hampshire Infantry: Bandmaster Gustavus W. Ingalls; Lt. Robert H. Allen; Chap. Henry Hill; Capt. Pierce L. Wiggin; Lt. Alfred J. Hill (*standing*); Capt. George W. Emmons; Capt. William H. Maxwell (*standing*); Capt. Ralph Carlton (*standing*); Lt. William H. Cornelius; Capt. Michael T. Donohoe; Lt. Walter Cody; Capt. Charles F. Dunbar; and Capt. Henry C. Handerson.

Many of these officers became casualties at Secessionville on June 16, 1862, when their regiment was repulsed in a charge. Allen was shot in the right hand, and his dog, Ned, a company favorite, was also wounded. Cody was shot in the right thigh, while Handerson was hit in the arm. All were more fortunate than Carlton, who was killed by a shell at the age of thirty-four, a month after returning from an extended leave for ill health. A soldier recalled seeing Carlton "conveyed past us on an old door, mangled and dying."[12] After a similarly bloody experience before Battery Wagner in July 1863, Chaplain Hill had the sad duty of returning home with the personal effects of those who had died. *Photo courtesy of MOLLUS, Mass., U.S.A.M.H.I.*

This photograph by Union military photographers Haas and Peale shows Lt. Paul Birchmeyer's battery of 12-pounder Wiards on Morris Island in the summer of 1863. A native of Syracuse, Birchmeyer had enlisted as a lieutenant during the fall of 1861 in the 3rd New York Light Artillery. Assigned to the siege of Battery Wagner, Birchmeyer's gunners participated in the reduction of that installation. They then moved to another position to take part in the bombardment of Fort Sumter. A pair of 200-pounder Parrotts were emplaced on mounds of sand only twenty feet behind Birchmeyer's new post; at their first discharge, the concussion knocked Birchmeyer to the ground. He had to be carried to the rear, and henceforth he complained of deafness and pain in his side.

In fact, his left eardrum had been ruptured, and his right was soon thereafter damaged by the firing of siege guns. He transferred to Battery H and commanded that unit in Virginia during 1864, incurring the reprimand of a court-martial for allowing his men to sleep without proper pickets in the lines before Petersburg. He left the service during January 1865, still complaining of deafness and pain in his head and ears as well as of congestion and other persistent symptoms from malaria contracted during his service in the Carolinas. *Photo courtesy of Library of Congress, no. B816-8028*

BATTERY F, 3RD NEW YORK LIGHT ARTILLERY
albumen print
Haas and Peale

Samuel A. Cooley
albumen print
Samuel A. Cooley

In this self-portrait (probably taken in 1864), Federal military photographer Samuel A. Cooley and his crew are mimicking the making of an exposure. To the right of the camera, with his hand on it, is Cooley. The man to the left of the camera has a wet-plate holder. The larger wagon behind him is outfitted for carrying photographic supplies and finished negatives. The buggy in front is outfitted for light travel and developing negatives in the field.

Cooley worked for Q.M. Gen. Montgomery Meigs in late 1864 and early 1865, primarily on the South Carolina and Georgia coasts. His work for the army in this period included an exhaustive record of buildings constructed or used by the Federal army at Hilton Head and Beaufort. At the same time, he maintained studios in both of those towns and on Folly Island, where he did a brisk business selling stereographs made from his military work and from the many photographs he made on his own. *Photo courtesy of MOLLUS, Mass., U.S.A.M.H.I.*

23

CHARLESTON, MARCH 1865
albumen print
George N. Barnard

Federal military photographer George N. Barnard arrived in Charleston during March 1865 and took some stark photographs of the ruined city. This image was published as an engraving in *Harper's Weekly* on July 8, 1865, and was included in a folio of Barnard's work printed in 1866.

In the center of the photograph, surrounded by scaffolding, can be seen the ruins of the Circular Church, a Congregational house of worship designed by noted architect Robert Mills. To the right, behind the ruined building with chimneys, is the South Carolina Institute Hall, its Renaissance-style appearance obliterated by fire. The latter, built in 1853 to promote agriculture and industry, had housed the Secession Convention in December 1860; the triumphant parade after the signing of the secession ordinance had begun at its entryway. These buildings were destroyed in the inferno that swept through this area of the city in December 1861. Other sectors were heavily damaged in the blaze that spread rapidly after the Confederate evacuation in February 1865. *Photo courtesy of Library of Congress, no. B8184-10,259*

These pictures were also included in the folio of George N. Barnard's work published in 1866. The exterior views of Fort Sumter, in the foreground of which can be seen Barnard's rowboat and crew on the sandbar, clearly shows the damage done to the post by Federal land and naval batteries. By the time that Sumter was evacuated by the Confederates in February 1865, more then 46,000 shells had been fired at it in 280 days of shelling from 1863 to 1865.

The photograph of the interior of the post reveals the extensive preparations made by the Confederates to repel an assault and to protect themselves from shells. The earth-filled baskets that are piled in such abundance are gabions, which, if maintained properly, reinforced the remaining masonry and prevented fragments of it from harming the garrison. Gen. Johnson Hagood, who visited Sumter in April 1864, discovered that the "bowels of the mass of debris" had been excavated into fairly secure galleries, barracks, hospital wards, magazines, arsenals, and a headquarters complex. He concluded that the improvements "had converted this wreck of an artillery fort . . . into an infantry post comparatively safe for its defenders."[13]
Photos courtesy of Library of Congress

FORT SUMTER, MARCH 1865
albumen print
George N. Barnard

FORT SUMTER, MARCH 1865
albumen prints
George N. Barnard

26

JOHN L. SHEPPARD
cabinet print
George N. Barnard

This print was made in Charleston by George N. Barnard during the 1870s, though with the repeated sale of the inventory of Charles J. Quinby's old establishment, it is impossible to say whether the former Union military photographer actually photographed John L. Sheppard, who was a Confederate veteran.

Sheppard had enrolled as a corporal in Company A of the 11th (Eutaw) Battalion, South Carolina Infantry, during February 1862, when he was twenty-one years of age. Promoted to sergeant in the fall of 1862, he was frequently hospitalized or confined to his quarters with an illness. In addition, he and five privates under his command were arrested for sleeping on picket duty and imprisoned in the Charleston municipal jail until Johnson Hagood ordered their release. Sheppard was subsequently promoted from third to second sergeant, but in June 1864 he was reduced to private and detailed to work in the quartermaster's department at Augusta, Georgia. He surrendered at the end of the war with Joseph E. Johnston's army in North Carolina. *Photo courtesy of University of South Carolina, Columbia*

27

Chapter 2

The Devil Is Unchained: Secession and Fort Sumter

South Carolinians had long considered secession, and in December 1860 their state left the Union. Within a few months they were joined by six more states, and after the fall of Fort Sumter, the last four states joined the new Confederacy. It was a triumphant season for the radicals who had advocated disunion for many years in South Carolina; only a few people publicly expressed doubts about the wisdom of sundering the Union and initiating what might be a disasterous Civil War. One of these was James J. Pettigrew, the cousin of staunch Unionist James L. Petigru. After the fall of Sumter, Pettigrew told supporters of secession that "the Devil is unchained at last, you have been talking fire a long time, now you must face it."[1] Ironically, he was actively involved in the siege of Sumter, became a Confederate brigadier general, and was mortally wounded in 1863 after leading a division in Pickett's Charge at Gettysburg.

Under the leadership of John C. Calhoun and the even more radical Robert Barnwell Rhett, many South Carolinians accepted that it might be necessary to leave the Union in order to protect their way of life, which was based upon slavery. South Carolina political leaders attempted to nullify federal laws in the early 1830s. They then took the lead in calling a convention of southern states in 1850 to consider secession, but their efforts were repudiated each time. For most of the 1850s, conservatives opposed to disunion, known as National Democrats and led by James L. Orr, gained support in South Carolina, but they were pushed aside in the hysteria that swept the South after John Brown's raid in October 1859, after which, support for secession in South Carolina became widespread.

The presidential campaign of 1860 provided an opportunity for the South Carolina secessionists to affirm their hold on the state. When the Democratic Convention met at Charleston in April 1860 and adopted a platform that did not demand federal protection for slavery, thirteen of South Carolina's sixteen delegates withdrew, along with representatives from three other southern states. Orr condemned the bolters, while Petigru and others praised Benjamin F. Perry, who had refused to leave his seat, for his opposition to splitting the Democrats. Most South Carolinians, however, supported the secessionists. Led by Rhett, the secessionists held a convention in June 1860 at Richmond, where they waited while the national party, reconvened at Baltimore, split into two factions and nominated Stephen A. Douglas and John C. Breckinridge for president. Having done that, delegates from seven slave states returned to Richmond, where the South Carolinians waited, and ratified the nomination of Breckinridge.

Through the summer and fall of 1860, the voters of South Carolina were told by their leaders that the election of a Republican to the presidency would be the prelude to sectional dominance by the North and should be the signal for leaving the Union. Gov. William H. Gist loudly urged secession, preferably in concert with other Southern states, if Abraham Lincoln won. All of the congressmen from South Carolina were no less outspoken. Even the previously moderate Orr, who had led the South Carolinians that bolted at Charleston, wrote to a friend that "no Black Republican President shall ever execute any law within our borders unless at the point of the bayonet and over the dead bodies of [our] slain sons."[2]

The news of Lincoln's election was greeted with celebration and plans for immediate secession in South Carolina. The moderates who had hesitated to commit themselves, such as Sen. James Chesnut, now endorsed leaving the Union. Secessionists pressed the legislature to authorize a convention to consider disunion. Rhett and Congressmen Lawrence M. Keitt and Milledge L. Bonham, joined by Edmund Ruffin of Virginia, addressed large crowds in Columbia, while pro-secession legislators introduced resolutions for a convention. Conservative members of the legislature fought in vain against more radical colleagues. Reports that Georgia had pledged her support swept aside the last reservations of many in the legislature, and on November 10, 1860, both houses voted for a convention to consider secession.

Most of the delegates elected to the convention were committed to secession. They convened at Columbia on December 17, 1860, and elected as chairman David F. Jamison, who declared the "greatest honor of his life" would be to sign an ordinance of secession.[3] In a single day at Columbia, the delegates unanimously endorsed secession, then decided to move to Charleston because smallpox was sweeping through the capital. They were greeted in the port city by cheering throngs and salvos of artillery. On December 20 they adopted an ordinance of secession—written by Orr and edited by Rhett—then assembled again that evening in the South Carolina Institute to affix their signatures before a cheering audience of three thousand. Crowds gathering outside the convention eagerly approved every announcement and gleefully joined in the triumphant procession that began in front of the Institute after the ordinance was signed. Only a few diehards did not share the sense of elation; Petigru, for example, told a secessionist that "South Carolina is too small for a republic, and too large for a lunatic asylum."[4]

A flurry of activity ensued after South Carolina left the Union. Commissioners were assigned to urge other slave states to secede, and Rhett led seven delegates—among whom were Chesnut, Keitt, and Congressman William P. Miles—to the convention at Montgomery, Alabama, where they helped organize the Confederacy. Gov. Francis W. Pickens, who had established his headquarters in the Charleston Hotel, created an unofficial cabinet that included Jamison. Pickens was also an ex officio member of the Executive Council, which included Chesnut managing military affairs and chairing the Council, former governor Gist directing finance, construction, and manufactures, and Attorney General Isaac W. Hayne supervising judicial matters and the police. Created to coordinate the war effort in South Carolina, the Council proved effective but controversial, and it was abolished on December 18, 1862, shortly after the secession convention adjourned for good.

The political leaders of South Carolina were not

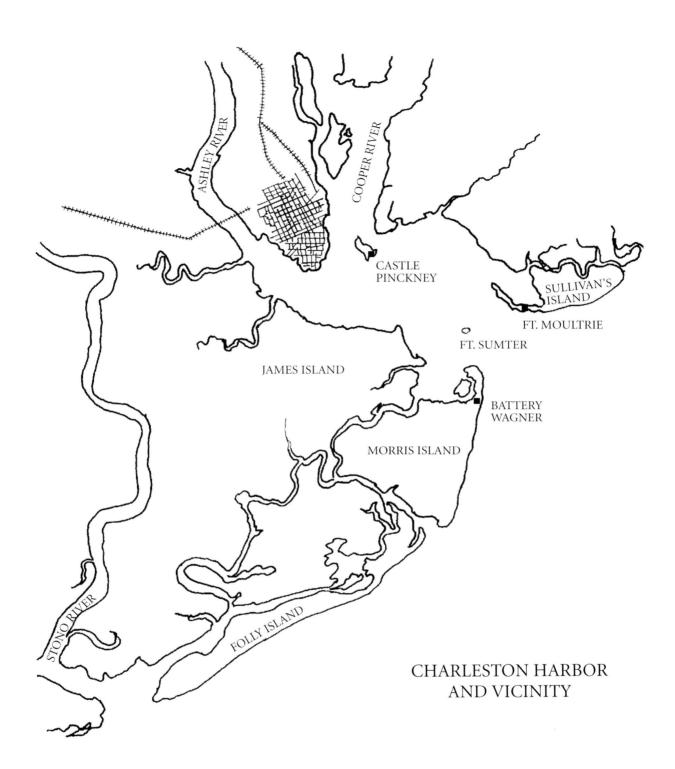

ASHLEY RIVER

COOPER RIVER

CASTLE
PINCKNEY

SULLIVAN'S
ISLAND

FT. MOULTRIE

FT. SUMTER

JAMES ISLAND

BATTERY
WAGNER

MORRIS ISLAND

STONO RIVER

FOLLY ISLAND

CHARLESTON HARBOR
AND VICINITY

the only ones preparing for the worst within the state. Shortly after South Carolina left the Union, Petigru visited the Federal garrison of Fort Moultrie on Sullivan's Island at Charleston "to express the deep sorrow and sympathy he felt for [them] in [their] trying position."[5] The aging Unionist need not have worried about the Federals. Their commander, Maj. Robert Anderson, a Kentuckian who had owned slaves and whose father had defended Moultrie against the British in the Revolution, had returned to the post. He had served there in the 1840s, after his predecessor angered Charlestonians by trying to move arms from the arsenal in the city to Moultrie. However, because the fort was undefendable, and because Anderson did not intend to sacrifice his men to political proprieties, he moved them during the night of December 26 from Moultrie to Fort Sumter, a new masonry work on an artificial island in the harbor.

The Federal move to Fort Sumter was accomplished without a major confrontation. Capt. Charles H. Simonton of the Washington Light Infantry, a Charleston militia company, had posted his men aboard two vessels to watch Anderson, but they failed to detect anything. Capt. John G. Foster, an engineering officer who had been sent to Fort Moultrie in September 1860 to repair the harbor defenses, commanded the crew left behind to spike the guns, burn their carriages, and cut down the flagpole. Meanwhile, Capt. Abner Doubleday, whose father was a congressman, led a company of the 1st United States Artillery to Sumter and expelled a force of Charleston laborers. Some of the latter brandished pistols, but all were driven at the point of bayonets to the parade ground and then placed outside on the wharf.

Anderson's move to Fort Sumter, while militarily astute, violated an agreement that South Carolina leaders thought they had with Pres. James Buchanan. Five of South Carolina's congressmen had visited the president on December 9 and had secured a pledge that he would not change the existing arrangement of the garrison at Charleston. Upon hearing that Anderson, who was not informed of this meeting, had moved to Sumter, Governor Pickens sent an aide, Col. James J. Pettigrew of the 1st South Carolina Rifles, to discuss the situation. Pettigrew's lieutenant colonel, Ellison Capers, accompanied him, but neither man could persuade Anderson to return to Moultrie.

After reporting to Pickens, Pettigrew was ordered to occupy both Fort Moultrie and Castle Pinckney, "an old-fashioned, half-moon fortification of brick" located on a small island across the Cooper River from Charleston.[6] Members of the 1st Battalion, South Carolina Artillery, found Fort Moultrie deserted and quickly began repairing the damaged guns, but Pettigrew encountered resistance at Pinckney. He led two companies from his regiment, one of which was the Washington Light Infantry, to the post, but Lt. Richard K. Meade refused to let him enter. A recent West Point graduate, Meade had been sent by Foster with a party of workmen to Pinckney after arriving at Moultrie on December 10, 1860. He had tried to teach them to work the artillery but they had refused, leaving only him and an ordnance sergeant with his wife and daughter as a garrison. Nevertheless, the doughty lieutenant argued heatedly with Pettigrew before surrendering his post.

Martial activity at Charleston undermined efforts to negotiate a peaceful transfer of power in South Carolina. After the state seceded, Orr, Robert W. Barnwell, and James H. Adams were ordered to speak with President Buchanan about transferring all Federal property in South Carolina to the state government. The news of Anderson's move arrived the day that they were to meet with the president, however, and their meeting was postponed for a day while Buchanan consulted with his cabinet. When they did meet, the president refused to order Anderson to withdraw from Fort Sumter, especially since South Carolina troops had occupied Fort Moultrie and Castle Pinckney as well as the arsenal, post office, and customs house in Charleston. After penning a condemnation of Buchanan, the commission suspended negotiations and prepared to leave Washington while Buchanan issued orders for supplies to be sent to Anderson in Sumter.

Meanwhile, the state troops in Charleston busily prepared for a fight. The 4th Brigade of Charleston, which included the 1st Regiment of Rifles, was the largest militia organization in South Carolina. On December 17, 1860, the legislature had augmented this force by authorizing the muster of ten regiments for twelve months' service. Four of the colonels of these regiments became Confederate generals—Johnson Hagood, Joseph B. Kershaw, Micah Jenkins, and Arthur M. Manigault—while James H. Rion also enjoyed a distinguished career as an officer. Adj. Gen. States Rights Gist reported in March that 8,836 men had enlisted and were organized as a division commanded by former congressman Milledge L. Bonham, now a major general in the provisional army of South Carolina. By that time, a regiment of six-month volunteers, led by Maxcy Gregg, had been raised by the secession convention, and the legislature had authorized an artillery battalion and yet another regiment of infantry under Roswell S. Ripley and Richard H. Anderson, respectively, to serve in Robert G. M. Dunovant's brigade within Bonham's division.

Faced with a growing host of enemies, Anderson pushed his men to prepare Fort Sumter for combat. A masonry work with walls sixty feet in height, it was designed to hold 146 guns in three tiers, the two lower ones being casemated and the upper one being open, or in barbette. Inside were barracks, officers' quarters, mess rooms, magazines, and hot-shot furnaces. Unfortunately for the Federals, there were only 15 guns mounted when they arrived; 66 guns were stored on the parade ground, where they were unusable. Anderson's troops worked feverishly and within a month 48 cannon were in position: 27 in barbette and 21 in the lower tier. In addition, 2 ten-inch rifles and 4 eight-inch rifles were emplaced as mortars in the parade ground. For all this ordnance, mounted within a work designed to hold a garrison of 650, Anderson had only 68 men, 9 officers, and 8 musicians, as well as 43 civilian workmen.

The first hostile shots in the siege of Fort Sumter were fired by the South Carolinians. At daybreak on January 9, 1861, the *Star of the West*, a small steamer hired by Buchanan's administration to carry supplies and reinforcements to Fort Sumter, was spotted trying to make its way into Charleston harbor. On Morris Island, a shot from a battery constructed and manned by cadets from the Citadel with assistance from the Zouave Cadets of Charleston, was fired across the bow of the *Star of the West*, but her captain raised the U. S. flag and refused to stop. Sixteen more shots, some from Ripley's batteries at Fort Moultrie, were fired at the vessel—a few of which hit their mark—before her flag was struck and she turned about and left. South Carolina authorities subsequently sank four hulks in the main channel to hinder other attempts to run past their batteries.

The *Star of the West* incident led to a reopening of negotiations. Anderson refused to fire at the South Carolinians; instead, after consulting with his officers, he sent an inquiry to Pickens, who offered no apologies. Unsure what to do, Anderson sent Capt. Theodore Talbot to Washington on January 9, 1861, to report and to receive instructions. Talbot returned ten days later with the approval of Federal authorities for Anderson's actions, but with no promise of further efforts at relief. Meanwhile, after yet another demand for surrender and threat to take Fort Sumter by force had been delivered to Anderson by South Carolina Secretary of War Jamison and Secretary of State Andrew Magrath, the latter suggested that negotiations for a transfer be resumed. Capt. Norman J. Hall, for the Federals, and Atty. Gen. Isaac W. Hayne, for the South Carolinians, were dispatched to Washington on January 11 to present views on the matter. Hall returned on February 10 after the president had flatly refused to consider Hayne's demand for the transfer or sale of Sumter—the last such demand forwarded by the government of South Carolina.

Matters began moving toward a climax after the appointment of a professional to take command of the volunteers gathering around Fort Sumter. The Confederate government sent an inspector to Charleston; the disarray he found there prompted them to appoint a career military officer, at Pickens' request, to take charge. Pierre G. T. Beauregard, who resigned his commission as a major in the U. S. Army in February 1861 and became a Confederate brigadier general several weeks later, reported to Pickens at the Charleston Hotel on March 3, 1861. The Creole officer had wanted an assignment near New Orleans, where he had resided for many years and where he had, as a curious bystander, inspected the damage to the *Star of the West* after her ordeal, but he dutifully went where he was assigned.

Beauregard was welcomed as a hero, especially by the women of Charleston, but he had been a student in Anderson's class on artillery at West Point, and he respected the major's skills enough to realize that the siege was far from won. Beauregard judiciously rearranged the batteries around Fort Sumter without treading too heavily on the toes of militia officers who had made the initial dispositions. Within a month he had four dozen guns emplaced in batteries supported by 3,700 troops and aimed at Sumter. Among the innovative arrangements employed were the use of an ironclad floating battery, anchored on the west end of Sullivan's Island where it could enfilade the postern entrance of Sumter, and an ironclad land battery on Morris Island, just 1,300 yards from the fort.

Anderson received some encouraging news while Beauregard labored. Capt. Henry J. Hartstene, a former navy officer who served as Beauregard's chief of naval operations, escorted his old friend,

Gustavus V. Fox, to visit Anderson in Fort Sumter on March 21, 1861, to discuss plans for relief. Fox had served in the navy for nineteen years before retiring to become a manufacturer in Massachusetts, and he had successfully proposed a plan for the relief of Sumter to Lincoln. Hartstene had been told by Pickens to keep a close watch on Fox, but the latter slipped away to talk privately with Anderson about the use of a small fleet to bring reinforcements. The major was encouraged, but he never received definite word that the scheme would be implemented. Capt. Theodore Talbot left again on April 4 to carry dispatches to Washington. He returned to Charleston four days later with a message for Pickens: Lincoln intended to allow Fox to reinforce Sumter. Pickens did not let Talbot rejoin his comrades in Sumter; instead, the officer was escorted to the railroad depot and put on a train headed north.

With Talbot's message in hand, Beauregard and Pickens asked Davis for instructions on April 9. The following day, Secretary of War Leroy Pope Walker told Beauregard to secure an evacuation of Fort Sumter or begin his bombardment. The general on April 11 sent three of his staff—James Chesnut, Roger Chisolm, and Stephen D. Lee—to Sumter with a surrender demand. They arrived at about three in the afternoon. Lt. Jefferson C. Davis, as officer of the day, escorted them to meet with Anderson, who after talking with his officers declined to surrender but explained that his men would soon be starved out. The three returned with Roger A. Pryor at eleven that evening to ask when Anderson expected to evacuate the post. The major replied that if he did not get assistance, he would have to leave in four days. Knowing that Lincoln would try to resupply Sumter, Beauregard sent a second surrender demand by Chesnut, Chisolm, Lee, and Pryor at about 1:30 on the morning of April 12. After waiting two hours, they were told there would be no capitulation. Chesnut then scribbled a notice that the South Carolina batteries would begin firing in an hour. Anderson was visibly shaken when Chesnut gave the note to him, but he escorted the pair to the wharf and politely bade them farewell.

Chisolm, Chesnut, Lee, and Pryor returned to Fort Johnson, an abandoned army post on James Island that had been refurbished by the South Carolinians. The honor of firing the symbolic first shot was offered to Pryor, a Virginia politician who had heatedly urged a bombardment of Fort Sumter, but he declined. Instead, an order was issued to Capt. George S. James, who touched off a mortar in Fort Johnson at 4:30 in the morning on April 12. The shell exploded directly over Sumter, signaling the many other batteries around the harbor to commence firing. Meanwhile, Chesnut and Lee rowed a small boat halfway back to Sumter to watch the drama that they had played such a large part in staging.

Fort Sumter's garrison did not reply for almost two hours, but at seven in the morning the Federals fired their first shot. Aimed by Captain Doubleday, it was directed at the ironclad battery on Morris Island. Like many others, the round bounced harmlessly off its target, which was constructed of heavy timbers covered with railroad iron angled back and covered with grease to deflect shells. As Doubleday wrote: "our balls bounded off the sloping iron rails like peas upon a trencher, utterly failing to make any impression."[7] Similarly, little damage was done by the gunners in Sumter to most of the Confederate positions. Anderson, seeing that Beauregard's batteries enfiladed his barbette guns, ordered his men to use only the 21 cannon emplaced in the lower tier of Sumter. A Federal private disobeyed orders and, knowing that the barbette guns had been loaded, singlehandedly fired them all and scrambled back to safety; but for the most part, Sumter returned a very small volume of fire against its besiegers.

Although the South Carolinians trained 18 mortars and 30 cannon on Fort Sumter from six different emplacements and fired a total of 3,341 shells, they did only slightly more damage than their opponents. Slightly less than 20 percent of the rounds hurled at Sumter hit the mark, and despite assertions to the contrary, most of these accomplished little because they were not heavy enough to penetrate the thick masonry walls. The only ones that came close were those from a Blakely rifled gun purchased in England by a Charleston planter and emplaced at Cumming's Point on Morris Island. Its shells bored deep into Sumter's walls, and a chance shot flew through the main gate. What forced Anderson to begin considering a surrender was the shooting by gunners commanded by Roswell C. Ripley on Sullivan's Island. A West Point graduate who served in the artillery, he directed the fire of several units, including a crew under Lt. Alfred M. Rhett, son of the secessionist radical, that served an eight-inch Columbiad at Fort Moultrie. Rhett's troops fired forty red-hot shot on the morning of April 13, setting Sumter's barracks ablaze. By lunchtime Sumter was almost untenable due to acrid smoke and the threat of a magazine explosion.

During the afternoon of April 13, the second day of Beauregard's bombardment, a Federal gunner in Fort Sumter was startled to see a face appear in an embrasure through which he was about to fire. After a short, heated discussion, the gunner pulled former U. S. senator Louis T. Wigfall, now a colonel on Beauregard's staff, through the opening. Wigfall had been out of touch with Beauregard for several days but on his own had decided to secure Anderson's surrender after Sumter's flag was cut down by a shell. Disregarding the replacement of the flag and Ripley's attempts to sink his boat with artillery fire (Ripley was allegedly incensed at Wigfall's interference), he had made his way to the besieged post. Lt. George W. Snyder escorted Wigfall to Anderson, who was asked to avoid useless bloodshed by capitulating.

Anderson was low on food and munitions, so he agreed to negotiate. A bedsheet was raised over Fort

Sumter when Wigfall departed. Soon other members of Beauregard's staff—Chesnut, Lee, Pryor, and former South Carolina congressman William P. Miles—arrived to ask why a white flag had been raised. Pryor haughtily helped himself to the contents of what appeared to be a liquor bottle and had to have his stomach pumped by the post surgeon, Samuel W. Crawford, but the other three spoke with Anderson. They were disappointed to learn that Anderson had not surrendered and was only willing to discuss terms. A formal agreement was reached after they conveyed Anderson's proposals to Beauregard, who sent David R. Jones, his chief of staff and the adjutant general of the South Carolina Provisional Army, to finalize matters.

Late in the afternoon of April 13, after a continuous bombardment of more than thirty-six hours, Anderson formally surrendered Fort Sumter. A boatload of Confederates, including Jones, Miles, Pryor, and Hartstene, spoke with him once more to arrange his evacuation. While final preparations were being made for a formal transfer of power, which Anderson requested, Beauregard ordered fire engines from Sullivan's Island and from the city of Charleston to be carried to Fort Sumter in order to put out the conflagration that threatened to ignite the powder magazines. This was accomplished only after more than twelve hours of hard work. At the same time, Hartstene directed the security for the evacuation, which was witnessed by thousands of Charlestonians ashore and in boats. Despite every precaution, the Federals suffered their first fatalities when a round exploded prematurely during their firing of a hundred-gun salute to their flag on April 14. One gunner was killed and a second was mortally wounded. Saddened, Anderson suspended the salute and embarked his men for the trip north.

In gratitude for Beauregard's efforts, the legislature of South Carolina adopted him as an honorary native son and extended to him the privilege of sending two boys to study at the Citadel. He sent his younger son, Henry T. Beauregard, and a nephew, James T. Proctor. The former studied for two years and the latter for one, and both subsequently joined South Carolina units. Within three weeks almost all evidence of the damage sustained by Fort Sumter during the bombardment had been eradicated: the walls were repaired, barracks were rebuilt, and gun carriages were restored. It was a giddy time for those who supported secession, but as Pettigrew had earlier asserted, the "Devil" had been "unchained" and terrible consequences would follow. In May 1861, Beauregard was ordered to report to Richmond, where he assumed command of the Confederate troops in Virginia, among whom were many South Carolinians who soon would receive their first baptism of fire.

GREENEVILLE

SPARTANBURG

CAMDEN

FLORENCE

COLUMBIA

AIKEN

HAMBURG

BRANCHVILLE

CHARLESTON

BEAUFORT

ST. HELENA SOUND

PORT ROYAL SOUND

SOUTH CAROLINA

ROBERT BARNWELL RHETT
carte de visite
E. and H. T. Anthony

Renowned by Southerners and reviled by Northerners as the "father of secession," Robert Barnwell Rhett briefly enjoyed the apex of his career when South Carolina seceded.[8] Born at Beaufort in 1800, his last name was originally Smith; he changed it to that of a more distinguished ancestor in 1837. He was an attorney who owned two plantations, on which lived 190 slaves. In 1860, he served in the legislature and as attorney general of his home state. He had served in the United States House of Representatives from 1837 to 1849 and in the Senate from 1851 to 1852. He used these offices to champion states' rights, and he briefly quit politics in 1852 after the secession movement appeared to collapse.

Through the 1850s he never ceased to agitate for disunion in the pages of the Charleston *Mercury.* He was vindicated in 1860 when he led the South Carolina delegation that met in Richmond to endorse the nomination of John C. Breckinridge for president, and he served on the committee that wrote the secession ordinance for his state. His demands that Fort Sumter be stormed ended after Gov. Francis Pickens offered to allow him to lead the charge, and he was further chagrined when his advice was largely ignored during the Montgomery convention that created the Confederacy. Becoming a bitter critic of Jefferson Davis, he lost his bid for a congressional seat in 1863. *Photo courtesy of Duke University*

After the election of Abraham Lincoln as president, secessionists were able to secure the passage of a resolution for a secession convention through the legislature. Their efforts were heartily supported by Gov. William H. Gist, who poses here with the officers of his escort. Gist is in the center of the front row; in the second row on the far right is 2nd Lt. Pressley Brown. The others, in no order, are Capt. William H. Casson, 1st Lt. Malcolm A. Shelton, and 3rd Lt. G. L. Dial.

Born at Charleston in 1807, Gist was elected governor in 1858, serving through the eve of secession. An active proponent of secession, he had become a respected political leader after overcoming difficulties in his early life—his unmarried mother had surren- dered custody of him to his father, he was expelled from South Carolina College during his senior year and did not graduate, and he was tried and acquitted for killing a man in a duel over a woman. He served eight terms as a legislator, during which he became a Methodist and a temperance advocate as well as a wealthy planter. As governor, Gist sent envoys, including his brother States Rights Gist, to ask other chief executives in the South to join with him in sundering the Union. He was a delegate to the seces- sion convention, which began in December 1860, and on the Executive Council of South Carolina, which directed military affairs. *Photo courtesy of University of South Carolina, Columbia*

WILLIAM H. GIST AND OFFICERS
OF THE GOVERNOR'S GUARDS
ambrotype

A former legislator, congressman, and minister to Russia, Pickens served as governor of South Carolina for two years and was succeeded by Milledge L. Bonham. Pickens' father had served as governor of the state from 1816 to 1818, and the son entered politics after completing his education at Franklin College, now the University of Georgia, and South Carolina College. He won respect as a state senator and as a U. S. senator for his unflinching support of states' rights and slavery.

After his return from Russia in 1860, Francis Pickens was selected to be governor of South Carolina on the seventh ballot by the legislature during December 1860. The solons put aside traditional concerns for a balance between upper and lower districts to select a chief executive who would support secession and not alienate other Southern states. Pickens had been known as a moderate, but on the eve of the election he gave a speech embracing more radical views, and so he became governor. His selection proved unfortunate for those who desired unity in the state because he often alienated associates with his manner. Writing in November 1861, Henry W. Ravenel declared that Pickens "has made himself so unpopular . . . that he would not probably get a vote if the election were held now." Ravenel added, "I meet with no one who has a word to say in his favor."[9] *Photo courtesy of University of South Carolina, Columbia*

Francis W. Pickens
carte de visite
Quinby and Company

40

Pres. David F. Jamison of the Secession Convention poses with David R. Jones, who became a Confederate major general, and ex-governor John H. Means. All three died in Confederate service.

Jamison attended South Carolina College and practiced law, but for most of his life he was a planter and prolific scholar. He served twelve years in the legislature, where he introduced the bill to found the Citadel. He relished being president of the convention and secretary of war for South Carolina, and he chaired a military court until yellow fever felled him in 1864.

Jones was born in South Carolina, but his parents moved with him to Georgia, where he was appointed to West Point. He enjoyed a successful army career that included combat in Mexico and a stint as an instructor at his alma mater. As chief-of-staff for Gen. Pierre G. T. Beauregard, he delivered the terms that were accepted by the garrison of Fort Sumter in April 1861. He led a brigade at First Bull Run, and then a division during the Seven Days and at Second Bull Run and Antietam. He left active service due to heart disease but was promoted to major general before he died on January 19, 1863.

Means, a graduate of South Carolina College who served as governor of South Carolina from 1850 to 1851, was an advocate of secession who held the rank of brigadier general in the militia. After serving as a delegate to the secession convention and on Beauregard's staff, he raised the 17th South Carolina Infantry. They were sent to Virginia shortly before Second Bull Run, where Colonel Means was killed by a shell fragment. *Photo courtesy of University of South Carolina, Columbia*

DAVID F. JAMISON, DAVID R. JONES, AND JOHN H. MEANS
albumen print
Quinby and Company

In December 1860, when the delegates met to debate secession, a smallpox epidemic was ravaging the populace of Columbia. They quickly adjourned to Charleston, leaving Robert W. Gibbes in charge of medical matters at the capital city. Gibbes, the former mayor of the capital and proprietor of the *South Carolinian,* had not practiced medicine for years, though he was a graduate of the Medical College of South Carolina and had taught at his other alma mater, South Carolina College. However, he was the surgeon general for his state and so he once more ministered to the sick in Columbia, his home town.

Though he was too old for military service—he celebrated his fifty-second birthday in 1861—he did serve as surgeon for the volunteers of his state as they mustered, and he tended the many wounded during the bombardment of Fort Sumter. In the summer of 1861 he accepted an appointment as an inspector of hospitals for the Confederate army. Although he soon resigned that post due to ill health, he did continue to serve as surgeon general of South Carolina until the end of the war.
Photo courtesy of University of South Carolina, Columbia

Robert W. Gibbes
carte de visite
Quinby and Company

The radical secessionists were well represented in the secession convention. Congressman Lawrence M. Keitt's brother was killed by his own slave in February 1860; seven months later Keitt wrote to a friend that if Abraham Lincoln won, "I'd cut loose through fire and blood if nescessary [*sic*]."[10] He resigned from Congress after Lincoln was elected, served on the committee that wrote the ordinance of secession, and attended the convention at Montgomery that organized the Confederacy.

A graduate of South Carolina College, he practiced law and served in the legislature and in Congress, in which he distinguished himself as an outspoken advocate of secession. In fact, when his fellow representative Preston S. Brooks assailed Sen. Charles Sumner in 1856, Keitt kept bystanders from interfering and was censured by the House. Keitt resigned his seat but was promptly reelected, serving until his resignation four years later.

After signing the Confederate Constitution, he raised the 20th South Carolina Infantry and commanded it at Charleston, where he won praise for his defense of Battery Wagner in the summer of 1863. He was the last Confederate commander of that post, directing its evacuation in September 1863. Promoted to brigadier general and ordered to Virginia in May 1864, he was mortally wounded at Cold Harbor. *Photo courtesy of University of South Carolina, Columbia*

LAWRENCE M. KEITT
carte de visite
Quinby and Company

43

WILLIAM P. MILES
carte de visite

Some of the radical delegates at the South Carolina secession convention later became prominent politicians in the Confederacy. Born on July 4, 1822, William P. Miles represented the Charleston district in the Confederate Congress during its entire existence. The chair of the committee on military affairs in the House, he was one of many who had also served in the United States Congress before the Civil War. During his first years in the Confederate Congress, he was often noted for his support of the Jefferson Davis administration, though he heatedly denied charges that he was a mouthpiece for the president. By 1864 he had decided that Davis was too obstinate to be a good chief executive.

Miles' path to political prominence was quite atypical. An 1842 graduate of Charleston College, he had taught mathematics at his alma mater until 1855, when his service during a yellow fever epidemic prompted the conservatives of the port city to nominate him for mayor in an effort to defeat the Know-Nothing candidate. Miles won and proved to be a popular reformer as mayor; among his innovations was a mounted police force to watch for slave unrest.

In 1857 he was elected to Congress, where he served until his resignation in 1860. After the secession convention and before taking his seat in the Confederate Congress, he was active in the negotiations for the surrender of Fort Sumter. *Photo courtesy of University of South Carolina, Columbia*

After adopting a secession ordinance, the delegates reconvened on the evening of December 20, 1860, to affix their signatures to a formal copy of the document. They chose to meet, because of its large seating capacity, in the South Carolina Institute Hall, a Renaissance-style building constructed in 1853 to house exhibits for the promotion of agriculture and industry. That night more than three thousand people jammed into the Institute, which was designed to hold about five hundred fewer, and cheered as the delegates signed their names. Leaving the heavily decorated main room, shown here, the crowd formed into a triumphant procession at the front entrance and made their way through the streets of Charleston. Sadly, the Institute was destroyed in the great fire that swept through the port in December 1861. *Photo courtesy of Library of Congress, no. B8184-4391*

Secession Hall, December 1860
albumen print
George S. Cook

45

Many Unionists became supporters of the Confederacy once it had been established; one of the most prominent was Richard Yeadon. An attorney and former newspaper publisher from Charleston who continued to write anti-secession editorials that appeared in the Charleston *Courier* up to the eve of the war, Yeadon was a well-known erstwhile Whig whose involvement in politics began shortly after his graduation from South Carolina College in 1820. He loudly condemned the secession convention and the South Carolina Executive Council, writing a number of columns opposing it and taking great pride in voting as a legislator for its abolition in December 1862.

However, though he opposed both nullification and secession and everyone who supported these issues, after his native state left the Union, he supported the Confederacy and provided funds for equipping troops and ships. Elected to the legislature in 1862 for a third term (he also served from 1856 to 1860), he steadfastly defended the policies of Pres. Jefferson Davis against those who criticized him, especially the followers of Rhett. Yeadon also became notorious for his offer of a ten-thousand-dollar reward for the capture of Benjamin F. Butler after Davis declared the Federal general to be an outlaw for his outrageous behavior in New Orleans. *Photo courtesy of Clemson University*

RICHARD YEADON
carte de visite
Quinby and Company

James L. Petigru
carte de visite
Quinby and Company

Once secession had been accomplished, only a handful of diehards in South Carolina continued to oppose disunion. Probably the best-known was James L. Petigru. He had passed the proverbial age of three-score-and-ten years by the time that South Carolina seceded, but the passage of time had not lessened his love for the Union nor his outspoken support of it. A native of Abbeville County, he had graduated from South Carolina College in 1809, and then practiced law in Charleston. He served as attorney general of South Carolina for eight years, beginning in 1822, and for a term in the legislature during the debate over nullification (which he loudly opposed). Otherwise, he was not successful in politics, nor did he achieve greater success in his efforts to establish himself as a planter.

His reputation as an effective defender of personal liberty and his popularity as a genial Unionist eccentric protected him from any serious harm during the secession crisis, but his residence on Sullivan's Island was leveled to make room for a battery to bombard Fort Sumter, and his Charleston home was destroyed by the fire that swept through the city in December 1861. He served a single term in the legislature and then died in 1863 at the age of seventy-four. *Photo courtesy of University of South Carolina, Columbia*

Because the secession convention was not dissolved until the fall of 1862, replacements occasionally had to be elected. Among them was John S. Preston, who reluctantly became the superintendent of the Confederate Bureau of Conscription in July 1863.

A native of Virginia, he attended Hampden-Sydney College, the University of Virginia, and the law school at Harvard College before marrying an aunt of Wade Hampton III. Preston served for eight years as a supporter of states' rights in the South Carolina legislature. He relocated to Europe in 1856, but returned in 1860 and again became immersed in South Carolina politics. He served as an envoy to his native state to urge secession, was an aide to Gen. Pierre G. T. Beauregard during the bombardment of Fort Sumter and at First Bull Run, and then became a delegate to the secession convention in July 1861 after James H. Adams died. In November 1861 Preston was assigned to organize recruits at Columbia; three months later he was given charge of the prison camp there, inheriting command of the conscript camp as well in April 1862. His performance in the latter capacity, repugnant as it was to him, led to his appointment as superintendent of the Bureau. He was efficient and clashed often with local officials, not the least of which were his old associates in South Carolina.
Photo courtesy of University of South Carolina, Columbia

MOSES S. HAYNSWORTH
quarter plate ambrotype

Most South Carolinians did not wait to be drafted. In fact, when their state seceded, many were already serving in the militia or quickly joined their local units. Born in 1845 at Darlington, Moses S. Haynsworth was a very young private in the Darlington Guards when they marched to Charleston to take part in the siege of Fort Sumter. His comrades, most of whom were older than he, were enlisted as Company A of the 8th South Carolina Infantry after Sumter fell, but Haynsworth stayed behind and in January 1862 was admitted to the Citadel. He became a corporal in Hugh S. Thompson's Company A of the Cadet Battalion, with which he served for the remainder of the war. *Photo courtesy of Citadel Archives, Charleston, South Carolina*

JOHN L. BRANCH
copy print

Few of the South Carolinians who served in the militia were fortunate enough to have educated officers such as John L. Branch, who was in the first class to graduate from the Citadel in 1846. He worked as an engineer and surveyor for Charleston and, when the war began, became the lieutenant colonel of the 1st Regiment of Rifles, South Carolina Militia, commanded by James J. Pettigrew. Branch commanded his companies on Sullivan's Island when Pettigrew was assigned greater duties in the spring of 1861.

After Pettigrew left for Virginia, Branch replaced him as colonel of the regiment—whose companies included the Washington Light Infantry and the Charleston Zouave Cadets. Branch aided in the building of harbor defenses and was in charge when his troops were forced to withdraw from Rockville by Federal warships during December 1861. He left the army when the 1st Regiment of Rifles was disbanded a few months later. The next December, he wrote to Jefferson Davis that he had considered joining the regular army as a private, but his health had failed and so he had hired a substitute instead. For months he had engaged in the production of soap and candles, as well as of oil for textile mills, but he wished to return to the army and take "a place in the great 'picture' (not yet complete) of Southern Independence."[11] His request was not granted. *Photo courtesy of Citadel Archives, Charleston, South Carolina*

GUSTAVUS W. KLINCK
quarter plate ambrotype

BENJAMIN T. GIBBES
carte de visite
George S. Cook

Almost completely undisciplined and often commanded by officers who knew little more than they about military drill, the militia and other recruits who gathered in 1861 were desperately in need of proper training. Gustavus W. Klinck, whose father was an import grocer in Charleston, was an eighteen-year-old cadet at the Citadel in the fall of 1861 when he was detailed to serve as an instructor, with the rank of second lieutenant, at Camp Butler near Charleston. Remaining with Hugh S. Thompson's Company A of the Cadet Battalion, Klinck became a cadet sergeant by the time the Citadel was evacuated in February 1865, when Federal forces occupied his hometown. A veteran of several campaigns in defense of Charleston, Klinck and his comrades marched to the North Carolina border before they were turned back and furloughed to go home. *Photo courtesy of Citadel Archives, Charleston, South Carolina*

According to official reports compiled long after the Civil War ended, 64,903 South Carolinians enlisted in the Confederate army, while another 6,180 joined reserve or home guard units. Of this total, approximately 23 percent (15,458) were killed, wounded, or captured. Many South Carolina families suffered wrenching losses in the conflict that began literally in their own backyards.

Disease claimed a large proportion of those who served in the army. When South Carolina left the Union, Surgeon General Robert W. Gibbes proudly announced that he had seven sons ready to fight for the Confederacy. Among them was his youngest son, Benjamin T. Gibbes. Born in 1846, he became a lieutenant in Company D, 16th South Carolina Infantry (Greeneville Regiment) in early 1864. He was posted in Georgia, but he did not receive a single paycheck before dying of typhoid fever at home in Columbia on March 14 of that same year at the age of "seventeen years and nine months." Allegedly the young soldier's last words were "I am not afraid to die."[12] *Photo courtesy of Clemson University*

52

FRANK H. HARLESTON, ALFRED S. GAILLARD,
AND WILLIAM E. STONEY
albumen print

The Citadel contributed most of its surviving graduates to the Confederate army. All three of these young men graduated from the Citadel in 1860 and were enlisted by the next year.

Frank H. Harleston, a Charleston native, worked as a civil engineer, then became a lieutenant in Company D of the 1st South Carolina Artillery and served in the ironclad battery during the bombardment of Fort Sumter. Promoted to captain during January 1862, he commanded his company in the ambush that compelled the USS *Isaac P. Smith* to surrender in the Stono River in January 1863. Three months later, he commanded one of the batteries in Sumter during its duel with the Federal fleet. On the night of November 24, 1863, he was mortally wounded while inspecting the obstructions placed around Sumter to block a Union assault.

Alfred S. Gaillard, a native of Fairfield, left the faculty of Hillsboro Military Academy in North Carolina to enlist as a lieutenant in Company G, 1st South Carolina Artillery, in October 1861 and then became captain of Company K in the same regiment in the summer of 1863. He commanded several posts at Charleston and was wounded during the reduction of Sumter by Union artillery in August 1863. He commanded Fort Johnson on James Island during a Federal attack in July 1864 but was wounded again and captured at Bentonville, North Carolina, in 1865.

William E. Stoney from Charleston became a lieutenant in the 1st South Carolina Rifles during December 1860, then, after the fall of Sumter, served in a series of staff positions, earning the rank of captain within two years. While serving as an aide to Gen. William B. Taliaferro, Stoney was shot in the thigh at Battery Wagner during the Union attack on July 18, 1863. He became inspector general for Johnson Hagood's brigade and was shot at Walthall Junction in May 1864. He lost a lung but recovered and fought at Town Creek and Bentonville before he was paroled with the remnant of Hagood's brigade in North Carolina in 1865. *Photo courtesy of Citadel Archives, Charleston, South Carolina*

WILLIAM P. BASKIN
copy print

The Cadets who attended the Citadel in Charleston and its allied school, the Arsenal Academy in Columbia, during the Civil War were not exempt from military service. The legislature created the Cadet Battalion in January 1861, enlisting the Citadel Cadets as Company A and those from the Arsenal as Company B.

Some of the cadets crewed three guns that fired on the *Star of the West* in January, then in November, were stationed at Wappoo Cut near Charleston. In June 1862 the Cadets manned siege guns on James Island during the Federal operations there, and a year later, when Gen. Quincy A. Gillmore began his campaign against Charleston, they were mustered again to patrol the streets after all adult males had been posted on the front lines. During June 1864 they returned to James Island, where they endured Federal artillery fire.

The climax of the Cadets' service in the Civil War occurred in December 1864, when they charged Union positions along the Tulifinny River and then assisted in repelling a Federal advance. Returning to James Island, they remained there until Charleston was evacuated on February 17, 1865. Cadet Sgt. William P. Baskin, a twenty-two-year-old senior, was with Hugh S. Thompson's Company A as it marched to the western part of the state and was allowed to go home rather than surrender. *Photo courtesy of Citadel Archives, Charleston, South Carolina*

The tremendous mobilization of the available military manpower in South Carolina entailed an expansion of the bureacracy that was responsible for organization and supply. Dozens of well-educated young men found themselves serving behind a desk for the duration of the war rather than standing in the ranks with a weapon. One such person was Gustavus A. Follin, a seventeen-year-old clerk presumably employed in his father's grocery store, was living with his parents in Charleston when the Civil War began. During 1862 he secured a position as a clerk in the adjutant general's office of South Carolina. He became an assistant adjutant general for the state, with the rank of lieutenant, in February 1863. *Photo courtesy of Clemson University*

GUSTAVUS A. FOLLIN
carte de visite
Richard Wearn

UNKNOWN AND WILLIAM S. SIMKINS
copy print of ambrotype

The first shots at Charleston were fired by South Carolinians. William S. Simkins, a nineteen-year-old cadet in his senior year at the Citadel, was on sentry duty on the beach at Morris Island when he spotted the *Star of the West* trying to make its way to Fort Sumter on January 9, 1861. After sounding the alarm, he joined the crew of the first gun to fire on the approaching ship. Seventeen shells in all were fired at the intruder from various batteries around the harbor; though only three shots hit the mark, the ship's captain quickly reversed his course and abandoned his feeble effort to supply the garrison at Sumter.

Born in Edgefield, Simkins was orphaned at a young age when his parents died of malaria or a similar

ailment at the family plantation near Monticello, Florida. Subsequently, he was raised by his maternal grandparents in Beaufort, South Carolina. He entered the Citadel in 1857; three months before his graduation he joined other cadets on Morris Island.

Simkins enlisted as a lieutenant in Company D of the 1st Battalion, South Carolina Artillery during the summer of 1861. Two years later he served as acting inspector general for Johnson Hagood and then spent most of the summer of 1864 sick on leave or in his quarters. He was paroled at Greensboro, North Carolina, in April 1865. *Photo courtesy of Citadel Archives, Charleston, South Carolina*

After the *Star of the West* incident, South Carolina officials tried to force Maj. Robert Anderson to transfer Fort Sumter to them. When he refused, South Carolina attorney general Isaac W. Hayne met with Pres. James Buchanan to discuss a cession or sale of the contested property. Buchanan refused to agree to terms, and Hayne returned home empty-handed.

This was not the first time Hayne had been involved in South Carolina's conflict with the federal government over sovereignty. During the nullification crisis he supported his uncle, Gov. Robert Hayne, in his advocacy of states' rights, and he served as secretary of the Nullification Convention. He became attorney general of South Carolina in 1848 and supported the secessionists in their agitation two years later. By 1860, when he served as a delegate to the secession convention, he was recognized as "one of the most influential men in the state."[13]

Hayne served as attorney general throughout the Civil War. Two of his sons—he had eleven children—joined the Confederate army, and one was killed at Cold Harbor in June 1864. *Photo courtesy of University of South Carolina, Columbia*

ISAAC W. HAYNE
carte de visite

While the South Carolinians blustered and negotiations broke down in Washington, Maj. Robert Anderson had his men hard at work in Fort Sumter preparing for the worst. When they occupied the post on the night of December 26, 1860, they found only fifteen of its eighty-one guns mounted. In a month they had thirty-three more guns in place, twenty-one in the lowest tier and twenty-seven in the uppermost level, or in barbette.

This view of the northwest casemate clearly shows the simple block and tackle used by the Federal garrison to lift the heavy cannon from the parade ground, where they were found, onto the uppermost tier. Ironically, the construction of an enfilading battery by the Confederates made it too dangerous for the guns on the upper level to be fired, and Anderson ordered his men not to use them. A daring private, knowing the guns were loaded, crept upstairs during the bombardment in April 1861 and touched them off. Also visible are a hot-shot oven, the barracks that caught fire and forced Anderson to capitulate, and piles of flagstones removed from the parade ground and stacked to protect gunners in the lowest tier from shell splinters. *Photo courtesy of University of South Carolina, Columbia*

Fort Sumter, April 1861
albumen print
James M. Osborn and F. E. Durbec

ROBERT ANDERSON AND STAFF
albumen print
George S. Cook

George S. Cook persuaded a reluctant Maj. Robert Anderson to pose with his officers at Fort Sumter on February 8, 1861. In the back *(left to right)* are Capt. Truman Seymour, Lt. George W. Snyder, Lt. Jefferson C. Davis, Lt. Richard K. Meade, and Capt. Theodore Talbot. Sitting in the front *(left to right)* are Capt. Abner Doubleday, Maj. Robert Anderson, Surgeon Samuel W. Crawford, and Capt. John G. Foster.

All but Snyder, Meade, and Talbot became generals for the Union. Snyder fought at First Bull Run, and then died at Washington in November 1861. Meade, a Virginian whose father was minister to Brazil, left Fort Sumter before it fell because his mother was ill; he joined the Confederate army and died during July 1862

at Petersburg. Talbot, a Kentuckian who had served in the west, was a major when he died of lung disease at Washington in April 1862.

Several of these officers later returned to South Carolina. Seymour returned as the commander of a division and was wounded in the attack on Battery Wagner in July 1863. Sent to Virginia in early 1864, he was captured in the Wilderness and, ironically, confined in Charleston. Foster took charge of the Department of the South in May 1864, remaining until February 1865. Finally, Davis led the XIV Corps during General William T. Sherman's march through the Carolinas. *Photo courtesy of Library of Congress*

When Gen. Pierre G. T. Beauregard arrived at Charleston to assume command of the troops besieging Fort Sumter, he found a number of militia officers already in charge of various units. Among them was Robert G. M. Dunovant, adjutant and inspector general of South Carolina and a brigadier general in Milledge L. Bonham's division of the state provisional army. Beauregard assigned Dunovant to command all infantry on Sullivan's Island.

A native of Chester County and a graduate of South Carolina Medical College, Dunovant had military experience and political ties. He had moved to Texas to practice medicine but returned during the war with Mexico to raise a company; he won a gold medal and became lieutenant colonel of the Palmetto Regiment. Staying in Edgefield, he married a sister of Preston S. Brooks, served in the legislature, and attended the secession convention. In July 1861 he became colonel of the 12th South Carolina Infantry, which served on Hilton Head during the debacle at Port Royal in November 1861 and was shelled by Federal gunboats a few months later at another post. Angry at the promotion of others whom he considered inferior, Dunovant resigned his commission in April 1862, though he repeatedly asked to be made a brigadier general of reserves. In 1864 he again served in the legislature. *Photo courtesy of University of South Carolina, Columbia*

ROBERT G. M. DUNOVANT
carte de visite
Quinby and Company

60

Capt. John R. Hamilton of Charleston, formerly in the U. S. Navy, designed this floating battery whose appearance was criticized by many who saw it. The South Carolina Executive Council gave him twelve thousand dollars and three weeks to build it; it was not yet complete when Gen. Pierre G. T. Beauregard arrived, but he approved the contraption and procured the two layers of railroad iron necessary to complete it. Originally, it was planned to anchor the floating battery within a hundred yards of the main gate of Fort Sumter, but the militia refused to man it, certain that it would be sunk. Instead, the unseaworthy vessel was towed late at night on April 10, 1861, by two tugs to an anchorage off the west end of Sullivan's Island. Positioned behind a stone breakwater to deflect ricochet shots, it fired upon the postern entrance of Fort Sumter, which faced Charleston.

The strange craft was about a hundred feet long and twenty-five feet wide and was constructed of pine timbers and palmetto logs. Its cannon, two 42-pounders and two 32-pounders, were counterweighted by sandbags on the other side, and it had its own hospital in an attached shed. However ungainly, the battery proved invulnerable to Sumter's fire—a Union gunner recalled that "shots were seen to bounce off its sides like peas"—while its guns "left telling marks" on the walls of the fort.[14] *Photo courtesy of University of South Carolina, Columbia*

FLOATING BATTERY, APRIL 1861
albumen print

JAMES CHESNUT
carte de visite
Richard Wearn

The official notification that Gen. Pierre G. T. Beauregard would commence a bombardment of Fort Sumter was written and given to Maj. Robert Anderson early in the morning of April 12, 1861, by James Chesnut, who had joined Beauregard's staff less than three days earlier. After returning to Morris Island to issue orders for the signal gun to be fired, Chesnut and Stephen D. Lee rowed halfway back to Sumter to watch the action.

Born in 1815 as the youngest of thirteen children, Chesnut graduated from Princeton and studied law under James L. Petigru. He served seven terms in the legislature and was a delegate to the Nashville Convention in 1850 before being elected to the U. S.

Senate in 1858. He resigned two years later to become a delegate to the secession convention, where he was on the committee that drafted the ordinance of secession.

As a member of the Provisional Confederate Congress, he helped draft a permanent constitution and then chaired the executive council of South Carolina. When the latter body was abolished in December 1862, he became an aide-de-camp with the rank of colonel for Jefferson Davis. In April 1864 Chesnut was made a brigadier general and assumed command of the reserves in his home state for the campaign against William T. Sherman. Mary Boykin Chesnut was his wife. *Photo courtesy of University of North Carolina , Chapel Hill*

Capt. Abner Doubleday of the 1st United States Artillery in Fort Sumter recalled that during the bombardment in April 1861, Maj. Roswell S. Ripley, "being a man of talent, and a skillful artillerist, . . . did us a great deal of harm."[15] A native of Ohio, Ripley graduated from West Point in 1843. He taught there and then fought Mexicans and Seminoles before leaving the army in 1853 and settling in Charleston, his wife's hometown, where he worked as a representative for a firearms company. A major of ordnance for the militia in 1860, he assumed command of all the artillery on Sullivan's Island for the siege of Sumter.

Appointed a brigadier general in August 1861, he commanded the coastal defenses of South Carolina until he was superseded by Robert E. Lee in the fall of 1861. He quarreled with Lee and then criticized John C. Pemberton until he was transferred, at his own request, to the Army of Northern Virginia. He led a brigade of Carolinians during the Seven Days and at Second Bull Run, South Mountain, and Antietam, where he was hit in the throat by a minié ball that was deflected by his cravat.

Criticized for his poor performance at South Mountain, he returned to South Carolina, where he supervised the defense of Charleston against Federal attacks during 1863 and 1864. Many Charlestonians blamed him for the loss of Battery Wagner—one, Henry W. Ravenel, wrote in his diary that Ripley was "considered incompetent for his dissipated habits."[16] In July 1864 he was removed from command after being accused of drunkenness during the Federal landing on James Island. After the evacuation of Charleston in February 1865, he joined Joseph E. Johnston in North Carolina, where he surrendered.
Photo courtesy of F. Bruce Kusrow

ROSWELL S. RIPLEY
carte de visite
Quinby and Company

JOHN P. THOMAS
copy print

John P. Thomas in this photograph wears the uniform of a faculty member of the Arsenal Academy in Columbia, a freshman preparatory school for the Citadel in Charleston. He held the commensurate rank of captain in the Cadet Battalion and commanded the crew of the Blakely gun positioned on Morris Island during the bombardment of Fort Sumter. Abner Doubleday recalled that shells from this piece, unlike those from any other, almost punched through the walls of Sumter.

Born in Fairfield County, Thomas graduated first in his class from the Citadel in 1851 at the age of eigteen. He was a professor of literature and history at the Arsenal Academy from 1853 until October 1861, when he became the academy's superintendent. In March 1863 he raised a battalion, among which were nine Protestant ministers, to defend Charleston. They served for a month and then again in July 1863 of the same year. During 1864 he remained a captain in the Cadet Battalion and superintendent of the Arsenal Academy, though he later recalled that he also held the rank of colonel in a home defense regiment at that time.

As Gen. William T. Sherman's troops approached Columbia, Thomas led the Arsenal Cadets out of the city and marched them to Spartanburg, where they joined cadets from the Citadel. He did not furlough the last of them to return home until May 1865. *Photo courtesy of Citadel Archives, Charleston, South Carolina*

When Gustavus V. Fox visited Maj. Robert Anderson at Fort Sumter to discuss plans for supplying the garrison, he was accompanied by an old friend, Henry J. Hartstene. A native of South Carolina, Hartstene had resigned his commission in the U. S. Navy and assumed command of the three small vessels of the South Carolina naval force. He was apparently unaware of what Fox was doing; while Fox and Anderson discussed a scheme in the latter's office, other Union officers debated the disposition of the floating battery with Hartstene. Fox, however, kept his ships outside the harbor during the bombardment of Sumter, much to the scorn of Hartstene, who declared, "One bold officer in command of a navy barge armed with a boat howitzer could have easily cleared the way for a hundred barges with men and supplies. . . ."[17]

Hartstene supervised the evacuation of the Sumter garrison, then remained in his home state. He served as a naval aide at the Battle of Pocotaligo in October 1862 and subsequently became a commander in the Confederate navy. Serving briefly at Savannah, he returned to Charleston as the captain of the CSS *Stono*, a captured gunboat formerly known as the USS *Isaac P. Smith*. The *Stono* ran aground on the night of June 5, 1863, while trying to run the blockade; by 1864 Hartstene was stationed overseas. *Photo courtesy of University of South Carolina, Columbia*

HENRY J. HARTSTENE
carte de visite
Quinby and Company

Chapter 3

For the Duration: South Carolinians in the Army of Northern Virginia

Soon after the capture of Fort Sumter, South Carolinians by the hundreds made their way to the front in Virginia. When Gen. Pierre G. T. Beauregard arrived at Manassas in June 1861 to take command, he found the troops there under the command of Milledge L. Bonham, the former commander of the South Carolina army who had served under him during the bombardment of Sumter. Bonham, now a brigadier general in the Confederate service, was left in command of a brigade that included four South Carolina regiments, but others were assigned to brigades led by David R. Jones and Nathan G. Evans, both of whom were also from South Carolina. While none of these four officers would serve for the duration of the war in Virginia, thousands of South Carolinians did, fighting in all the major campaigns and sadly stacking their weapons for the last time at Appomattox in April 1865.

Along Bull Run, Bonham's brigade was assigned to watch Mitchell's Ford, Jones' troops were posted at McLean's Ford, and Evans was on the left near the Stone Bridge. Skirmishers from the 4th South Carolina Infantry, in front of the Stone Bridge, claimed the honor of the first shots fired by the Confederate army at First Bull Run on July 21, 1861. Beauregard assumed command on the left and threw reinforcements—including Bernard E. Bee's brigade and Wade Hampton's legion—into combat as they arrived. Despite being reinforced, the Confederates were forced back until most of the units, including those commanded by Bee and Evans, dissolved into a confused and demoralized mass. Only stubborn fighting by Hampton's South Carolinians, who suffered heavy casualties, protected the rest from disaster.

A counterattack by the Virginia brigade led by Thomas J. Jackson allowed the Confederates to regain the initiative. It was while rallying his men for a counterassault in which he would be killed that Bee immortalized Jackson with the line, "There is Jackson, standing like a stone wall."[1] Beauregard directed a series of charges, allegedly demanding to be allowed to carry the palmetto flag of the Hampton Legion after the color bearer fell. South Carolinians from Bonham's brigade arrived on the left, adding weight to Confederate attacks that finally routed the Federals.

After First Bull Run, pursuant to orders from Richmond to brigade troops from the same state whenever possible, four South Carolina regiments remained in Bonham's brigade while four others were assigned to Jones' brigade. Bonham resigned in early 1862, so command of his troops fell to Joseph B. Kershaw, formerly the colonel of the 2nd South Carolina Infantry. At the same time, Jones was promoted to major general and relinquished command of his original brigade to South Carolinian Richard H. Anderson, a West Point graduate who had fought in Mexico and against Indians in the West, and who briefly commanded the defenses of Charleston after Beauregard's departure for Virginia in 1861.

Gen. George B. McClellan landed his Federals on the Peninsula in April 1862, and the Confederates slowly fell back as the Union army pushed toward Richmond. South Carolinians under Kershaw and Anderson fought well on May 4 and 5, 1862, at Williamsburg, where the Confederates lost half as many casualties as the Federals. Charged with managing all troops present on his front, Anderson turned over his brigade to Col. Micah Jenkins of the Palmetto Sharpshooters, who handled his assignment with a "fiery zeal" that "won many plaudits."[2] Hampton's performance also elicited praise and a promotion to brigadier general, which he declined for unexplained reasons.

The Confederate defenders of Richmond lashed back at Seven Pines on May 31, 1862. After other assaults failed, Anderson's brigade of South Carolinians attacked "like demons possessed" late in the afternoon.[3] Anderson directed one column and entrusted the other to Jenkins. The latter led his Palmetto Sharpshooters, the 6th South Carolina Infantry, and the 27th Georgia Infantry toward Fair Oaks through a heavy fire. The Confederates pushed the Federals out of two defensive lines, then stalled before a third. The 5th South Carolina Infantry arrived in time to help Jenkins hold his position. One of Jenkins' South Carolina companies, 47 strong, bagged 139 prisoners at Seven Pines, but at a horrific cost. Casualties exceeded 50 percent among Jenkins' units.

Gen. Joseph E. Johnston was badly wounded at Seven Pines and relinquished command of his army to Gen. Robert E. Lee, who renamed it the Army of Northern Virginia and began preparing to drive McClellan away from Richmond. Troops were gathered from all over the Confederacy, including a brigade of South Carolina and Georgia troops led by Gen. Roswell S. Ripley, who earlier served under Lee at Charleston. Although the removal of units increased fears in South Carolina, their service in Virginia was needed. In the second of the Seven Days—at Mechanicsville on June 26, 1862—Ripley's brigade took part in an assault against the Federal right along Beaver Dam Creek, where the Confederates suffered horrendous casualties.

Lee continued to pound McClellan as the Seven Days progressed. When Ambrose Powell Hill's division led the Confederate attack at Gaines' Mill on June 27, 1862, a South Carolina brigade commanded by Maxcy Gregg formed the vanguard. They scattered the Federals assigned to impede their advance in a rush described by Hill as "the handsomest charge in line I have seen during the war," but they stopped before a large body of Union troops posted behind a boggy stream known as Boatswain's Swamp.[4] Gregg's men charged again and again, but neither they nor other Confederates could dislodge the Federals until a push by the entire Army of Northern Virginia, including Hampton's Legion and Anderson's South Carolina brigade, compelled the Union army to withdraw.

As McClellan retreated down the Peninsula, South Carolinians remained in the forefront of Lee's pursuit. Kershaw's brigade of South Carolinians, supported by Capt. James F. Hart's battery from South Carolina and a Virginia battery, led the advance at Savage Station on June 29, moving forward until darkness and a thunderstorm stopped the fight. At Frayser's Farm on June 30, Anderson took command of James Longstreet's division, which led the attack on the Union position. The assault itself was led by Anderson's brigade, commanded by Jenkins. When the Confederates began to give ground before Federal reinforcements, parity was restored by the timely charge of Gregg's brigade, spearheaded by Samuel McGowan's 14th South Carolina Infantry.

The South Carolinians paid a heavy price for the laurels earned during the Peninsular Campaign. The brigades of Anderson, Gregg, and Ripley suffered the macabre distinction of being among those with the heaviest casualties in the Army of Northern Virginia. At Gaines' Mill, for example, Gregg lost almost a third of his troops; of his regiments, the 1st South Carolina Rifles suffered the greatest casualties of any Confederate unit engaged (315 of the 537 men present). Ripley's brigade advanced during the ill-advised Confederate assaults at Malvern Hill until they were mown down with canister, while Kershaw's troops also made no headway before nightfall ended the slaughter.

After the Seven Days, Anderson was promoted to major general and given command of the division previously led by another South Carolinian, Benjamin Huger, who had performed without distinction during the Seven Days and who had been blamed for the loss of Roanoke Island in North Carolina to Union forces. Anderson's brigade was given to Jenkins, who was promoted upon the advice of Lee himself. In preparation for an advance into Maryland, Lee also acquired two brigades that contained South Carolina troops led by Nathan G. Evans and Thomas F. Drayton. The former was not posted to any division, but the latter was attached to Jones' command.

While Lee was preparing to march north, portions of his army, including Gregg's brigade, fought under the command of Jackson in the Shenandoah Valley. The South Carolinians' sad condition led to conflicts between Gregg and Jackson, who was known as "Old Blue Light" to many South Carolinians. By late August 1862 all of Gregg's regimental commanders had been arrested by Jackson because their troops had stolen food or burned fence palings in their campfires in defiance of orders. The officers were released as impending battles demanded their services, but little was done for their men. However, a fast march by Gregg's troops, a third of whom had no shoes, allowed them to take part in the sack of a Federal commissary at Manassas where, according to McGowan, they "regaled themselves upon delicacies . . . which they were in good condition to enjoy. . . ."[5]

Gregg's South Carolinians redeemed themselves at Second Bull Run. On August 29, when Gen. John Pope tried to crush Jackson's solitary divisions, Gregg anchored the left of the Confederate line. During their fifth assault on his men, Union attackers penetrated a gap between Gregg's right flank and the next brigade. A quick counterattack by McGowan's 14th South Carolina Infantry in tandem with Georgia troops repulsed the Federals after an exchange of volleys at less than thirty yards. When the Union troops charged again, Gregg's men were forced out of the railroad cut in which they had taken cover. Having spent their last cartridges, they fought with bayonets while Gregg rallied them with an ancestor's Revolutionary War scimitar in his hand, crying, "Let us die here, my men, let us die here!"[6] After seven hours of combat, Gregg's troops retired behind a screen of reinforcements.

Longstreet's arrival on August 29 set the stage for a Confederate victory the next day. Pope renewed his attacks against Jackson on August 30, ignoring Longstreet. Late in the afternoon, Longstreet ordered his artillery to open on the Union left flank; the enfilading fire of Confederate guns, including the South Carolina units in Charleston native Stephen D. Lee's battalion, shredded the Federal lines and facilitated an attack by almost the whole of Longstreet's command against Pope's flank. Only nightfall saved Pope from a total disaster.

Second Bull Run was a Confederate triumph, but South Carolina's losses were not slight. In all, 1,714 casualties were reported among South

Carolina units. Gregg's brigade on the first day lost 613 in killed and wounded, including every field officer except Gregg and a subordinate. On the second day, Jenkins' brigade suffered more than 400 casualties; among the wounded was Jenkins himself. Four South Carolina colonels in Longstreet's command, including former governor John H. Means, were killed. Nor was the bloodshed over for South Carolinians when Pope retreated; Gregg lost another 104 casualties when Jackson attacked the Union rearguard in a rainstorm at Ox Hill on September 1, 1862.

Lee marched into Maryland, but shortly after he did so, a copy of the orders for the disposition of his scattered army fell into the hands of McClellan, who promptly moved toward Turner's Gap near South Mountain in an attempt to divide the Army of Northern Virginia. Hampton, now a brigadier general of cavalry, harried the Union troops to win time for Confederate infantry to reach the gap first. When McClellan did attack at Turner's Gap on September 14, the Confederates, among whom were a number of South Carolinians, including Evans' and Drayton's brigades, withstood his assaults despite heavy casualties (the 17th South Carolina Infantry lost 43 percent of those engaged), then withdrew in good order after sunset.

While South Carolina units were fighting at South Mountain, the brigades of Kershaw and Gregg were participating in the seige of Harper's Ferry under the command of Jackson. Gregg's men did not suffer a casualty during the investment of the Union stronghold, but Kershaw's troops, led by the 7th South Carolina Infantry, had to drive Federal defenders from their positions along Maryland Heights on September 13 so that Confederate guns could be placed there to shell the town. Although Kershaw lost 196 casualties, he was ordered to move on, and it was Gregg's men who again dined on Union stores after the garrison capitulated.

Kershaw's troops rushed to the town of Sharpsburg, where Lee made a stand against McClellan. They arrived on September 17 in time to lead a counterattack to the left of the Confederate center, where a Union assault threatened to shatter Jackson's command. In the center of the Confederate perimeter, Federal troops pressed forward until halted by a battery from Macbeth, South Carolina. Advancing in a crossfire that detonated one of their caissons, these gunners unlimbered close to the Federals and fired seventy rounds of canister in a few minutes, driving their enemy back. A counterattack in which Evans' brigade participated restored the Confederate line. On the right, Jenkins' and Drayton's brigades of Longtreet's command held their ground until Ambrose Powell Hill's division, led by Gregg's brigade, arrived and pushed the Union attackers back for the last time.

Lee's army survived the crisis at Sharpsburg, but its losses were terrific. Kershaw's men suffered horrendous casualties: of 45 men from the 8th South Carolina Infantry that reached the field, 23 were shot, while 140 casualties were reported among the 263 members of the 7th South Carolina Infantry. In the center, the 17th South Carolina Infantry in Evans' brigade lost 19 of the 59 effectives who fought. Among the South Carolina generals, Gregg, Anderson, and Ripley were wounded. The first, however, reentered the battle mounted on an ambulance horse, and he directed the rearguard during the retreat across the Potomac River, refusing even to abandon an ambulance whose driver had left the occupants to their fate. At Gregg's insistence, the ambulance was pulled by hand across the river before he directed a charge that chased pursuing Federals into the water.

The South Carolina infantry had little to celebrate during the fall of 1862, but Hampton's cavalry enjoyed themselves. On the morning of October 10, Matthew C. Butler's 2nd South Carolina Cavalry led the way as Confederate troopers crossed the Potomac River and occupied Chambersburg, Pennsylvania, before nightfall. Hampton, appointed "Military Governor," burned military stores there the next day and directed the rear guard until the command recrossed the Potomac, losing not a single man. On November 27, Hampton's troopers captured a Federal post in northern Virginia, two weeks later they snatched four dozen prisoners and seventeen wagons, and on December 17 they bagged 157 prisoners and twenty wagons loaded with army stores, all without the loss of a single Confederate. When, during late December, Jeb Stuart himself led a raid, in which Hampton's South Carolinians rode, behind Ambrose E. Burnside's army, he found the pickings slim. Disappointed, he blamed the scarcity of victims on the depredations by Hampton.

South Carolina infantry played a prominent role in the crushing defeat of Burnside's army at Fredericksburg on December 13, 1862. After the repulse of Union attacks on the Confederate right, the Federals engaged in a series of spectacularly bloody, and futile, assaults against Lee's left, which was securely anchored behind a stone wall at the base of Marye's Heights. Kershaw's brigade stood in reserve until ordered to reinforce the Confederates at the wall. Kershaw realized that the path to the wall was swept by Federal gunfire, but "he rode out into the fire with no more hesitation than he would have shown on his way to a political barbecue in his native South Carolina."[7] The South Carolinians conducted a spirited defense of that virtually impregnable post; no Union soldier got closer than thirty yards.

The Confederate victory at Fredericksburg was bittersweet for South Carolina. During the Union attack against the Confederate right, Federals swept through the woods that separated a pair of frontline brigades and surprised Gregg's troops who, being held in reserve, had stacked arms. Some fled because they were unable to reach their weapons and were leaderless because of the mortal wounding of Gregg, who mistakenly believed the new arrivals were retreating Confederates and ordered his men not to shoot at them. More of Gregg's brigade, however, rallied and, with reinforcements, drove the Federals back. Gregg pulled himself erect with the aid of a

tree to urge forward the Confederate attack and then was taken to a nearby house. He dictated a telegram to Gov. Francis W. Pickens, declaring that he was proud to die for the "independence of South Carolina."[8] He worried that his conflict with Jackson would be unresolved, but Jackson visited him to insist that there was no offense on his part. Gregg's body lay in state at Richmond and then was sent to Columbia for burial.

After Gregg died, command of his brigade was offered to Hampton, but he refused it, and the honor went to McGowan, who first led his new command in battle at Chancellorsville. On May 2, 1863, Jackson, accompanied by his staff, was approaching that town when he heard the sound of gunfire. Upon inquiring, he was told by Capt. Alexander C. Haskell of South Carolina—a staff officer for Gregg and now McGowan—that Henry Heth, the ranking brigadier general present, had insisted upon probing the Federal lines in the nearby woods and that he, Haskell, had volunteered the 14th South Carolina Infantry and the 1st South Carolina Rifles for the task. The South Carolinians had dashed into the trees and were skirmishing when Jackson arrived. Stonewall told Haskell to hold his position until dark, when his troops would be relieved.

The South Carolinians actually remained in position until early morning, when they joined Jackson's flanking march. The general himself passed nearby during the operation, but when McGowan's brigade stood to cheer him, they were stilled by the sternness of his gaze. With other troops, the South Carolinians were led to the right flank of Joseph Hooker's army, arriving in place during the afternoon of May 2, 1863. McGowan's men served as a reserve for Jackson's attack that evening, which drove the right flank of the Federals for some distance.

While Jackson was conducting his flank march, Kershaw's brigade was among those harassing Hooker's front. On May 3, the South Carolina troops of McGowan and Kershaw were in the front lines as the two halves of Lee's army fought to reunite in Hooker's front. McGowan's attack began about sunrise, but the South Carolinians advanced only a hundred yards before they were repulsed. About their assault, Heth later wrote that he could not recall any unit enduring a more destructive fire. After other Confederates took the Union breastworks, McGowan's men advanced, suffering 448 casualties in all. McGowan himself was severely wounded in the initial attack. The reunion of Lee's army was accomplished by Anderson, who maneuvered his division to effect a linkage. The Confederates pushed Hooker's forces beyond Chancellorsville and then Kershaw's troops and others defeated a Union detachment pressing the Confederate rear at Salem Church.

Concerned with Lee's obvious preparations to invade the North again, Hooker ordered a reconnaissance in force. When Federal troopers attacked Jeb Stuart's pickets along the Rappahannock River on June 9, the largest cavalry battle of the Civil War, known as Brandy Station, began. The 1st South Carolina Cavalry delayed the Union advance on the right until a brigade took their place, while a section from Hart's Battery stalled the Federals on the left long enough for reinforcements to arrive. The 1st South Carolina Cavalry raced to the left in time to join in an attack, led by Hampton, that repulsed the Federals. Changing fronts, Hampton's brigade, with Hart's Battery and others, led another attack that secured the field for Stuart. Meanwhile, the 2nd South Carolina Cavalry took part in a fierce battle, in which Matthew B. Butler lost his foot, against a third Union column. The Federals suffered 936 casualties; the Confederates lost 523, including Hampton's brother Frank, lieutenant colonel of the 2nd South Carolina Cavalry, who was mortally wounded as he led a charge.

After Brandy Station, Stuart was pressed hard during June 1863 at Aldie, Middleburg, and Upperville. In the fighting at Middleburg, Hart's Battery lost the first gun ever captured from Stuart by the Federals, though the general assured them that its loss was more than offset by the casualties it had inflicted. Hampton's men fought well, and Hampton himself won glory for his impetuous charge at Upperville with only five squadrons against a much more numerous Union host. When Stuart once more decided to conduct a raid, South Carolinians rode in the vanguard and Hart's was among the batteries assigned to accompany the column. Skirmishing often, the Confederates captured many wagons and inflicted many casualties, but they were not where Lee needed them most: at Gettysburg.

On June 30, 1863, James J. Pettigrew's brigade, marching to Gettysburg to capture a stockpile of shoes reported to be there, encountered Union cavalry outside the town and withdrew without a fight. Early the next morning Ambrose Powell Hill ordered Heth's division, led by Pettigrew's troops, forward, to be followed by W. Dorsey Pender's division. Among Pender's division was McGowan's South Carolina brigade, now commanded by Col. Abner Perrin because of McGowan's wound at Chancellorsville. The South Carolinians spearheaded an attack that pushed the Federals through Gettysburg with a loss of more than 5,000 prisoners. The 1st South Carolina Infantry was the first Confederate regiment to plant its colors in the town, despite the fact that every color sergeant in that regiment was killed that day. Perrin maintained his position at the foot of Cemetery Hill for the next two days, then withdrew with the remainder of the Army of Northern Virginia. In all, 654 of McGowan's (Perrin's) men were lost in the Gettysburg campaign.

On the right, Lafayette McLaws' division of Longstreet's corps, which included Kershaw's South Carolina brigade, was ordered on July 2 to drive the Union defenders from the peach orchard before the gap between Little Round Top and Cemetery Ridge. The attack, pushing through the orchard and a wheat field, reached Little Round Top but was stopped by Union reinforcements. In the bitter fighting, Kershaw lost 630 men, about half of the effectives that he had. A company of the 2nd South Carolina Infantry, which had anchored the left flank of Kershaw's attacking line, lost all but four of the forty men present that day.

No South Carolina units took part in the climactic assault upon the Union center on July 3, but Pettigrew, a Charlestonian, took command of Heth's division after that officer was wounded, and he led them in the attack. As his men, many of them suffering from wounds inflicted in the first day's fighting, approached Cemetery Ridge to the left of George E. Pickett's division, they were mowed down by a storm of small arms and artillery fire from their front and flank. Pettigrew, though his horse was shot from under him and he was badly wounded, pressed his attacks against the Federal line until his units were too badly shattered to continue.

Confederate cavalry was conspicuously ineffective at Gettysburg, and they fought hard to regain their reputation in the fall of 1863. Hampton's brigade had been the first of Stuart's troopers to reach Gettysburg, on July 1, and they had fought with Federal cavalry there. Hampton suffered two saber cuts to the head as well as a shrapnel shot through the body, but, promoted to major general, he soon took command of a cavalry division. Among his new brigadier generals was Butler, who was promoted despite the loss of his foot at Brandy Station. South Carolina troopers fought with distinction in Virginia that October; Stuart praised the 1st South Carolina Cavalry after they forced detachments from Judson Kilpatrick's division to retreat. The 1st South Carolina Cavalry also led the attack at Buckland several weeks later, when Kilpatrick was routed and several hundred Federals were captured in what the Confederates derisively called the Buckland Races.

By the time that the Army of the Potomac advanced in May 1864, Longstreet had returned with his corps to the Army of Northern Virginia from Tennessee. They were sorely needed. On the first day in the Wilderness, May 5, McGowan's brigade, from Ambrose Powell Hill's corps, charged, gaining ground and capturing many Federals, including Brig. Gen. Truman Seymour, a veteran of the Fort Sumter bombardment in April 1861 and of the Battery Wagner assault in July 1863. He now returned to Charleston, but this time as a prisoner. That evening McGowan did not entrench because he expected Longstreet's troops would replace his men. At dawn on May 6, a Union assault pushed McGowan back until two divisions from Longstreet, one commanded by Kershaw, arrived. Kershaw had his regiments screen the retreating Southerners and personally led a counterattack that checked the pursuing Federals until a Confederate flank attack drove their foes beyond their original starting point.

An opportunity for another blow at the Federals was missed when South Carolina lost her second general. Kershaw was riding with Longstreet, Micah Jenkins, and others, discussing a counterattack, when they were mistakenly fired upon by Confederates. Kershaw prevented them from firing a second volley, but Longstreet and Jenkins were wounded, the latter mortally. With a bullet lodged in his brain he lingered for hours, urging his South Carolinians forward in his delirium, and then died without apparently knowing what had happened. Meanwhile, Lee delayed the attack until order could be restored; during the delay, Kershaw's troops and others repulsed a Federal attack. When the Southerners moved forward, the Union line broke, but the attackers could do little more than plant their flags on the captured fieldworks.

Col. John Bratton of the 6th South Carolina Infantry was promoted in Jenkins' place, while Anderson assumed command of Longstreet's corps until his recovery. Ordered by Lee to send troops south to block the flanking movement of Gen. Ulysses S. Grant, Anderson told Kershaw's division and another to march before midnight on May 7, 1864. Among these troops were Bratton's brigade and Kershaw's brigade, now led by John W. Henagan. Their departure was hours ahead of schedule, but

Anderson reasoned that his men would be unable to sleep in the burning Wilderness. His decision proved fortunate; a courier delivered a plea from Stuart for support as Anderson's men approached Spotsylvania Courthouse shortly after sunrise on May 8. Henagan's troops rushed forward and fought viciously with the Federal V Corps. When night fell, the Confederates held the crossroads at Spotsylvania.

After the opposing forces sparred for several days, Grant ordered an assault by the Union II Corps against the salient known as the Mule Shoe in the center of the Confederate line. More than 20,000 Federals punched a hole in the Southern perimeter at dawn on May 12, in a cold rain, and captured more than 2,000 prisoners before being halted by Confederates in a second, incomplete line of entrenchments. One of the units in these works was McGowan's South Carolina brigade. Both McGowan and his second-in-command were disabled by wounds during the desperate fighting, but part of the Mule Shoe was recaptured by the South Carolinians. They held their ground, sometimes less than a dozen paces from their opponents, despite Federal demands for surrender and small arms fire that cut at least one stout oak tree in half. Before they were withdrawn seventeen hours later, behind the screen provided by Bratton's brigade, more than 320 of McGowan's men were killed or wounded, and 117 were reported missing.

After more probing at Spotsylvania, Grant moved south again in an attempt to get around Lee's flank. The two armies arrived almost simultaneously at the crossroads near Cold Harbor on June 1. Lee ordered an assault, but Kershaw's old brigade, led by Lawrence M. Keitt, colonel of the newly arrived 20th South Carolina Infantry, was routed and Keitt was mortally wounded. Union attacks that same day had little more success, and both armies fought with no effect on June 2. Just before daylight on June 3, three Federal corps assailed the Southern lines; in no more than eight minutes, about 7,000 Union soldiers were killed,

wounded, or missing, while the Confederates lost less than a fourth of that number. During this grim clash, Kershaw's division held a salient, repulsing a series of charges.

Meanwhile, southeast of Richmond, reinforcements from South Carolina had halted an inept advance by Gen. Benjamin F. Butler toward the Confederate capital. The 21st and 25th South Carolina Infantry arrived at Walthall Junction, between Richmond and Petersburg, on May 6 and, reinforced by elements of the Richmond garrison, blocked Butler. The rest of Johnson Hagood's brigade arrived the following day; during the ensuing fortnight the South Carolinians played a prominent role in bottling up the Federals in the Bermuda Hundred, where they were effectively out of the war. Hagood's brigade was particularly distinguished at Drewry's Bluff on May 16, driving back their opponents and capturing five guns. Ironically, in this campaign the South Carolina troops were again commanded by Pierre G. T. Beauregard, and they often faced their old foes, the Union X Corps, which had operated along the coast of their home state earlier in the war.

Union and Confederate cavalry fought almost continuously while the infantry was locked in their grisly square dance through northern Virginia. Troopers from the 4th and 5th South Carolina Cavalry fought alongside two Virginia brigades at Haw's Shop on May 29, 1864, inflicting 344 casualties before withdrawing. The South Carolinians, newcomers to Virginia and still stinging from the welcoming taunts of veterans, dismounted and fired volleys with their Enfields into the startled Federals before Hampton intervened and led his troops from the field. South Carolinians fought at Hanover Courthouse on May 31 and then, with reinforcements that included other units of Hampton's division, futilely tried to keep Union troopers from destroying railroads in the area.

As the summer progressed, the Confederate cavalry remained almost constantly engaged. A thrust south by Gen. Philip H. Sheridan was repulsed at Trevilian Station on June 11 and 12 through the combined efforts of Hampton's and Fitzhugh Lee's divisions, under the overall command of the former. Bolstered by a South Carolina brigade led by Martin W. Gary (whose command was organized around the mounted infantry of the Hampton Legion), Hampton in late June won again at Nance's Shop and then almost captured a Union cavalry force sent to cut the railroad lines supplying the defenders of Petersburg and Richmond. Although the Union raiders destroyed sixty miles of track, Hampton could boast that he had captured more than 2,000 prisoners in three weeks of campaigning while losing only 719 of his own men.

Grant moved the bulk of his army south of the James River in mid-June 1864, compelling Lee to commit his infantry to the trenches before Petersburg. When Kershaw moved his division into the line on June 18, Bratton's South Carolina brigade defended the sector south of the Appomattox River under continuous fire for a week until relieved by Stephen Elliott, Jr.'s, brigade, which had been led by Evans until he was disabled. Bratton's men did not leave the trenches; instead, they were sent to another area where the pressure was not as intense. At the same time, Hagood's brigade fought to hold the sector along the City Point Road, where many of them were killed by incessant artillery and small arms fire.

During late July, the 18th and 22nd South Carolina Infantry and an artillery battery were settled into a salient in the trenches northeast of Petersburg. The Confederates were aware that the Union troops facing them had been constructing a tunnel toward their position for a month, but they had not been able to nullify that threat by digging countermines. Uneasy, they dug a line of entrenchments across the base of their salient. Shortly before five in the morning on July 30, about eight thousand pounds of black powder, packed into the end of the Union tunnel, exploded under the slumbering South Carolina regiments, opening a huge crater. Over 330 South Carolinians were lost in the explosion, and most of the remainder were too dazed to respond as Federals attacked. Elliott was badly wounded leading a counterattack, but his troops established a new line and, with reinforcements, forced the Union attackers to retreat. In all, Elliott lost 677 South Carolinians that day, over half of the total number of Confederate losses.

To draw Confederates out of the trenches before Petersburg and to assist in the attack to be undertaken when the mine exploded under Elliott's regiments, Grant ordered a surprise attack north of the James River. The Federal assault on July 27 was unexpectedly met and stopped by Kershaw's division, which had been sent into the area to shield the Confederate capital. Sheridan's cavalry was ordered to proceed toward Richmond the next day, but it was hit hard by Kershaw's troops. The latter suffered heavy casualties from the repeating carbines of the Federal troopers and had to withdraw in haste, but Sheridan was forced to abandon his raid. A probe by Federals in this same area in August was repelled by a Confederate force that included the infantry brigades commanded by McGowan and Bratton, which suffered heavy casualties, and the cavalry brigade led by Butler.

As the months dragged on at Petersburg, there were few successes to provide the Confederates with hope. Federal losses exceeded those of Lee's units, but the former could be replaced while the latter could not. Hagood's brigade led an assault by Ambrose Powell Hill's corps on Union trenches along the Weldon Railroad, south of Petersburg, on August 21. The South Carolinians drove the Federals back to their main line, but more than two-thirds of the former became casualties. Four days later, Hill's corps and Hampton's cavalry defeated a Union force at Ream's Station on the Weldon Railroad and captured 2,150 prisoners, but not before the Federals destroyed several miles of track.

In fighting along the Darbytown and New Market roads north of the James River during the last week of September and the first two weeks of

October, Lee failed to reestablish a defensive perimeter lost to Federal attacks. These efforts cost Confederate units dearly, including the South Carolina brigades of Bratton and Martin W. Gary. The former, for example, was ordered on September 30 to recapture a work on New Market Road that had been taken by the Federals. Bratton tersely reported that the number of his men who lay dead near the Union lines testified to their earnest attempt to carry out their orders; of his 1,294 officers and men who fought that day, 377 were killed or wounded. Another 190 from Bratton's brigade were killed or wounded in an assault on October 7, in which Bratton was disabled by a wound.

Hampton scored a brief triumph in September when his men captured twenty-five hundred head of cattle for Lee's army after a well-managed skirmish south of the James River near City Point. Among the troopers who participated in this raid were about a hundred South Carolinians. Their euphoria was short lived because, on October 1, 1864, John Dunovant, a brigadier general from South Carolina, was killed in fighting along Hatcher's Run. In a pitched battle on October 27, Hampton's cavalry, supported by two infantry divisions, blocked elements of three Union corps pushing north to cut the Southside Railroad, the last line connecting Petersburg with the rest of the Confederacy. Again, the cost was heavy, including the death of Lt. W. Preston Hampton and the wounding of Lt. Wade Hampton, two of the three sons of the general who served in the Confederate army. Among the seriously wounded, too, was James F. Hart, whose South Carolina battery had won praise from Lee himself during August 1864.

In August 1864, Kershaw's division marched with others under the overall command of Anderson to join the small army led by Jubal Early into the Shenandoah Valley to divert Federal troops from Petersburg. After a month, an overconfident Early allowed the South Carolinians and others to return to Petersburg. When Early subsequently was badly defeated, Kershaw rejoined his small army. With his confidence restored, Early attacked Sheridan's army at Cedar Creek on October 19, 1864. The surprised Federals fled in confusion, then rallied to drive the Confederates from the field. The Confederates lost most of their artillery and wagon train, as well as 2,910 casualties; Kershaw's old brigade, under James Conner, reported losses of 205. The Confederates had lost the Valley.

As the war entered its last year, a number of South Carolinians were sent away from Petersburg to bolster defenses elsewhere, but many were present at Appomattox. Hagood's and Conner's infantry brigades and Butler's troopers returned to the Carolinas, where Hampton assumed command of all cavalry. However, when Richmond was evacuated, Gary's brigade was the last unit to leave on April 3, pushing through milling throngs of hysterical citizens. Six days later, most of them surrendered at Appomattox Courthouse, though Gary escaped to North Carolina. Col. Robert M. Sims, a graduate of the Citadel who had begun the war as a captain in the 9th South Carolina Infantry, had the sad duty, as Longstreet's adjutant general, of bearing one of the last flags of truce at Appomattox. He galloped into the Union lines, waving a white towel trimmed in red, to convey a request to Sheridan for a truce until the results of the conference between Lee and Grant could be known. Within a few hours the Confederates capitulated; soon thereafter, the South Carolinians began walking home.

MILLEDGE L. BONHAM
carte de visite
Hix and Fitzgerald, Columbia

When Gen. Pierre G. T. Beauregard arrived at Manassas to take command, he found the troops there in the charge of Milledge L. Bonham, who had resigned from the U. S. Congress to take up the sword once more. A noted attorney and alumnus of South Carolina College, Bonham commanded state troops in the Seminole and Mexican wars and then became a major general in the militia. He also served in the legislature before taking the congressional seat of his cousin, Preston Brooks, following Brook's death. Appointed commander of the South Carolina army after secession, he had served under Beauregard during the bombardment of Fort Sumter and did so again at First Bull Run.

Bonham fought well at First Bull Run, though he did err in ordering James Longstreet not to pursue the retreating Federals. He resigned his commission as a brigadier general after only seven months at that rank—perhaps upset that he had been passed by for promotion—and was succeeded as commander of his brigade by Joseph B. Kershaw. He was quickly elected to the Confederate Congress and served from February 1862 until January 1863, when he resigned to become governor of South Carolina. In February 1865 he again became a brigadier general in Confederate service, and he surrendered with Joseph E. Johnston in North Carolina. *Photo courtesy of University of South Carolina, Columbia*

BERNARD E. BEE
carte de visite

As the Confederate lines during the first battle at Manassas gave way before Union reinforcements during the afternoon of July 21, 1861, Thomas J. Jackson ordered his Virginia brigade forward as the nucleus for a new Confederate line. Struggling to rally his South Carolinians, Gen. Bernard E. Bee earned a measure of immortality by referring to the Virginian's unwavering line as a "stonewall," a nickname that stuck with Jackson and his brigade for the duration of their service. Unfortunately, Bee never knew that he had such an impact on history; mortally wounded later that afternoon, he died the next day.

It is interesting to speculate what influence Bee might have had on the course of the war if he had lived, for the Charleston native was a graduate of West Point who had risen to the rank of captain in an army career that included distinguished service in Mexico, for which he was presented an engraved sword by the South Carolina legislature, and campaigns on the frontier against both Indians and Mormons. He had been promoted to brigadier general while serving in the Shenandoah Valley on June 17, 1861, the same day as David R. Jones, also from South Carolina. He had been a brigadier general of the Confederacy for less than five weeks when he was killed at the age of thirty-seven. *Photo courtesy of University of South Carolina, Columbia*

Samuel J. Hester was the captain of Company D in the 7th South Carolina Infantry, which was sent to Virginia in June 1861 and assigned to the brigade commanded by Milledge L. Bonham. Posted at Mitchell's Ford during First Bull Run, the regiment remained in their trenches under Union artillery fire until the Federal withdrawal began and then swept forward to press their retreating foes. The next day, July 22, they were assigned to retrieve arms and ammunition left on the field by the panic-stricken Federals.

An Abbeville County planter, Hester, at the age of forty, had recruited his company, which mustered for state service on April 15, 1861, at Abbeville and entered Confederate service the following June. He resigned after the regiment was reorganized in May 1862. In 1863 and 1864 he served in Company I of the 1st South Carolina State Troops, a six-month regiment that served as provost guards in Charleston beginning in September 1863. *Photo courtesy of University of South Carolina, Columbia*

SAMUEL J. HESTER
carte de visite
Quinby and Company

JAMES H. BURNS
sixth-plate ambrotype

A number of South Carolinians served in units organized in other states; an entire company, for example, enlisted in a Mississippi regiment when they feared that they might be assigned to garrison duty on the South Carolina coast. They sought a glorious career in the military, but many paid a higher cost for glory than they expected to be assessed.

One such "expatriate" was James H. Burns, a native of Kershaw County who graduated from the Citadel in 1861 at the age of twenty and then became a drillmaster for the 6th North Carolina Infantry. When the regiment was organized a month later, Burns was listed in Company E as a lieutenant. The regiment,

after a series of forced marches, reached the field at First Bull Run just in time to be thrown into the charge on Henry House Hill, where it suffered heavy casualties that included the death of its original colonel.

Burns's regiment was also in the thick of the fighting in the Seven Days and at Second Bull Run, Antietam, South Mountain, and Fredericksburg. Promoted to captain in December 1862, Burns took an extended leave in early 1863 and then returned to the regiment in time for Chancellorsville. He was killed at Gettysburg on July 1. *Photo courtesy of Citadel Archives, Charleston, South Carolina*

The carnage at First Bull Run made it clear that the Confederacy would need a well-organized military medical corps. Samuel P. Moore, a Charleston native who had served as a physician in the army for thirty-six years before his resignation in 1861, was appointed surgeon general on July 30 of that same year. He soon established boards to examine credentials and assign doctors, and he also served as president of the "Association of Army and Navy Surgeons," which was organized in August 1863 at Richmond. Under his strict supervision, a journal occasionally appeared, intended to educate both hospital and field surgeons. He was denounced as autocratic by his critics, but his work was indispensable.

He was always struggling to obtain enough supplies, as well as personnel and hospitals, and so he developed a great interest in medicinal substitutes, especially from indigenous plants. He supervised the publication of a number of medical works, but none so useful as the one on thera-peutic properties of plants commonly found in the South. This work was written by Francis P. Porcher, the former surgeon in charge of the city hospital in Charleston and longtime member of the faculty of the South Carolina Medical College. *Photo courtesy of National Archives*

SAMUEL P. MOORE
copy print

THOMAS A. EVANS
carte de visite

A number of South Carolina physicians served with the Army of Northern Virginia, but few as faithfully as Thomas A. Evans, a physician from Anderson. He was thirty-four years of age when he enlisted as surgeon of the 1st South Carolina Rifles in July 1861. He held the rank of major (he wears the single star of a major in this photograph) and was the acting chief surgeon of

Gen. Cadmus M. Wilcox's division when he surrendered at Appomattox in 1865. With the exception of two brief leaves of absence, in the spring of 1862 and the fall of 1863, Evans had been on continuous duty since the summer of 1861. *Photo courtesy of University of South Carolina, Columbia*

JOHN A. CRAWFORD
sixth-plate ambrotype

After the initial excitement of combat at First Bull Run, many South Carolinians found themselves assigned to mundane garrison duty. Unfortunately for the Confederacy, peaceful duty did not mean a cessation of casualties; many units in Virginia and elsewhere lost a number of men to disease.

A native of Columbia, John A. Crawford enlisted during June 1861 as a private in Company A (a horse artillery unit) of the cavalry battalion of Hampton's Legion. By September his company was on the Virginia coast, at Freestone Point in Prince William County, digging emplacements for rifled guns. Using the latter, as well as howitzers, the company engaged several Union ships in the next few months with little result and few casualties.

During this time, more men in Crawford's company were felled by disease than by Federal shells. Crawford himself was briefly hospitalized for gonorrhea at Williamsburg, Virginia, in May 1862 and then was discharged during October 1862 upon a surgeon's certificate of disability. *Photo courtesy of University of South Carolina, Columbia*

The Confederacy adopted a conscription act in April 1862 that drafted recruits and compelled those already enlisted to remain in service; however, they were also allowed either to transfer or to reorganize their original units. In the ensuing reelections of officers, many officers lost their commissions.

Among those who lost their military rank but remained active in public life was Robert A. Fair, lieutenant colonel of the 7th South Carolina Infantry. Before the war, Fair had been a wealthy attorney in Abbeville. He was elected at the age of thirty-two as a lieutenant colonel and was sworn in as such on April 15 by Nathan G. Evans, then a major in the South Carolina militia.

Fair's regiment, after its arrival in Virginia during June 1861, had been assigned to the brigade commanded by Milledge L. Bonham. Posted at Mitchell's Ford during First Bull Run, they endured Union artillery fire until late in the afternoon, when they took part in the haphazard pursuit of the fleeing Federals.

Fair resigned in May 1862 after the conscription act necessitated a reorganization of his regiment, which remained in northern Virginia. He began a four-year term as a legislator for Abbeville County in November 1862, during which time he also served as a private in the 5th South Carolina Reserves. *Photo courtesy of University of South Carolina, Columbia*

ROBERT A. FAIR
carte de visite
Quinby and Company

JAMES W. ADAMS
quarter-plate ambrotype
Richard Wearn

The conscription act implemented by the Confederacy during the spring of 1862 was necessary to replenish the depleted ranks of Confederate armies on all fronts, but it disrupted a number of families in South Carolina, as it did throughout the South.

James W. Adams was conscripted into Company C of the 2nd South Carolina Infantry, which was popularly known as the Palmetto Regiment, at Columbia on July 1, 1862, after that regiment suffered heavy casualties in the Seven Days' Battles. During his term of service more than a third of the regiment's effectives who fought at Antietam were killed, wounded, or captured, and many more were lost at Maryland Heights just a few days later.

Adams left the regiment on sick leave during early October and died on November 15, 1862, at a hospital in Virginia. He was only thirty-two years of age. *Photo courtesy of Museum of the Confederacy, Richmond, Virginia*

JOHN BRATTON
cabinet print
W. A. Reckling, Columbia

Of the 521 members of the 6th South Carolina Infantry present for duty at Seven Pines on May 31, 1862, 269 became casualties. Among the casualties was Col. John Bratton, who ironically had graduated from South Carolina College and South Carolina College's medical school and had been a practicing physician before the war.

Originally enlisted as a private in the 6th South Carolina Infantry, Bratton was elected lieutenant of Company C before they departed for Virginia in July 1861, arriving, as he wrote on the back of this print, "in time to hear the last gun, but not in time to take part in the fight." It was just before departing from Charleston that the original of this image was taken.

Elected colonel of his regiment after it was mustered into Confederate service, he received his baptism of fire in a "hot little action" at Dranesville, Virginia, in December 1861. He was shot and captured at Seven Pines, then was exchanged after being held for a few months in Fortress Monroe. Two years later, following the Battle of the Wilderness, he became a brigadier general in place of Micah Jenkins, whose brigade he had earlier led during the Tennessee campaign in the fall of 1863. Nicknamed "Old Reliable," he remained with James Longstreet's corps of the Army of Northern Virginia until its surrender at Appomattox. *Photo courtesy of University of South Carolina, Columbia*

86

AUGUSTUS M. SMITH
carte de visite

On May 27, 1862, in the battle of Gaines' Mill, the 1st South Carolina Infantry formed the right flank of Maxcy Gregg's brigade as it charged and drove the Federals from their position. The regiment came under heavy fire; one volley swept away the entire color guard. Among the many casualties was Lt. Col. Augustus M. Smith, who was mortally wounded and died two days later. Sadly, his wife just one month earlier had given birth to a son, whom the lieutenant colonel never met.

Smith had been perhaps the wealthiest planter in Abbeville County in 1860, owning more than two hundred slaves who worked on his plantation there and on another in Arkansas. He served as the grand marshal of the secession meeting held at the county seat in November 1860 and then traveled to Charleston as a lieutenant in a militia company. Shortly after the mustering of Gregg's first regiment of volunteers in April 1861, Smith was appointed its adjutant and promoted to major. After Daniel H. Hamilton took command of the regiment in the fall of 1861, Smith replaced him as lieutenant colonel. *Photo courtesy of University of South Carolina, Columbia*

Capt. Henry J. Smith was mortally wounded at Antietam while in command of Company D (Gist Rifles) of the Infantry Battalion in Hampton's Legion. He died a few days later, after his troops had returned safely to northern Virginia.

During June 1861, when he was twenty-five years of age, Smith, an attorney at Williamson in Anderson County, enrolled in the Gist Rifles at Columbia. He led these men at First Bull Run, where the legion's stand bought time for the Confederate army to rally, as well as during the Seven Days, when the legion lost more than a third of the men it had engaged. Emerging unscathed from these engagements, as well as from the bloody fighting at Second Bull Run, Smith led his weary company into Maryland, where he fell during the desperate struggle along Antietam Creek. *Photo courtesy of University of South Carolina, Columbia*

HENRY J. SMITH
cabinet print
Bundy of Hartford, Connecticut

A graduate of South Carolina College and born in Society Hill, David G. McIntosh was a first lieutenant in Company B (Darlington Guards) of Maxcy Gregg's first regiment of six-month volunteers. After this unit reorganized in July 1861, his company became the "Pee Dee" Battery, which was attached to Ambrose Powell Hill's division. Captain McIntosh led his gunners in the Seven Days and at Second Bull Run. He then rushed three guns to the front and suffered the indignity of having them captured at Antietam, though they were quickly retaken by Confederate infantry.

McIntosh's gunners were stationed on Prospect Hill during the Battle of Fredericksburg; they suffered heavy losses but did not retire until their ammunition was exhausted. Subsequently promoted to major, McIntosh led a battalion at Chancellorsville, where his batteries punished Union infantry and artillery alike while suffering relatively heavy casualties themselves. The same was true at Gettysburg, the Wilderness, and Spotsylvania.

Before Petersburg, his employment of howitzers for indirect fire on Union troops in their trenches proved grimly successful. McIntosh also won renown when he led a battery into the no man's land between the trenches on June 22, 1864, and disrupted a Union column long enough for Confederate infantry to move through a gap and capture seventeen hundred prisoners. For his exploits, McIntosh became a lieutenant colonel in the spring of 1865. He left the Army of Northern Virginia before its surrender at Appomattox and briefly joined Jefferson Davis's party of refugees before returning home. Edward McIntosh, his younger brother, wears the uniform of a private in the Darlington Guards of the South Carolina militia. He served as a lieutenant in the Pee Dee Battery and remained with it until the fall of 1863, when he was assigned as assistant quartermaster to the battalion commanded by his brother, who had requested the transfer. He remained with the artillery of the Army of Northern Virginia through the end of the war. *Photo courtesy of U.S.A.M.H.I.*

DAVID G. MCINTOSH
AND EDWARD MCINTOSH
copy print

William W. Higgins was a forty-year-old slaveholder living in Abbeville County when the war began. He enlisted as a first lieutenant in Company G of the 1st South Carolina Rifles in 1861 and then the following year endured an unforgettable baptism of fire at Gaines' Mill and was killed December 13, 1862, at Fredericksburg.

The 1st South Carolina Rifles earned the sarcastic nickname, "the Pound Cake Regiment," because of the light duty that its members enjoyed on Sullivan's Island in 1861 and early 1862. In March of the latter year Higgins and his companions were ordered to Virginia. There they soon got an introduction to the harsh realities of war: 59 percent of those engaged at Gaines' Mill were killed, wounded, or reported missing. More than 100 men were lost at Second Bull Run, and no less than 170 at Fredericksburg. *Photo courtesy of University of South Carolina, Columbia*

WILLIAM W. HIGGINS
carte de visite
Quinby and Company

MAXCY GREGG
carte de visite
Richard Wearn

Maxcy Gregg seemed to lead a charmed life, but his luck ran out at Fredericksburg in December 1862. The death of the wealthy South Carolina bachelor was widely mourned.

Gregg had tied for top honors in his class at South Carolina College, of which his grandfather had been the first president. While practicing law in Columbia, he studied both science and classical literature and also became a major in a South Carolina regiment raised for the Mexican War. He was never in combat, but he was slightly wounded while serving as a second in a duel; the contents of his vest pocket deflected the bullet.

He supported secession at the Nashville convention in 1850 and ten years later was on the committee that drafted the South Carolina secession ordinance. He then commanded a regiment of six-month volunteers on Morris Island during the bombardment of Fort Sumter and eleven days later arrived in Richmond to a hero's welcome, though some of his troops refused to leave South Carolina.

He missed First Bull Run because his regiment's enlistments expired, but he became a brigadier general and was wounded in an attack at White Oak Swamp in the Seven Days. Reinforced, Gregg's brigade fought again at Second Bull Run and Antietam, where his handkerchief once more trapped a bullet. *Photo courtesy of Museum of the Confederacy, Richmond, Virginia*

RICHARD R. KIRKLAND
albumen print

The day after the futile Union charges against the Confederates behind the stone wall on Marye's Heights at Fredericksburg, the Southerners could see and hear thousands of wounded Federals on the field before them. Sgt. Richard R. Kirkland of Company G (Camden Volunteers) in the 2nd South Carolina Infantry, who was only nineteen years of age, asked his general, Joseph B. Kershaw, for permission to carry water to the suffering Federals trapped between the lines. Kershaw had known Kirkland's family in Camden before the war; he agreed, but reluctantly informed the younger man that no white flag could be shown. Assuming the risk of being shot, Kirkland climbed over the wall and spent an hour and a half carrying water to the wounded Federals sprawled thickly on the ground.

Kirkland was not harmed at Fredericksburg, and he was promoted to lieutenant for his performance at Gettysburg just a few months later. Tragically, however, he was mortally wounded in a charge at Chickamauga during September 1863. A marker placed at Fredericksburg by the Camden chapter of the United Daughters of the Confederacy commemorates him as the "Hero of Fredericksburg" and the "Angel of Marye's Heights." A fountain was also built in Camden in memory of Kirkland. *Photo courtesy of University of South Carolina, Columbia*

SAMUEL MCGOWAN
carte de visite

After the tragic death of Maxcy Gregg at Fredericksburg, Samuel McGowan was promoted to command his brigade. The son of Irish Presbyterian immigrants and a graduate of South Carolina College, he had served for thirteen years in the South Carolina House of Representatives and was a delegate to the secession convention. After distinguished service in the Mexican War, he also became a major general in the militia on the eve of the Civil War.

McGowan commanded a brigade during the bombardment of Fort Sumter and served as an aide to Gen. Milledge L. Bonham at First Bull Run, and then took charge of the 14th South Carolina Infantry. He participated in every major engagement of the Army of Northern Virginia from the Seven Days onward, except when he was disabled by wounds received on the Peninsula, at Second Bull Run, Chancellorsville (the first engagement in which he commanded a brigade), and Spotsylvania. He surrendered with his troops at Appomattox. *Photo courtesy of University of South Carolina, Columbia*

ALEXANDER C. HASKELL
copy print

One of the first units engaged at Chancellorsville in May 1863 was Samuel McGowan's South Carolina brigade. Skirmishers from that unit under the command of Capt. Alexander C. Haskell were engaged when Gen. Thomas J. Jackson arrived, and they remained in the forefront of his attack, even after Haskell and McGowan suffered wounds that kept them out of the Gettysburg campaign.

Haskell was one of seven brothers who fought for the South (among whom was William T. Haskell, whose picture is included in this work). He enlisted in 1861, the year after he graduated from South Carolina College, as a lieutenant in Company I, 1st South Carolina Infantry, which was recruited by Maxcy

Gregg. He then was promoted to Gregg's staff as an assistant adjutant general.

Haskell's wound at Chancellorsville was his second; his first came at Fredericksburg in December 1862. He subsequently commanded the 7th South Carolina Cavalry and was wounded for a third time at Cold Harbor when seven balls hit him or his horse. One ball was never removed, but he recovered in ten days and rejoined his unit. In October 1864 he lost his left eye in the fighting along the Darbytown Road, but he was present for the surrender at Appomattox, where he was chosen by Robert E. Lee to lead the cavalry to its final mustering out. *Photo courtesy of University of South Carolina, Columbia*

As the acting commander of the 14th South Carolina Infantry, Maj. Edward Croft led his regiment at Gettysburg and allegedly was the first Confederate to enter that town. Shot on the slopes of Cemetery Hill, he almost died, but he was returned to Virginia in an ambulance with a faithful black servant in attendance.

Born in 1835 in Edgefield County, Croft was a roommate of future governor Hugh S. Thompson at the Citadel and graduated with him from that institution in 1856. Croft then settled near Aiken as a planter, though he remained active in the militia. In 1861 he raised and commanded the Ryan Guards, who became Company H of the 14th South Carolina Infantry.

Croft's company served at Port Royal during November 1861, losing eleven members when a shell exploded in their midst. The company then traveled to Virginia and fought during the Seven Days. Severely wounded at Gaines' Mill on May 27, 1862, Croft was subsequently promoted to major of his regiment.

While convalescing after Gettysburg, Croft was captured but quickly exchanged, and he took command of his regiment once more, now as a lieutenant colonel. He was again wounded at Gravelly Run on March 31, 1865, but he was with his troops at Appomattox. He was one of four brothers who served in the Confederate army. *Photo courtesy of Citadel Archives, Charleston, South Carolina*

EDWARD CROFT
carte de visite
George S. Cook

WILLIAM T. HASKELL
carte de visite
Quinby and Company

Capt. William T. Haskell of Company H in the 1st South Carolina Infantry, mustered by Maxcy Gregg in the summer of 1861, had this photograph taken during February 1863, when he was home with the distasteful duty of chasing deserters. Returning to Virginia, he assumed command of a picked battalion of sharpshooters for Samuel McGowan's brigade. On the evening of July 2, 1863, at Gettysburg, Haskell's troops led the way as the Federals were driven from the road in front of Cemetery Hill. Mortally wounded while deploying his men to hold what they had won, he was buried on the field.

Twenty-six years of age, he was one of seven brothers from Abbeville County who fought for the Confederacy, another one of whom was killed that same month on Morris Island during the Federal campaign against Charleston. Four (including Alexander C. Haskell, whose picture is included in this work) surrendered at Appomattox. William T. Haskell graduated from the University of Virginia in 1860 and then together with his brother Alexander C. Haskell enlisted in Gregg's first regiment of six-month volunteers at the onset of the war. He remained with Gregg after the reorganization of his regiment, fighting on the Peninsula, at Second Bull Run, and at Fredericksburg before accepting command of the sharpshooter battalion. *Photo courtesy of University of South Carolina, Columbia*

JAMES J. PETTIGREW
sixth-plate tintype

On the morning of July 14, 1863, while preparing for a rearguard action at Falling Waters on the Potomac River after the defeat at Gettysburg, Pettigrew was walking with other officers among their troops, who had stacked arms, when they were attacked by Federal cavalry. Mortally wounded, Pettigrew died three days later.

A native of North Carolina, Pettigrew had graduated from the University of North Carolina in 1847 and then settled in Charleston, where he studied law under his cousin, James L. Petigru. After a term in the legislature, he traveled to Italy in 1858 to join the Sardinian army but arrived too late to take part in their war against the Austrians.

After his return to South Carolina in 1859, he was elected colonel of the 1st Regiment of Rifles in the state militia. He occupied Castle Pinckney after Maj. Robert Anderson's withdrawal to Fort Sumter. He then was ordered to Morris Island and finally to Sullivan's Island. Following the fall of Sumter, he raised a regiment for Confederate service, but authorities in Richmond refused to accept it. He briefly joined Hampton's Legion and then accepted command of a North Carolina infantry regiment. Promoted to brigadier general in February 1862, he was shot, bayoneted, and captured at Seven Pines. Exchanged, he was again wounded while leading Henry Heth's division in "Pickett's Charge." *Photo courtesy of University of North Carolina, Chapel Hill*

DANIEL H. HAMILTON
carte de visite

After the bitter defeat at Gettysburg, declining morale took its toll on the Army of Northern Virginia. Among the South Carolina officers who left was Col. Daniel H. Hamilton, who had played an active role in the war from the outset. A former U. S. marshal for the District of Columbia, Hamilton served as an envoy from Gov. Francis W. Pickens to Pres. James Buchanan and then became lieutenant colonel of Maxcy Gregg's six-month regiment of volunteers. Later he commanded the 1st South Carolina Infantry, which Gregg also recruited and which served for the duration in Samuel McGowan's brigade.

When numerous recommendations for his promotion to brigadier general were rejected, including a petition endorsed by the South Carolina congressional delegation, Hamilton in late June 1863 took a leave of absence, ostensibly due to malaria. After Gettysburg, he was assigned at his own request to command the troops on Sullivan's Island. In the fall of 1863 he asked to have his regiment transferred to him. He argued that volunteer recruitment and conscription had failed to refill its ranks, which had been reduced to a third of their original number, but that if his regiment were posted in its home state, more men would enlist. Upon Robert E. Lee's advice, Hamilton's request was denied, and so he resigned from his command in January 1864. *Photo courtesy of University of South Carolina, Columbia*

ALESTER G. TRADEWELL
sixth-plate ambrotype

During the winter of 1863–1864, the Federal forces constantly pressed the Confederate defenders of Richmond. Corp. Alester G. Tradewell, a member of Company B in the Cavalry Battalion of the Holcombe Legion, was captured on January 19, 1864, in James City County and was imprisoned at Fort Monroe and Point Lookout.

This image was taken by an unknown photographer in 1862, the same year that Tradewell enlisted as a private in Company B at the age of eighteen. He was promoted to corporal during the fall of 1862 and assigned to work as a clerk for Gen. Arnold Elzey in Richmond, but he returned to active service in April 1863.

While Tradewell was imprisoned, his unit became Company D of the 7th South Carolina Cavalry after the Holcombe Battalion and other commands were consolidated during March 1864. After he was exchanged in November 1864, he returned to active duty and served with his new regiment, which was among the last to leave Richmond in April 1865, and surrendered at Appomattox. *Photo courtesy of the University of South Carolina, Columbia*

MICAH JENKINS
copy print

While preparing for a counterattack in the Wilderness on May 6, 1864, Gen. Micah Jenkins was accidentally shot by Confederate troops. He lingered for a few hours, deliriously urging his men forward, and then expired. His corps commander, James Longstreet, who was wounded at Jenkins' side, recalled that he was one of the most highly regarded officers in the Army of Northern Virginia.

Born on Edisto Island in 1835, Jenkins graduated first in his class from the Citadel. With Asbury Coward, he established the King's Mountain Military School and then was elected colonel of the 5th South Carolina Infantry. His troops served at First Bull Run in David R. Jones' brigade, and then Jenkins organized the "Palmetto Sharpshooters" from among transfers of his own and other South Carolina regiments.

He was praised for his performance on the Peninsula (where he briefly led Richard H. Anderson's brigade), and he became a brigadier general in July, taking over Jones' command after he was promoted. Badly wounded at Second Bull Run, Jenkins quickly recovered and fought at Fredericksburg. His brigade remained in southeastern Virginia during the Gettysburg campaign, but they marched to Tennessee under Longstreet during the fall of 1863. Jenkins again temporarily commanded a division at Knoxville, but after returning to Virginia, he led a brigade in the Wilderness. *Photo courtesy of Library of Congress, no. USZ62-62493*

100

Brig. Gen. Abner Perrin allegedly declared that he would come out of the fighting at Spotsylvania as a "live major general or a dead brigadier."[9] Tragically, it was as the latter; he was shot seven times while leading a counterattack on horseback into the salient known as the Mule Shoe on May 12, 1864.

Perrin was a captain in the 14th South Carolina Infantry commanded by Samuel McGowan during the disastrous engagement with Federal forces at Port Royal in 1861. Although his prior military experience consisted only of a stint as a lieutenant in a regular army regiment during the Mexican War (on the eve of the war he was practicing law in Columbia), he led his company in the Seven Days, at Cedar Mountain, Second Bull Run, Harper's Ferry, Sharpsburg, and Fredericksburg.

Promoted to colonel of the 14th South Carolina in February 1863, he assumed command of the brigade when McGowan was wounded in the Battle of Chancellorsville and led them at Gettysburg, where his troops, the first to enter the town, remained at the foot of Cemetery Hill for the rest of the battle. Confirmed as a brigadier the following September, he won recognition for his performance in the Wilderness, a week before he was killed. *Photo courtesy of Library of Congress, no. B812-292*

Abner M. Perrin
copy print

Enrolled at the age of twenty-eight as a lieutenant in Company F, 1st South Carolina Rifles, George W. Fullerton, a native of Pickens County working as a clerk at Pendleton in 1860, became the captain of his company in June 1862, after his predecessor was killed during the Seven Days. He led his company at Second Bull Run and then was wounded on December 13, 1862, of that year at Fredericksburg and hospitalized.

A few months later he futilely petitioned James L. Orr, his former commander (now serving in Congress), to secure a position for him in the Treasury Department because his failing health could no longer endure military service. Fullerton returned to duty with his regiment, which again suffered severe casualties in the fighting at Chancellorsville and took part in the debacle at Gettysburg. A dozen members of the regiment were killed during the Wilderness campaign; among them was Fullerton, who died on May 12, 1864, at Spotsylvania. *Photo courtesy of University of South Carolina, Columbia*

GEORGE W. FULLERTON
carte de visite

While the Army of Northern Virginia fought in the Wilderness, a smaller force of Confederates blocked a Federal thrust at Petersburg. Among the South Carolinians killed at Drewry's Bluff on May 16, 1864, was John L. Hart, a planter and former carriage maker from Darlington County who was serving as a lieutenant in Company B (Wild's Rifles) of the 21st South Carolina Infantry. This unit originally mustered during November 1861 in the Pee Dee region of South Carolina, and it had remained on the coast of its home state until it was transferred to Virginia as part of Johnson Hagood's brigade before the fight at Drewry's Bluff.

Hart, who was active in the militia, originally enlisted as a sergeant at Darlington on Christmas Day in 1861, when he was thirty-six years of age, but he became a lieutenant when his company mustered the following month. An ardent Baptist who was always trying to convert his comrades, Hart was absent on sick leave or on detached service as an overseer of the slaves working for the engineers at Fort Johnson on James Island for almost all of 1862 and 1863, while his unit served in Battery Wagner. He rejoined his regiment in January 1864 and was present when they were sent from Charleston to Virginia. His troops participated in the repulse of two Union assaults at Walthall Junction on May 6 and then marched to Drewry's Bluff. *Photo courtesy of Darlington County Historical Society, Darlington, South Carolina*

JOHN L. HART
copy print

A native of Colleton and a graduate of the Citadel, Capt. Thomas E. Raysor of the 11th South Carolina Infantry, assigned to Johnson Hagood's brigade, survived the fighting at Drewry's Bluff but was captured in June during the continuous struggle for the defenses of Petersburg. After an involuntary tour of many of the detention centers for prisoners of war maintained by Federal authorities in the east, he was finally imprisoned at Fort Delaware until the end of the war.

Raysor had graduated from the Citadel during 1861,

at the age of twenty-one, and enlisted at Hilton Head as a lieutenant in Company H of the 11th South Carolina Infantry. A year later he was elected captain of his company, which fought at Pocotaligo in October 1862 and then campaigned in north Florida and served during the siege of Charleston in 1863. In early 1864 they were sent to Virginia as part of Hagood's brigade to bolster the defenses of Richmond. *Photo courtesy of Citadel Archives, Charleston, South Carolina*

Cavalry units as well as infantry were transferred from South Carolina to Virginia in the spring of 1864. Equipped primarily with Enfield rifles, the South Carolina troopers usually fought dismounted. Their rapid, accurate firing convinced many Union officers that they faced infantry, but at the same time the relatively immobile Confederates also suffered heavy casualties.

William L. Kirkland enlisted in November 1862 at Pocotaligo as a private in the Charleston Light Dragoons, an independent cavalry company that was incorporated into the 4th South Carolina Cavalry as Company K during December 1862. They were sent in the spring of 1864 to Virginia, where they joined the brigade commanded by Matthew C. Butler, a South Carolinian feared by the Federals for his hard-hitting tactics.

Soon after their arrival in Virginia, portions of the 4th South Carolina Cavalry and other Confederate units were attacked by Union troopers at Haw's Shop on May 28, 1864. The Southerners suffered substantial casualties and grudgingly gave ground after Federal reinforcements arrived. Of the thirty-six members of the Charleston Light Dragoons present, half were killed or wounded. Kirkland's femur was fractured by a minié ball; he survived an amputation but died three weeks later, at the age of thirty-six. *Photo courtesy of University of South Carolina, Columbia*

William L. Kirkland
carte de visite
Quinby and Company

During the evening of June 11, 1864, the first day of the cavalry battle at Trevilian Station in Virginia, Sgt. Maj. James O. Sheppard became convinced that he would be killed the next day. He sought out a friend and made him promise to make sure that his horse was returned to his father in South Carolina. Just as he had anticipated, Sheppard was killed on June 12.

Sheppard was one of the thirty-six Citadel cadets who left that institution in June 1862 and, the next month, organized as the 16th Battalion, South Carolina Partisan Rangers. Twenty years old at the time, Sheppard had studied for two and one-half years before deciding to join the army along with his classmates. In the fall of 1862 other companies were added to create the 6th South Carolina Cavalry.

Sheppard was promoted from corporal to sergeant major during early 1863 while his company was still in South Carolina, where it fought with Federal gunboats and troops along the coast, but his application for a commission as lieutenant, which Johnson Hagood endorsed, was ignored. In the summer of 1864 the regiment was sent to Virginia, where the members of the Cadet Company, in which Sheppard served, participated in many of the major cavalry engagements of that theater, including the battle in which their sergeant major lost his life. *Photo courtesy of U.S.A.M.H.I.*

JAMES O. SHEPPARD
carte de visite
Quinby and Company

The grandson and namesake of the South Carolina statesman, John C. Calhoun of the 4th South Carolina Cavalry was singled out in a memoir written by Gen. Matthew C. Butler for his role in recapturing wagons taken by Union troopers led by Gen. George A. Custer during the fighting at Trevilian Station in June 1864.

Calhoun had originally enrolled as a lieutenant in the 10th Battalion of South Carolina Cavalry. He became captain of his company and then remained at that rank after his troops joined with others during late 1863 to create the 4th South Carolina Cavalry. Transferred in 1864 from South Carolina to Virginia, Calhoun's regiment was assigned to Butler's brigade.

Two months after Trevilian Station, during August 1864, the young captain was hospitalized with gonorrhea and "contusio"; he remained confined until he was given leave to return home with broken-down horses in December 1864. On April 3, 1865, a letter from the head-quarters of the 4th South Carolina Cavalry asked Calhoun to return to duty, which seemed unlikely in light of his persistent illness, or to resign. Otherwise, a superior would be under the "harmful necessity of requiring that you be dropped in accordance with instructions from Brig. Hd. qrs. as your place needs to be filled." There is no record of a reply. *Photo courtesy of University of North Carolina, Chapel Hill*

JOHN C. CALHOUN
carte de visite
Quinby and Company

STEPHEN ELLIOTT, JR.
carte de visite

On July 30, 1864, two South Carolina regiments under the command of Stephen Elliott, Jr., became the victims of a Union mine that exploded underneath their trenches at Petersburg. Many South Carolinians were literally buried, and Elliott was wounded while leading a counterattack to establish a new defensive perimeter.

The son and namesake of an Episcopal bishop (who served as chaplain of the 11th South Carolina Infantry), Elliott graduated from South Carolina College and managed a plantation at Beaufort, where he was born, before the war. He commanded the Beaufort Volunteer Artillery, which was organized during the Revolution, when the war began. They served during the bombardment of Fort Sumter and then were sent to Port Royal where twelve men, including Elliott, were wounded during the Union attack in November 1861.

Remaining upon the South Carolina coast, he led a number of raids, sank a Federal vessel with a mine, and, using his guns, captured the USS *George Washington*, a steamer, in April 1863. In September 1863 he took command of Fort Sumter, where he remained until the next May, when he went to Virginia as the commander of the Holcombe Legion. Promoted to brigadier general, he was given Nathan G. Evans' old brigade at Petersburg.

Elliott went home to recuperate but took charge of a brigade created to oppose William T. Sherman's invasion of the Carolinas. He surrendered with Joseph E. Johnston's army during April 1865. This photograph was "recolored" by William P. Hix, a photographer associated with Richard Wearn in Columbia. *Photo courtesy of University of South Carolina, Columbia*

While the survivors of two South Carolina regiments scrambled out of the Crater, and Gen. Stephen Elliott, Jr., struggled to organize a counterattack to repulse a Union charge, Maj. Wade Hampton Gibbes and a subordinate manhandled a gun into position and disrupted a Federal column with enfilading fire. Gibbes was seriously wounded, but his efforts won time for the Confederates. The son of South Carolina surgeon general Robert W. Gibbes, the younger Gibbes was a former student at the Citadel and an 1860 graduate of West Point who resigned his commission as a cavalry lieutenant in January 1861. This portrait was obviously taken of him during 1860, because he is wearing the uniform of a lieutenant in the U. S. Army.

He commanded the mortar battery posted on James Island during the bombardment of Fort Sumter and then was sent to western Virginia. He was assigned to Norfolk in 1862 and by the summer of 1863 he was a major in charge of the artillery at Wilmington, North Carolina. Returning to northern Virginia, he commanded a Virginia artillery battalion during the Petersburg campaign in 1864. A classmate of George A. Custer at West Point, Gibbes escorted Custer when he presented his surrender demand to Gen. James Longstreet at Appomattox and was scornfully rejected. *Photo courtesy of University of South Carolina, Columbia*

Wade Hampton Gibbes
albumen print
W. H. Allen, Lawrence, Massachusetts

Disease exacerbated the losses suffered by the Army of Northern Virginia during the summer of 1864. Not a few veteran combat officers spent those critical months in the hospitals around Richmond or at home, suffering from illnesses that accomplished what Federal bullets had not been able to do.

Andrew H. Ramsay, a native of Scotland, was a forty-year-old postmaster at Edgefield in 1860. He enrolled as a lieutenant in Company E of the 1st South Carolina Rifles during July 1861, and he became captain of his company in August 1862 after it had suffered heavy losses at Gaines' Mill and Second Bull Run.

He led his company during the Maryland campaign and at Fredericksburg in 1862 and during the operations of 1863. He returned late from a furlough in April 1864, presumably after his fourth and last child was born, and was charged with being absent without leave. When he tendered his resignation, it was accepted but later rejected, so he returned to active duty. However, he was in the hospital at Richmond or on sick leave during most of the summer of 1864, suffering from general debility (dyspepsia and chronic dysentery). *Photo courtesy of University of South Carolina, Columbia*

ANDREW H. RAMSAY
carte de visite
Quinby and Company

110

As the South Carolina units were depleted in the savage fighting before Petersburg in the summer of 1864, new recruits were sent forward as quickly as they could be enlisted. Thomas J. Holland enlisted during July 1864, prior to his eighteenth birthday, as a private in Company G of the 2nd South Carolina Reserves and then was transferred to Company F, 7th Battalion, South Carolina Infantry (Enfield Rifles), under the command of Maj. James H. Rion. This unit was then in Virginia as part of Johnson Hagood's brigade.

Holland joined his new company in the trenches at Petersburg and quickly found himself involved in heavy fighting. Of 175 men in the battalion who charged the Union positions along the Weldon Railroad on August 21, 124 were killed, wounded, or captured; more were lost in other desperate engagements at Fort Harrison and on the Darbytown Road during September and October.

In November 1864 the battalion was sent to North Carolina along with the remainder of Hagood's brigade. More defeats at Wilmington, Kinston, and Bentonville reduced the brigade to about 500 effectives, or less than one-fourth of its original number. The remnant, including Holland, was consolidated into a small regiment under Rion's command and was paroled at Greensboro in May 1865. *Photo courtesy of U.S.A.M.H.I.*

THOMAS J. HOLLAND
copy print

GOODMAN JEFFERIES
carte de visite
George S. Cook

Ordered by Pres. Jefferson Davis to make one last offensive effort to break the siege at Petersburg, Gen. Robert E. Lee issued directions that led to the abortive Confederate assault at Fort Stedman on March 25, 1865. The initial charge reached the Federal lines, but a counterattack trapped a number of Lee's men before they could retreat. Lee lost about 3,500 troops, more than half of whom were captured. The attempt did not slow the tightening of the Union grip on the Confederate capital.

Among those taken prisoner at Fort Stedman was Capt. Goodman Jefferies, a prosperous slaveholder from Union County who had advanced from first lieutenant to captain of Company F in the 18th South Carolina Infantry. He mustered his company himself in December 1861 in "Davises Old Field" in Union County and then became their captain in September 1862 after his predecessor died. The regiment served on the South Carolina coast until the spring of 1864, when it was ordered to Virginia.

During the siege operations before Petersburg, Jefferies was hospitalized for a fever. He then rejoined his company in time for the assault on Fort Stedman. He was imprisoned at Old Capitol Prison and then at Fort Delaware until after the end of the war. *Photo courtesy of University of South Carolina, Columbia*

The last Confederate units to leave Richmond during April 1865, making their way through milling throngs of distraught citizens as the city burned, were the 7th South Carolina Cavalry and some detachments of Hampton's Legion, under the overall command of Martin W. Gary. Among the troopers in the ranks of the 7th South Carolina Cavalry was Aaron D. Burton, a native of Newberry County who, in December 1861, had joined Cavalry Company C (Newberry Rangers) of the Holcombe Legion, which in 1864 became Company E of the 7th South Carolina Cavalry in Gary's brigade.

Burton had endured hard and frequent fighting in his career as a cavalryman, which soon would be over. In the fall of 1862 he suffered the indignity of being sent home to South Carolina to procure a new horse, his own having been captured. He emerged unscathed from the bloody skirmishing before Petersburg in May 1864 and then was wounded at Cold Harbor. Still only a private, he recovered and rejoined his company in time to surrender with the Army of Northern Virginia at Appomattox. *Photo courtesy of Gary Tarpley*

AARON D. BURTON
copy print

Chapter 4

Implementing the Anaconda Plan: Port Royal and Charleston, 1861–1863

Soon after the Civil War began, the Federal government initiated its "Anaconda Plan" to starve the South into submission. Such a strategy entailed the capture of points along the southern coast where Union blockaders could be refitted, as well as the closure of principal ports. A planning board, chaired by Rear Adm. Samuel F. Du Pont, advised the acquisition of Port Royal, South Carolina, for the South Atlantic fleet, as well as the closing of Charleston. During November 1861 Du Pont led a successful attack on Port Royal that began with a naval bombardment to reduce shore fortifications and ended with a landing by troops. Subsequent attempts to take Charleston by similar methods, however, failed utterly and Du Pont resigned, having accomplished only a portion of what his planners had envisioned at the outset of the war.

Gen. Thomas F. Drayton—a West Point graduate who had left the army before the war to manage several plantations, including his ancestral home of Fish Hall on Hilton Head Island—commanded the Confederate defenses at Port Royal. He located his headquarters near Fort Walker, which was built on Hilton Head less than a mile from Fish Hall

and boasted twenty-three guns. Across the sound, on Phillip's Island, was Fort Beauregard, which mounted twenty guns. Together these two makeshift fortifications were expected to defend the waterways and the Charleston and Savannah Railroad. Drayton was the president of the latter and had supervised the construction of that important link between the two port cities. Now, wearing a military uniform once more, he was responsible for preventing the Federals from capturing or damaging that line.

On November 7, 1861, a Union fleet of seventeen ships moved into Port Royal Sound. Their commander, Du Pont, was aboard the lead ship, the USS *Wabash*, a steam frigate carrying 46 guns, more than both of the Confederate forts combined. Ironically, General Drayton's brother, Percival Drayton, captained another Union warship, the USS *Pocahontas*. The Federal vessels, which carried approximately 175 guns, circled, firing three broadsides apiece into Forts Walker and Beauregard—commanded by Colonels William C. Heyward and Robert G. M. Dunovant, respectively. The Federals then withdrew for a long-range bombardment, out

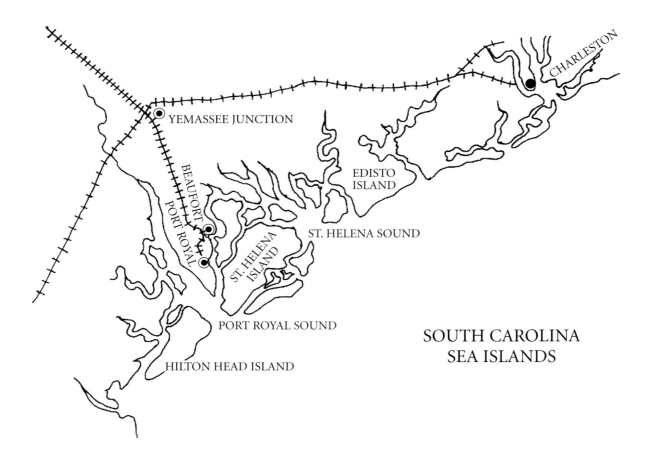

of reach of most of the Confederate artillery. After four hours of gunfire, during which the *Wabash* alone fired almost nine hundred shots, General Drayton ordered Heyward to abandon Fort Walker, which was being battered by enfilading fire from three Union ships, one of which was the *Pocahontas.* Dunovant soon followed suit with the garrison at Fort Beauregard.

The capture of Port Royal provided the Federals with a base for operations along the South Carolina coast. Transports unloaded more than twelve thousand troops commanded by Gen. Thomas W. Sherman, who established his headquarters on Hilton Head. Of these, only the 79th New York Infantry had been in combat, and that was at the Union defeat at First Bull Run. Their original colonel had been killed in that battle, and their new commander, Gen. Isaac I. Stevens, had been recently promoted to command the 2nd Brigade. In spite of their inexperience, the Federal numbers impressed the Confederates, who quickly abandoned the surrounding area. An arsenal at Beaufort was destroyed by a Union landing party on November 9, 1861, and the 2nd Brigade under Stevens returned to occupy the town on December 11. They found the town deserted except for a white man who was either drunk or demented; a Union officer recalled that he "seemed quite dazed."[1]

Sherman hesitated to move inland, in part because of inadequate water transport, but on the night of December 31, 1861, Stevens' 2nd Brigade, supplemented by the 47th and 48th New York Infantry and an assortment of volunteers, made their way around Port Royal Island, traveling in abandoned planters' flatboats and escorted by four warships. The Union troops pushed aside the

Confederates positioned to resist their landing on the mainland and then halted. Their orders did not authorize a raid upon the Charleston and Savannah Railroad. After setting some houses afire with shells from the escorting warships, the Federals retired, carrying with them four dead and seventeen wounded.

Such operations, minor as they were in scope, were still nerve-wracking to the Confederate officer assigned to defend the South Carolina coast. In November 1861, after a disastrous campaign in western Virginia, Gen. Robert E. Lee superseded Gen. Roswell S. Ripley as commander of the coastal defenses of South Carolina, taking charge of those in Georgia and eastern Florida as well. Lee established his headquarters at Coosawhatchie, at the head of the Broad River upon the Charleston and Savannah Railroad, which he intended to defend from the Federals downriver at Beaufort. He divided the coastline into five districts and assigned them to Generals Ripley, Drayton, Arthur M. Manigault, Nathan G. Evans, and John C. Pemberton.

Lee's subordinates commanded perhaps seventeen thousand troops, with which they had to defend the entire South Carolina coast. Lee realized that to hold every island and inlet was impossible, so, with the support of the government in Richmond, he ordered all sea-island garrisons back to the mainland (thus abandoning many estates and making inland refugees of their residents) and began preparing a defense of key points and interior lines. He labored tirelessly, directing the strengthening of forts such as Sumter and Moultrie and the blocking of river mouths so that Federals could not use the waterways to reach inland railroads such as the Charleston and Savannah, which Lee intended to use to convey his scanty troops to any point that was threatened.

Reassigned to other duties in Richmond, Lee left South Carolina on March 3, 1862. He had constructed many new fortifications and raised a substantial number of troops, but he realized that there was, as he wrote to his wife during February 1862, "more here than I can do, & more, I fear, than I can well accomplish."[2] He was frustrated by the continual raids of the Federals based at Port Royal on the surrounding coast; with the small number of men available to him and the length of the convoluted shoreline, he could do nothing to prevent the raiding. He left the headaches and frustrations of defending South Carolina in the hands of Pemberton as the new commander of the department.

After capturing Port Royal, Federal strategists in South Carolina began to discuss the capture of Charleston itself. The city had little intrinsic military importance, apart from the use of its harbor by blockade runners, but its fall would have been a great propaganda victory because it was considered the locus of the secession movement. Beginning in 1862, the Federal government exerted a great deal of effort to take the port, but the number of men and ships devoted to the task never proved to be enough.

Much of the reason for Charleston's impregnability lies in its location. The city is situated between the Ashley and Cooper rivers. Its harbor stretches to the east, bounded on the south by James Island, whose Atlantic side is screened by Morris and Folly islands. Morris Island's northern tip marks the southern extremity of the entrance into Charleston harbor; the northern limit is marked by Sullivan's Island. Midway between these two points is Fort Sumter, on a small artificial island in the main channel leading into the harbor. Defensive installations on Sullivan's, James, and Morris islands, as well as in the city itself, had made it relatively easy to surround Fort Sumter with artillery and compel the surrender of its Federal garrison in April 1861. Supplemented with other fortifications, these posts amid a tangle of waterways and swamps presented Union attackers with a series of almost insurmountable obstacles.

Initially, Federal efforts focused on closing Charleston harbor. At the beginning of the war, there were six channels through which ships could reach the wharves. Several of these were soon blocked with defenders' obstructions, but others remained open. On December 20, 1861, exactly one year after South Carolina left the Union, the Federals sank twenty-five old whaling ships filled with blocks of granite in an ill-advised attempt to obstruct the main channel. Lee angrily reported that, "This achievement, so unworthy any nation, is the abortive expression of the malice and revenge of a people which they wish to perpetuate by rendering more memorable a day hateful in their calendar."[3] During late January the Federals sank more stone-filled vessels in Moffit's Channel. Like the first group, these hulks also disintegrated in the strong submarine currents, providing no obstacle to ships attempting to enter the harbor.

Closing Charleston harbor was left to the Union fleet. They had some success; a Charleston vessel, the *General Parkhill*, was the first blockade runner captured during the Civil War—on May 15, 1861, as she made an approach to her home port. However, most of the runners learned to enter the harbor along its northern side through the Beach Channel, close to Sullivan's Island under the guns of Fort Moultrie and other batteries. Steaming full-speed in the darkness to evade Union patrols, a number of vessels ran aground on Sullivan's Island, but most of them slid safely into the harbor. Blockade running at Charleston was mostly done by small vessels owned by companies operating in that city, which had the greatest number of such firms of any Southern city. George A. Trenholm of Charleston became the most profitable and influential sponsor of blockade runners in the South, and his financial acumen was recognized when he was appointed secretary of the treasury for the Confederacy in July 1864.

Charleston and Wilmington remained the chief refuges for blockade runners along the Atlantic coast until late in the war. Trade at the former city declined during the Union campaigns in the summer of 1863, but revived a year later. The Richmond *Dispatch* in late 1864 reported that in just two months 6 million pounds of meat, 2 million pounds of saltpeter, 1.5 million pounds of lead, 546,000 pairs of shoes, 316,000 blankets, 69,000 rifles, and 43 cannon had been imported through Charleston and Wilmington. The closing of the latter port, where most blockade runners operated, in January 1865 renewed interest in Charleston, but it was too late.

The Confederate defenders of Charleston realized that the failure of Union efforts to close the harbor meant that attempts to take the city itself would be made. After Pemberton assumed command, many South Carolina units were sent to Virginia or Mississippi to reinforce Confederate armies there. Frustrated by the reduction of his forces, Pemberton in late April 1862 elected to commit the majority of his remaining troops to a defense of Charleston. He abandoned the defensive works at the mouth of the Stono River, south of Charleston, and at the harbor of Georgetown, to the north of the port city, and assigned only a few companies of cavalry to defend the Charleston and Savannah Railroad. James Island became the key to defending Charleston, and Pemberton strengthened his lines at that point.

Stevens learned of Pemberton's withdrawals and urged Sherman to act, but Sherman did nothing. Gen. David Hunter replaced Sherman as the commander of the Department of the South during April 1862. He brought reinforcements and transports with him and made plans to attack Charleston. On May 13, 1862, the black crew members of the CSS *Planter*, led by Robert Smalls, piloted the little steamer out of Charleston harbor and turned it over to the Federals, along with information about Confederate positions in the area. Smalls, as pilot of the *Planter*, did good service in the Union fleet. One of his first duties was to lead the way as Union warships on May 20, 1862, took possession of the mouth of the Stono River. By early June, divisions led by Stevens and Gen. Horatio G. Wright, under the overall direction of

Gen. Henry W. Benham as the commander of the northern district of the Department of the South, had landed on the southern end of James Island, where they were protected by gunboats in the Stono River.

The Union troops on James Island endured Confederate raids and long-range artillery fire while their commanders bickered. The 100th Pennsylvania Infantry of Stevens' division were the first to encounter the Confederates. On June 3 they were attacked by South Carolinians commanded by Lt. Col. Ellison Capers. The Confederates drove the Federals back, but reinforcements from the 28th Massachusetts Infantry and the 8th Michigan Infantry forced Capers to retire. In the meantime, Stevens and Benham argued. Stevens participated in this operation, which was Benham's idea, despite grave misgivings and his own preference for launching an attack to sever the Charleston and Savannah Railroad, for which he had been preparing for months. Stevens had no confidence in either Benham or Hunter, both of whom were superior to him in rank. In a letter to his wife he referred to them as "imbeciles" and further denigrated Benham as "an ass—a dreadful man, of no earthly use except as a nuisance and an obstruction."[4]

Benham insisted upon a frontal assault on the Confederate lines, and he outranked Stevens. At dawn on June 16, 1862, six Union infantry regiments attacked a small earthwork at Secessionville, which anchored the left end of the Confederate defenses on James Island. Pemberton had methodically reinforced his posts after the Federals landed. The Confederate commander at Secessionville, Col. Thomas G. Lamar, had portions of his 2nd South Carolina Artillery and the 22nd South Carolina Infantry, along with the Charleston and Pee Dee battalions, in his earthwork. In nearby supporting positions were the 24th and 25th South Carolina Infantry, as well as companies from Johnson Hagood's 1st South Carolina Infantry and Louisiana and Georgia detachments.

The Federal assault column at Secessionville was led by the 8th Michigan Infantry, followed by the 7th Connecticut, 28th Massachusetts, 100th Pennsylvania, 79th New York, and 46th New York. Lamar himself aimed and fired a 10-inch Columbiad, whose load of canister tore a tremendous hole in the Union ranks. The Federals still pressed on, reaching the earthwork and engaging in hand-to-hand combat, during which Lamar was seriously wounded, before being repulsed. At the same time, an advance by infantry companies from the 3rd New Hampshire, 45th Pennsylvania, 97th Pennsylvania, 6th Connecticut, and 47th New York, as well as the 3rd Rhode Island Heavy Artillery and the 1st New York Engineers, was driven back by a counterattack organized by Hagood. The Federal forces at Secessionville suffered 683 casualties, many of them lost to friendly fire from Federal gunboats along the Stono River. The Confederates lost less than a third of that number. Federal casualties in certain units were horrifying: the 8th Michigan Infantry lost 185 of 534 engaged, while the 79th New York lost 110 of 484.

Benham had ordered the disastrous attack on Secessionville in defiance of orders not to conduct an offensive and despite the protests of Stevens and others. Hunter ordered his arrest for disobedience, and Abraham Lincoln revoked Benham's commission as a brigadier general. Although Benham was later reinstated, he was not allowed to resume a field command. Hunter evacuated James Island by the end of June, convinced that the Confederate defenses could not be taken with the men he had. In July 1862, Stevens and his 2nd Brigade were transferred to Virginia, where he was killed while leading his beloved 79th New York Infantry in a rearguard action at Chantilly in September. He was carried from the field by men of the 79th New York Infantry and 28th Massachusetts Infantry, both of which had fought, against his wishes, on James Island in June.

The transfer of Stevens' 2nd Brigade and other

Union troops from South Carolina refocused attention on the recruitment of local blacks into the Union army. After the Federal occupation of Port Royal, thousands of blacks made their way to Union lines. Sherman had been authorized to arm the males for military service, but he chose not to do so. Instead, able-bodied blacks were put to work gathering contraband left by whites who had fled, including a crop of sea island cotton worth hundreds of thousands of dollars. After Hunter, a dedicated abolitionist, succeeded Sherman, he declared on May 9, 1862, that South Carolina, Georgia, and Florida were under military law and that all slaves in these states were free. Three days later, he began recruiting the 1st South Carolina Colored Infantry from among the sometimes reluctant blacks on the coast, for which an executive order from Jefferson Davis provided that Hunter would be executed if captured. The Radicals in Congress supported Hunter's bold move, but President Lincoln did not, and the involuntary enlistments alienated much of the black community as well as the white superintendents assigned to care for them. After a single review, the regiment was disbanded on orders from Washington, though a single company remained in camp.

Lincoln refused to endorse the precipitate mustering of a black regiment at gunpoint in South Carolina during the summer of 1862, but mounting casualties increased public support in the North for recruiting freedmen. In October, after the promulgation of the preliminary Emancipation Proclamation, Gen. Rufus Saxton began the recruitment of five thousand black troops at Beaufort. By the first day of December 1862, almost five hundred men had been enlisted into the reconstituted 1st South Carolina Colored Infantry, for which the company from Hunter's original black regiment served as a nucleus. Thomas Wentworth Higginson, formerly a captain in the 51st Massachusetts Infantry, became their colonel. Higginson—a native of Massachusetts, a graduate of Harvard College, and an ordained minister—

had reservations about assuming command of a regiment for which official support could again be withdrawn and which might never be assigned to combat duty. He was, however, a committed abolitionist, and so he became the commander of the first black regiment from South Carolina.

A second regiment of blacks was mustered in South Carolina soon after the first. James Montgomery, a former ally of John Brown, became the colonel of the 2nd South Carolina Colored Infantry, organized in early 1863, and subsequently led one of the most notorious operations undertaken by Union troops on the Atlantic coast: the burning of Darien, Georgia. He loaded five companies of his own regiment, eight companies from the 54th Massachusetts Colored Infantry (accompanied by their colonel, Robert G. Shaw), and the 3rd Rhode Island Artillery on board two transports and a gunboat. As they approached Darien, which was not defended, on June 11, Montgomery told Shaw of his intention to burn the town, just as he had earlier destroyed the community of Ashepoo and the surrounding countryside in South Carolina. Shaw was aghast and refused to participate; only one of his companies took part in the complete destruction of the town. Subsequent protests and expressions of disgust by the Massachusetts colonel were ignored by Hunter, and the controversy ended only after Shaw's death on the parapet of Battery Wagner in July 1863.

Gen. Pierre G. T. Beauregard was sent back to South Carolina during the fall of 1862. He reorganized the coastal garrisons into three districts, commanded by Generals States Rights Gist, Johnson Hagood, and William S. Walker. At the same time, Hunter was replaced as commander of the Department of the South with Gen. Ormsby M. Mitchel. As Stevens had urged months earlier, Mitchel tried to sever the Charleston and Savannah Railroad. On October 22, 1862, about 4,500 Federals led by Gen. John M. Brannan landed at Mackey's Point on the Broad River and marched toward Pocotaligo. They were attacked by a Confederate force of about one-tenth their number, commanded by Walker. The latter was driven back to Pocotaligo, but, reinforced and protected by the deep channel and marshy banks of Pocotaligo Creek, they stood their ground and forced Brannan to withdraw. A Union detachment, ferried to their destination in the *Planter*, did remove a few rails from the railroad before they were chased away by South Carolina cavalry, but little more was accomplished. The Union troops suffered 340 casualties; Walker lost less than half that number.

Beauregard scored other victories against the Federals trying to invest Charleston during the next few months. After Pemberton ordered the removal of Confederate troops from the mouth of the Stono River, Union gunboats patrolled that waterway up to Fort Pemberton, which was on James Island. Beauregard determined to capture at least one of these vessels. Masked batteries—with companies from the South Carolina Siege Train, the Palmetto Light Artillery, and the 1st South Carolina Artillery—were emplaced on the Stono River during the night of January 29, 1863, and two companies from the 20th South Carolina Infantry were assigned to support these guns. On the afternoon of January 30 the USS *Isaac P. Smith,* a veteran of the Port Royal expedition with nine guns, steamed upriver and was caught in a crossfire from the Confederate batteries. Disabled, the ship was surrendered and refitted as the CSS *Stono* and captained by Henry J. Hartstene.

Before dawn on January 31, 1863, the day after the *Isaac P. Smith* was captured, the only Confederate ironclads at Charleston, the CSS *Palmetto State* and the CSS *Chicora,* slipped out of the harbor and attacked the Federal fleet anchored outside. Both of these rams had been constructed in Charleston; the *Palmetto State* mounted three guns, while the *Chicora* had six. The *Palmetto State* damaged a Union steamer, the USS *Mercedita,* by ramming her and then firing a shell into her at close range, forcing the Federals to surrender. The *Chicora* pumped ten shells into the USS *Keystone State,* setting it afire. The remainder of the Union blockaders easily evaded the lumbering Confederate vessels, which triumphantly anchored near the mouth of the harbor to wait for the return of high tide to float them over the bar. The crippled Union vessels were towed to safety so damage to their fleet was minimal, but after this engagement, more ironclads, especially monitors, were hurried south to reinforce the Union blockaders.

The newly arrived Union ironclads received their baptism of fire in April 1863 when the Federal fleet commanded by Du Pont (now an admiral) engaged Fort Sumter in response to ill-advised orders from Washington. Du Pont requested that Hunter—who had resumed command of the Department of the South after Mitchel died of yellow fever at Beaufort on October 30, 1862—occupy Folly and Morris islands while the Union ships assailed the batteries, but that operation was not initiated. Instead, on the afternoon of April 7, Du Pont's warships steamed without support toward Fort Sumter, whose band, at the request of post commander Alfred M. Rhett, serenaded them from the parapet with "Dixie."

The USS *Weehawken,* a monitor, led the attack, pushing a large wooden raft fitted with chains and grappling hooks for detonating torpedoes. After the raft was shot loose from its moorings and the *Weehawken* itself was hit by fifty-three shells, the battered monitor withdrew. The *New Ironsides,* an armored frigate that served as Du Pont's flagship, ran aground, while the *Keokuk* (piloted by Smalls), a lightly armored craft with two fixed turrets, was carried close to Sumter by unexpectedly strong tides. The *Keokuk* challenged Sumter's guns, which were handled by the 1st South Carolina Artillery, for forty minutes and then was scarcely able to steam out of range. Hit ninety times, it sank the next morning near Morris Island, and its two eleven-inch rifles were salvaged by the Confederates.

Du Pont stopped the unequal fighting after two and one-half hours. He reported to Hunter that the monitors were completely useless for assaulting a fort because five of the eight engaged were wholly or partly disabled. At the same time, Confederate losses were slight and their damaged fortifications were repaired within two days. The principal problem was the disparity in firepower: the Union warships fired only 139 shells, while the Confederates estimated that they fired more than 2,200 shells from Fort Sumter and other installations. The monitors were quickly repaired, but Du Pont's mind was made up: they were of little use for offensive maneuvers. He had never approved the harbor assault, and he was determined that he would not again have to participate in such an operation. At his own request he was relieved in July 1863 and departed from the South Carolina theater.

To add insult to the injury of the disaster at Charleston, on the morning of April 9, 1863, the Federal steamer *George Washington* was set afire and destroyed in the Coosaw River by a shot from the Beaufort Volunteer Artillery commanded by Stephen Elliott, Jr. The round, fired from a field-piece wheeled to the edge of the water, pierced the wooden hull of the gunboat and penetrated the boiler. Fire spread rapidly; the white flag was raised and the surviving crew members made their way through neck-deep water to Port Royal Island, where many of them were retrieved from the marshes by members of the 1st South Carolina Colored Infantry.

By the summer of 1863, it had become apparent that Fort Sumter and the other fortifications defending Charleston would not be as easily silenced as those at Port Royal in November 1861. Despite great efforts to recruit a sizable Federal army that included blacks to isolate the port city by cutting its rail lines and to strip Charleston of its defenses by bombardment, little had been accomplished beyond the capture of Port Royal and the raids of Federal forces on the surrounding countryside. Du Pont was not alone in believing that the Confederate installations could not be reduced by naval forces; it would now be left to others to try their luck against the stubborn defenders of Charleston.

THOMAS P. PELOT
copied from illustration for Douglas Featherstone,
"Thomas Postell Pelot: South Carolina Patriot,"
[Columbia, South Carolina] *State Magazine*,
May 30, 1954

At the outset of the war a bitter struggle ensued for control of the southern coastline. One early victory for the Confederacy was won by Thomas P. Pelot, a South Carolina native who commanded the *Lady Davis,* a raider outfitted at Charleston. In May 1861, Pelot's ship, which carried twelve infantrymen under the command of Capt. Stephen Elliott, Jr., captured a larger Union vessel, the *A. B. Thompson,* and brought it into Beaufort, South Carolina.

Appointed to the United States Naval Academy by John C. Calhoun, Pelot was commissioned as an acting midshipman in 1849, prior to his thirteenth birthday. He resigned from the navy in 1861 and took command of the *Lady Davis,* but he was subsequently posted primarily in Savannah. There he commanded the *Savannah, Atlanta, Oconee, Resolute,* and *Georgia*—the last an ironclad. A lieutenant temporarily without a ship during the summer of 1864, he led a boarding party that used rowboats to capture the USS *Water Witch,* a steamer with four guns, on the night of June 3. Pelot was the first to board the Union warship. He bested the Federal captain in a "sword duel," but within minutes the doughty Confederate was shot and killed, though his men took the ship. A colleague wrote, "In his death the country has lost a brave and gallant officer, and society one of her highest ornaments."[5] *Photo courtesy of University of South Carolina, Columbia*

SAMUEL F. DU PONT
copy print

The Federal fleet assigned to blockade the South Carolina coast needed a base for refitting. Flag Officer Samuel F. Du Pont commanded the fleet that successfully reduced the Confederate works at Port Royal on November 7, 1861, and unloaded more than ten thousand troops to occupy the region. Du Pont had chaired the planning committee that selected Port Royal as one of the first sites on the Atlantic coast for an invasion. For the successful culmination of his plans, he was appointed a rear admiral and received the official thanks of Congress.

A nephew of the founder of the well-known U. S. chemical corporation, Du Pont had already served fifty-six years in the U. S. Navy by the time that he led the fleet at Port Royal. He was only twelve years of age when he became a midshipman in 1815. Promoted to captain forty years later, he was in charge of the Philadelphia Navy Yard when the war began.

Next on his list of personal conquests was to have been the capture of Charleston, but the defenses of that harbor proved much more difficult to defeat. When he allowed his fleet of ironclads, in which he had little faith, to challenge Fort Sumter during April 1863, the Union ships were battered and had to withdraw. Du Pont was relieved of command at his own request a few months later, and he served on boards and commissions until his death in June 1865. *Photo courtesy of Library of Congress, Biographical File*

THOMAS F. DRAYTON
carte de visite
George S. Cook

The Civil War deeply divided many families when brothers chose opposing sides. Gen. Thomas F. Drayton was in charge of the defenses at Port Royal; his brother, Percival Drayton, commanded a ship, the USS *Pocahontas*, in the Union fleet that drove the general from his works.

A graduate of West Point, Thomas F. Drayton had left the army in 1836 to manage his plantation in South Carolina. He also served in the militia and legislature and was president of the Charleston and Savannah Railroad, whose construction he directed. Appointed a brigadier general for the Confederacy in September 1861, he commanded the district that included the installations at Port Royal, which were near his plantation and railroad.

After losing Port Royal, Drayton was transferred to Virginia in 1862 and given command of a brigade, which participated in the battles of Thoroughfare Gap, Second Bull Run, South Mountain, and Antietam. Although he had been a classmate of Jefferson Davis at West Point and remained his lifelong friend, his inefficient performance at the latter two engagements could not be ignored, and he was assigned to court-martial duty. Later he was given command of a brigade in the District of Arkansas and supervised the Sub-District of Texas. *Photo courtesy of University of South Carolina, Columbia*

Comdr. Percival Drayton of the USS *Pocahontas* entered the engagement at Port Royal late due to problems with the machinery of his ship. Eager to prove that his delay was not due to a lack of loyalty to the Union, he moved close to Fort Walker while his gunners fired more than seventy enfilading shots in just an hour at the troops led by his brother, Gen. Thomas F. Drayton.

Younger than the general by four years, Commander Drayton had become a midshipman at the New York Naval School in 1827 at the age of fifteen. He rose steadily in rank while serving with the Pacific, Mediterranean, and Brazil squadrons. At the outset of the war he was stationed in Philadelphia, where he had resided for over thirty years and which he considered to be his home. By that time he was noted not only for his leadership, but also for his scholarship, as he had mastered several languages.

After the fall of Port Royal, Commander Drayton remained on duty in South Carolina, participating in the occupation of the Stono River area. During July 1862 he became a captain and took charge of the USS *Passaic*, a monitor, which he commanded in the futile attack on Fort Sumter in April 1863. Highly praised by Federal authorities and condemned by the legislature of his native state for his performance, he left South Carolina when he was assigned as fleet captain of the West Gulf Squadron. *Photo courtesy of National Archives*

PERCIVAL DRAYTON
copy print

Josiah Bedon
copy print

When Federal warships approached Port Royal on November 7, 1861, and began a punishing bombardment of the Confederate defenses, among the units defending Fort Walker was Company C (Summerville Guard) of the 11th South Carolina Infantry, under the command of Capt. Josiah Bedon. After hours of futile defiance, they and other Confederates were withdrawn, and Port Royal was occupied by Union troops.

Bedon subsequently became a first lieutenant in the 2nd Battalion of South Carolina Sharpshooters and served in Virginia until he was wounded in the foot at Seven Pines during May 1862. Reenlisting in Company K (Charleston Light Dragoons) of the 4th South Carolina Cavalry, he remained on the coast of his home state until early 1864, when his unit was ordered to eastern Florida.

He traveled once more to Virginia when his troopers were ordered there in the spring of 1864. After their arrival at Petersburg, they served at Drewry's Bluff on May 16, 1864. Union officers who encountered them were convinced that the 4th South Carolina Cavalry were infantry because they fought dismounted and with Enfield rifles, delivering a terrific volume of fire. Their immobility in battle, however, led to greater casualties. Bedon was killed at Haw's Shop on May 28, just weeks after his return to Virginia. *Photo courtesy of Confederate Relic Room, Columbia, South Carolina*

USS *WABASH*
albumen print

The *Wabash*, technically known as a "screw-frigate," with forty-six guns, served as Flag Officer Samuel F. Du Pont's flagship during the bombardment and occupation of Port Royal in November 1861. The unarmored wooden vessel survived thirty hits from Confederate batteries, which stripped away "everything from her halyard to her spanker boom." At the same time, her crew fired 888 shells at the two Confederate emplacements, many of which passed over their intended targets but enough of which landed to compel a hasty evacuation. Comdr. John Rodgers of the *Wabash* was the first to raise the Union flag over the abandoned headquarters of Gen. Thomas F. Drayton.

The *Wabash* remained on the South Carolina coast after the victory at Port Royal, and it participated in a number of other operations. This photograph was taken from the deck of the USS *Weehawken*, a single-turret monitor, at Port Royal in 1863. *Photo courtesy of U.S.A.M.H.I.*

Enoch Q. Fellows
copy print

When the 3rd New Hampshire Infantry came ashore at Port Royal in November 1861, it was commanded by Enoch Q. Fellows, a former student at West Point who had risen to the rank of brigadier general in the New Hampshire militia. Appointed at the age of thirty-six as colonel of the regiment during August 1861, after serving in a three-month unit, Fellows directed the campaigns of the 3rd New Hampshire on the South Carolina coast for the next five months.

Fellows won a reputation as a strict disciplinarian and became the first commandant of the Federal post on Hilton Head Island, which was occupied soon after the landing at Port Royal. His service in South Carolina was disrupted by the occupation of Edisto Island on March 29, 1862, by Confederates under the command of Nathan G. Evans, who killed or captured about two dozen men from the 55th Pennsylvania Infantry. Fellows posted detachments from his own regiment to secure the island, which they did under his personal command.

In April 1862 Fellows took an extended leave from his duties in South Carolina. He never returned; instead, he resigned to take command of the 9th New Hampshire Infantry at the request of the governor of his home state a few months later. *Photo courtesy of MOLLUS, Mass., U.S.A.M.H.I.*

After the Federals occupied Port Royal and the surrounding area, the harbor proved to be as useful as they had anticipated for sheltering the diverse fleet assembled for the blockade of the southern coastline. In this photograph can be seen three vessels at anchor. Journalist James Gordon Bennett in 1861 donated a 160-ton yacht, the *Rebecca*, to the Federal government for use as a revenue cutter. Outfitted with two bronze 6-pounder rifles and a brass 12-pounder, the vessel was commanded by Bennett's son and namesake, who became a lieutenant in the customs service.

The *Rebecca* was one of the fastest private sailing vessels of the time. When it sailed into Port Royal during February 1862 after a cruise off Long Island, many Union officers mistook it for a bold Confederate blockade runner. They quickly learned their mistake, but their embarrassment was smoothed over by the lavish entertainment and the news from the North provided by those aboard the *Rebecca*, which was photographed at anchor near an unidentified dispatch boat and a monitor of the *Passaic* class. The vessel's career proved short-lived: on April 29, 1862, it was withdrawn from service, and Bennett resigned twelve days later.[6] *Photo courtesy of Library of Congress, no. B8184-7149*

USS *Rebecca* at Port Royal
copy print

FLOATING MACHINE SHOP
albumen print

The Federal government expected to use Port Royal not only as a staging ground for other invasions along the Atlantic coast, but also as a place where the blockading fleet could be maintained or even repaired without returning to a northern port. Part of this effort, which proved successful, was undertaken through the use of floating machine shops such as this one.

Built on two old whaling ships, the *Edward* and the *India*, this rig was photographed at Port Royal in 1863. The two aged hulks were requisitioned by Rear Adm. Samuel F. Du Pont from among those chosen to be filled with stones and sunk in the main channel of Charleston harbor during December 1861. They then were lashed together with chains and anchored. Aboard one was a well-equipped machine shop; on the other were spacious storerooms, furnaces, and crew quarters. This contraption was not attractive and certainly was not seaworthy, but it made it unnecessary for ships in the Union blockading fleet to travel to a northern port for repairs. *Photo courtesy of MOLLUS, Mass., U.S.A.M.H.I.*

JOHN W. PATRICK
carte de visite
George S. Cook

The successful establishment of a Federal enclave on the South Carolina coast at Port Royal forced the enlistment of several militia units into regular Confederate service. John W. Patrick originally joined the Washington Artillery when it was attached to the 4th Brigade, South Carolina Militia, and served on Morris Island at Cumming's Point during the bombardment of Fort Sumter. This company was mustered into regular service during February 1862 at Adams Run, which was located near Charleston.

Patrick and his comrades spent the next three years moving from point to point on the coast south of Charleston, frequently engaging Federal gunboats. In the summer of 1863, shortly after this photograph was taken, Patrick was posted with an advance detachment on John's Island, and then, after the Union drive stalled, he returned to Charleston and was assigned to the quartermaster's department.

Following the evacuation of Charleston in February 1865, he marched with the rest of that city's garrison to North Carolina. He was paroled with the remainder of Gen. Joseph E. Johnston's army at the end of the war. *Photo courtesy of University of South Carolina, Columbia*

On Gregg G. Richards' cap can be seen the crossed cannons and "PG" of the Palmetto Guards, or Company A of the 18th Battalion, South Carolina Infantry, also known as Manigault's Battalion or the South Carolina Siege Train. After the capitulation of Fort Sumter, the Palmetto Guards, which at that time served in the 17th South Carolina Militia, split in two, half going to Virginia and half remaining in South Carolina as a garrison for the captured Federal post. The latter were enlisted into Confederate service at Pocotaligo in February 1862, but they remained on the coast of their home state for most of their term of enlistment.

During Gregg's second year of service his company took part in the capture of the USS *Isaac P. Smith* on January 30, 1863, dueled with the USS *Pawnee* two months later, served on James Island during the Federal operations the following summer, and participated in the abortive attack on the USS *Marblehead* on Christmas Day, 1863. Sent to Florida in February 1864, they returned to the South Carolina coast during April. They fought their last engagement with Federals on James Island on February 10, 1865, and then evacuated the Charleston area with the rest of the garrison a week later and marched to North Carolina. Curiously, Richards was paroled at Hartwell, Georgia, on May 17, 1865. *Photo courtesy of University of South Carolina, Columbia*

Gregg G. Richards
carte de visite
Quinby and Company

133

Capt. Edwin S. Hitchcock led Company G of the 7th New Hampshire Infantry into action on June 16, 1862 at Secessionville. Several hundred yards from the Confederate works his regiment blundered into a ditch that bunched the onrushing troops into a mass that made an easy target for the Southern defenders. The Federals continued forward, however, until ordered to withdraw. Shot in the right thigh and the upper lip, Hancock was "evidently dying when last seen" during the retreat; apparently his body was not recovered, and so he was interred in an anonymous grave.

Hitchcock had enlisted at the age of twenty-seven at New Haven in September 1861 as the captain of Company G of the 7th Connecticut Infantry. His regiment was among those that landed at Port Royal in November 1861 and then conducted reconnaissances to Hilton Head. In early June 1862 they disembarked on James Island where, after two long weeks of enduring constant mosquitoes and sporadic Confederate artillery fire, the Union forces massed for the assault on the earthwork at Secessionville in which Hitchcock was killed. *Photo courtesy of MOLLUS, Mass., U.S.A.M.H.I.*

EDWIN S. HITCHCOCK
albumen print

GEORGE H. DAVIS
copy print

Pvt. George H. Davis of Company I, 3rd New Hampshire Infantry, advanced with his regiment during the assault at Secessionville in June 1862 until they found their way barred by a wide, soft-bottomed creek across their front. Despite repeated attempts, in which they suffered heavy casualties, the members of the 3rd New Hampshire Infantry were unable to reach the Confederate works.

A native of Winchester, New Hampshire, Davis had enlisted in Company I of the 3rd New Hampshire Infantry during August 1861. After his arrival in South Carolina with his regiment at Port Royal in November 1861, Davis saw plenty of action. In addition to the frustrating attack at Secessionville, his regiment also

fought at Pocotaligo the following October. They swept a small Confederate force from the southern tip of Morris Island on July 10, 1863, but they were bloodily repulsed eight days later in the attack on Battery Wagner. They then settled down for an extended siege.

Promoted to corporal, Davis reenlisted on Morris Island in January 1864 and then was transferred with his regiment to Virginia for the Bermuda Hundred campaign, during and after which they served as mounted infantry. Wounded three times in May 1864, he was promoted to sergeant before he was discharged during July 1865 at Goldsboro, North Carolina. *Photo courtesy of U.S.A.M.H.I.*

JOHN M. MOONEY
carte de visite
A. G. Keet, Harrisburg,
Pennsylvania

Pvt. John M. Mooney, a Pennsylvania-born farmer, landed with Company F of the 45th Pennsylvania Infantry on James Island in early June 1862 and then took part in the failed assault on June 16 at Secessionville, where they were repulsed during an attack intended to provide support for the main assault column. They left James Island a few weeks later and did not return before being transferred to Virginia.

Mooney had enlisted at Equinunk as a private in Company F, 45th Pennsylvania Infantry, in October 1861 when he was twenty-one years of age. He emerged unscathed from the fighting on James Island in 1862, but he was shot in the left leg on May 6, 1864, in the Wilderness. He lay on the field untended until the next day and remained in hospitals or at home on furlough until the war's end, though he was officially assigned to the Invalid Corps. *Photo courtesy of U.S.A.M.H.I.*

William McCarty, a native of Pennsylvania, holds the colors of the 97th Pennsylvania Infantry. Stationed at Hilton Head, his regiment took part in the expedition to Florida in the spring of 1862 and then returned to participate in the operations on James Island in the summer of that year. Casualties were light in the preliminary skirmishes on June 10, but the Union troops suffered terribly in the failed assault on Secessionville six days later. By July 7 the 97th Pennsylvania Infantry, together with all other Federal units, had been evacuated from James Island.

McCarty had enlisted at West Chester as a corporal during September 1861 at the age of twenty-five. He did not do well in the James Island campaign and was reduced to the rank of private. He was, however, restored to the rank of corporal in October of that year after being wounded during the late summer. In July 1863 his regiment again ventured onto James Island for a week and then participated in the siege of Battery Wagner that ended successfully in September.

He became a sergeant during December 1864 (and at this time may well have become the color bearer for his regiment). He was wounded once more on January 15, 1865, at Fort Fisher in North Carolina, but he remained in the army and mustered out at Weldon, North Carolina, on August 28, 1865. *Photo courtesy of U.S.A.M.H.I.*

WILLIAM MCCARTY
copy print

CEMETERY AT BEAUFORT, 1862
albumen print

The South Carolina climate proved as deadly for
northern soldiers as bullets fired by Confederate
troops. Many Federals succumbed to a variety of
diseases endemic to the marshy coastal regions;
among them was Gen. Ormsby M. Mitchel, who
served as commander of the Department of the South
for only a few months before he was felled by yellow
fever at Beaufort on October 30, 1862. His body was
taken to New York for burial, but the bodies of many
Union soldiers were interred near where they fell.
This burial ground for United States troops was laid
out in five hours at Beaufort, where there were a
number of military hospitals. The bodies were later
reinterred in the national cemetery at that town.
Photo courtesy of Duke University

WARREN W. STRIBLING
sixth-plate ambrotype

Thousands of South Carolinians volunteered for the Confederate army after the fall of Port Royal and then discovered military life was often tedious. Warren W. Stribling, a thirty-five-year-old slaveowner, considered serving on a privateer but in November 1861 became a lieutenant in James L. Orr's 1st South Carolina Rifles. Within a month his company was reassigned, with others, to the 5th Battalion, South Carolina Rifles, which was reshuffled in the spring of 1862 to become the 2nd South Carolina Rifles.

During this time Stribling was stationed at Charleston with his company. His health declined, and he was made more miserable by homesickness and his concerns for his family. This photograph may be among a group that he mailed to his wife, Emily, after he visited Charleston in December 1861. He wrote to her on February 1, 1862, that he longed "for the time to come when I can say that I am free; if it ever does come I never will be bound again by my own consent."[7]

He remained on the coast through the summer of 1862, but by January 1863 he had become a contractor, repairing rifles for an armory in Athens, Georgia. He still complained about having to drill as a reservist in Company B of the 23rd Battalion, Georgia Infantry, but his employer organized a band and even gave him a clarinet to occupy his idle hours. *Photo courtesy of University of South Carolina, Columbia*

ALFRED J. HILL AND WILLIAM L. DODGE
albumen print
Henry P. Moore

Lt. Alfred J. Hill is in the forefront of this idyllic photograph of camp life for Federal officers at Hilton Head in 1862. A veteran of the Mexican War, in which he was a sergeant in the 9th United States Infantry, Hill forfeited a military pension and enlisted at Concord in August 1861 as the adjutant for the 3rd New Hampshire Infantry. He resigned at North Edisto in April 1862 at the age of fifty-nine, explaining that a fall from his horse had left him virtually an invalid, and that his deteriorating eyesight also hindered his activities.

Behind Hill, in the tent, is Pvt. William L. Dodge, who was about twenty years of age when this photograph was taken. He also enlisted in August 1861 at Concord in Company F of the 3rd New Hampshire Infantry. He was detailed as a clerk in June 1862 on James Island, after his company fought at Secessionville, and then in September was sent to Hilton Head as a recruiter. In January 1863, while still on recruiting duty at Hilton Head, he became a sergeant major, in time for the clash on Morris Island during the summer of that year. He was promoted to lieutenant and assigned to Company F of the 3rd New Hampshire Infantry in January 1864 and then transferred to Company B in May. He was discharged in October 1864 after he contracted malaria at Petersburg. *Photo courtesy of MOLLUS, Mass., U.S.A.M.H.I.*

WILLIAM M. "TUCKER" MAYNADIER
copy print

Some of the Federal officers who enjoyed a quiet tour of duty on the South Carolina coast during the spring of 1862 later found service elsewhere to be much less pleasant. The son of a West Point graduate and career artillery officer, William M. Maynadier was appointed a second lieutenant in Company M of the 1st United States Artillery in May 1861. His father, a native of Maryland, was offered a commission in the Confederate army by Jefferson Davis himself, but he declined and the younger Maynadier followed his example, though many of their relatives fought for the South.

Maynadier was promoted to first lieutenant in Battery K a few months after the war began, and after a quiet term of service in South Carolina, his battery was transferred during early 1863 to Virginia, where he served on detached duty as an ordnance officer. He was detailed briefly to West Point in 1864 and then was captured on June 29, 1864, near Ream's Station, Virginia, along with others in his unit and four of their guns. While in prison he was promoted to captain and given command of Battery C, whose commanding officer had been killed at Cold Harbor. Upon his return to active duty, however, Maynadier was assigned to Benton Barracks, Missouri. *Photo courtesy of MOLLUS, Mass., U.S.A.M.H.I.*

NATHANIEL W. LORD
carte de visite
George S. Cook

Gen. John C. Pemberton assumed command of South Carolina in the spring of 1862 and ordered a contraction of the defensive perimeter at Charleston. The removal of units from forward posts proved more difficult than expected when Union gunboats attacked the withdrawing garrisons. When the Palmetto Guards of the South Carolina Siege Train were ordered to leave Battery Island in late May 1862, they had to flee with their four guns under Federal artillery fire across a causeway to James Island.

Nathaniel W. Lord, who enlisted in March 1862 as a private in Company A (Palmetto Guards), 18th Battalion of South Carolina Artillery, also known as the South Carolina Siege Train, was one of those who made his way to safety through a rain of shells. His company remained at Fort Pemberton for a few months, then camped in Charleston until the next spring, when they again fought with Union gunboats and troops on James Island.

After the Palmetto Guards campaigned in north Florida during the spring of 1864, Private Lord was furloughed upon the orders of a medical review board for 120 days. He was assigned to light duty upon his return and may have avoided the final engagements of his comrades at Charleston because there is no record of his surrender with them. *Photo courtesy of University of South Carolina, Columbia*

Early in the morning of June 16, 1862, Col. Thomas G. Lamar of the 2nd South Carolina Artillery, having supervised work details through most of the night, fell asleep upon the parapet of his earthwork at Secessionville on James Island. He was awakened by a sentinel and discovered that his pickets were being driven by several thousand Union attackers. With no time to issue orders, Lamar woke his sleeping troops by firing a ten-inch Columbiad, whose charge of grapeshot tore a huge hole in the Federal ranks. The Union soldiers were repulsed only after a hand-to-hand fight in which Lamar was shot through the ear and neck.

Lamar, a planter born in Edgefield County who had supported secession as a legislator and served on Morris Island during the bombardment of Fort Sumter, was commended by the Confederate Congress and chose to remain in the army. Interestingly, he was one of three officers detailed to investigate the duel in which Alfred M. Rhett killed his superior (Rhett later assumed command of his regiment). Lamar succumbed to malaria at the Charleston Hotel in October 1862, a little more than a year after he had originally enlisted as the captain of an independent artillery company. Thirty-five years of age at the time of his death, he left a tremendous estate, including a number of slaves, to his wife and nine children. *Photo courtesy of Clemson University*

Thomas G. Lamar
carte de visite
Quinby and Company

WASHINGTON LIGHT INFANTRY
albumen print

Among these musical members of the Washington Light Infantry is Lt. Richard W. Greer, who was killed at Secessionville. This Charleston militia company was mustered as Company B in the 11th (Eutaw) Battalion, South Carolina Infantry, in February 1862 and became the 25th South Carolina Infantry (Eutaw Regiment) the following June. Greer is on the far right; the others, who also fought at Secessionville, are (*seated, left to right*) Henry H. Williams, S. B. Woodberry, and Henry J. Greer.

Williams was a twenty-four-year-old hatter when he enrolled as a private. He left in October 1862 for four months on sick leave and then was hospitalized for whooping cough in July 1864 at Richmond. He then was furloughed and apparently did not return.

Woodberry, a clerk from Charleston, was thirty years of age when he enlisted as a private. In October 1862 he was detailed to work as a carpenter on gunboats being built in Charleston, and he remained there when his regiment left for Virginia despite the protest of Capt. Edward W. Lloyd that Woodberry was actually working as a clerk for the shipbuilding company. In February 1865 he was transferred to Company E, 2nd Regiment of Engineers.

Henry J. Greer was a nineteen-year-old clerk in Charleston when the war began. Mustered as a sergeant, he was cited for gallantry at Drewry's Bluff in May 1864. He then became a lieutenant in November of that year. *Photo courtesy of MOLLUS, Mass., U.S.A.M.H.I.*

BENJAMIN T. SHEPPARD
albumen print

Sheppard enlisted at Charleston in February 1862 as a private in Company A of the 11th (Eutaw) Battalion, South Carolina Infantry.

This battalion originally carried the colors of a South Carolina unit that fought at Eutaw Springs during the American Revolution, but they probably discarded it after they were merged with other organizations to become the 25th South Carolina Infantry (Eutaw Regiment) in June 1862. That was probably just as well; Johnson Hagood, alongside whose regiment they fought at Secessionville, described their treasured relic as a "piece of red damask without device, [which] looked as if it had once covered a piece of furniture."[8] The fighting at Secessionville proved to be the highlight of Sheppard's brief military career—he succumbed to "congestive chills" at the Citadel Square Hospital in November 1862. *Photo courtesy of University of South Carolina, Columbia*

145

Brig. Gen. Isaac I. Stevens, who stood an inch over five feet in height, during early 1862 commanded the Federal troops at Beaufort, where this image was taken in March of that year. In June, despite his protests, his troops participated in the futile assaults at Secessionville that resulted in heavy casualties.

A native of Massachusetts, he graduated first in his class from West Point and won several brevets during the Mexican War. In 1853 he directed the survey for the Northern Pacific Railroad and then became the governor of the Washington Territory. He served as Washington Territory's delegate in Congress and then was campaign manager for John C. Breckinridge and Joseph Lane, a friend, in 1860.

After First Bull Run he took charge of the battered 79th New York Infantry, which was on the brink of mutiny; when he became a brigadier general in September, the 79th New York requested a transfer to his brigade. Stevens participated at Port Royal and Secessionville, where he personally led three charges. He then returned to Virginia with his brigade. Given a division during the Second Bull Run campaign, he was killed at Chantilly on September 1, 1862. He was posthumously promoted to major general in recognition of his achievements, for which he was allegedly being considered to be the next commander of the Army of the Potomac. *Photo courtesy of Library of Congress, no. B8171-164*

Company F, 3rd New Hampshire Infantry
albumen print
Henry P. Moore

Sgt. Horatio C. Moore was twenty-one years of age when he joined Company F of the 3rd New Hampshire Infantry in August 1861. In the summer of 1862 he wrote to his parents that "We must clean out Charleston before we go home. I shall never be contented to go home till we get one or more victories on our flag."[9] Wounded at Secessionville, Moore died three days later aboard a transport carrying him to the hospital on Hilton Head.

Moore was among the members of Company F who posed for this photograph at Hilton Head in early 1862. From left to right are Sgt. David Wadsworth, Jr. (*stripes*), Pvt. John F. Ennis ("*F*" *on cap*), Pvt. Norman E. Cobb (*beret*), Cpl. George H. Gay (*map*), "Milton"

(*black*), Pvt. Caleb Davis (*over Gay's head, next to Stevens*), Pvt. Albert H. Stevens (*fez*), Pvt. George W. Emerson (*beard and musket*), Moore (*on washtub*), and Sgt. Thomas Nottage, Jr. (*on box*).

Moore was not the only member of Company F killed during the war. Gay became a sergeant and then was wounded on Morris Island in August 1863 and again at Bermuda Hundred in Virginia in May 1864. He was killed at the age of twenty-nine on the Weldon Railroad on August 16. Private Ennis was twenty-three years of age when he was wounded at Bermuda Hundred in June 1864 and died nine days later. *Photo courtesy of MOLLUS, Mass., U.S.A.M.H.I.*

Lt. David I. Gilfillan of the 100th Pennsylvania Infantry, which served in Isaac I. Stevens' brigade, was captured on James Island in June 1862 during a desperate charge at Secessionville in which his regiment advanced into a "perfect storm of grape, canister, nails, broken glass, and pieces of chains" fired from Confederate artillery.[10] He was imprisoned for several months at Columbia before being sent to Virginia for exchange, which took place in October 1862.

Gilfillan had advanced rapidly in rank after enlisting in August 1861 as a private in Company F of the 100th Pennsylvania Infantry, becoming a sergeant, then a sergeant major, and finally a second lieutenant. His regiment came ashore at Port Royal as part of the 2nd Brigade, led by Gen. Isaac I. Stevens, and occupied Beaufort on December 11, 1861.

Soon after the sanguine engagement at Secessionville, the 100th Pennsylvania Infantry transferred to Virginia. Gilfillan went home on leave and in February 1864 married Mary A. Rose at Titusville, Pennsylvania; at that time she was just sixteen years of age. He returned to his regiment and, while serving as an aide, was shot through the head and killed on June 2, 1864, at Cold Harbor. *Photo courtesy of U.S.A.M.H.I.*

JOHN M. KNOX
AND UNKNOWN
[WILLIAM T. KNOX?]
copy print of ambrotype

Among the victims of the humid summer climate of South Carolina were John M. Knox and his brother William T. Knox, who enlisted as privates in Company F, 76th Pennsylvania Infantry (Keystone Zouaves) in 1861. This portrait was made at Camp Cameron near Harrisburg, Pennsylvania, on November 5 of that year, shortly before they left for Port Royal.

Neither brother fared well in the summertime heat along the South Carolina coast. In July 1862 John wrote to their father that "we sweat more here in the shad [*sic*] doing nothing than we did up there in the harvest field."[11] Both of the brothers became seriously ill, but they continued to send money to their father,

who was partially blind and could not work. John soon recovered and assured their father that William would do so as well, but the latter died in the regimental hospital at Port Royal during late July 1862.

John remained with the regiment after his brother's death. The 76th Pennsylvania took part in the attack at Pocotaligo in October 1862 and was involved in the operations in the summer of 1863 against Battery Wagner. The regiment broke under fire; it then reached the parapet itself during the assault on July 11 and charged again in the second attack seven days later. Tragically, John died of wounds suffered at Cold Harbor in June 1864. *Photo courtesy of U.S.A.M.H.I.*

WILLIAM R. ATKINSON
copy print of ambrotype

The continued pressure of the Federal armies on the Confederate defenses at Charleston and elsewhere along the coast, as well as the fairly constant use of the latter city's harbor, made quick and reliable communications a necessity. Capable Signal Corps personnel were recruited from among the regular units serving on the coast.

One such individual was William R. Atkinson. Born in 1842, he had received a degree from South Carolina College in absentia, having already joined the Richland Volunteers on January 1, 1861, the day that they left Columbia for Charleston. Many members of that company, which mustered for only six months, later enlisted in other units. Atkinson was enrolled at Pocotaligo in February 1862 as a private in Company A (Palmetto Guard), 18th Battalion, South Carolina Artillery, also known as the South Carolina Siege Train. In May 1862 he transferred to Company G, 3rd (Palmetto) Battalion, South Carolina Artillery; there are many others with the same surname, so it appears he joined some of his relatives. During the late summer of 1862 Atkinson was detached to the Signal Corps by order of General John C. Pemberton. The next June he officially transferred to that branch of the service and served as a signal operator at Savannah and Charleston. Promoted to lieutenant, he surrendered in North Carolina at the end of the war. *Photo courtesy of University of South Carolina, Columbia*

150

COMPANY H, 3RD NEW HAMPSHIRE INFANTRY
albumen print
Henry P. Moore

Company H of the 3rd New Hampshire Infantry was assigned in July 1862 to picket duty on Pinckney Island. The lieutenant in charge took few precautions, despite the admonitions of Henry F. Hopkins before he was hospitalized with malaria. On the night of August 20, Confederates led by Capt. Stephen Elliott, Jr., surprised the picket, killing five and capturing thirty-two.

These members of Company H, only one of whom was captured on Pinckney Island, posed at Hilton Head in early 1862. Left to right are Lt. John F. Langley, Pvt. Josiah F. Hunt, Pvt. Walter A. Lawrence, Sgt. Stephen S. Fifield, Sgt. Henry F. Hopkins, and an unidentified person. Langley resigned on July 3, 1862, claiming he suffered from rheumatism. Hunt, a shoemaker before he enlisted, was captured on Pinckney Island. His fellow private, Lawrence, was not with him because he was wounded at Secessionville and died in the hospital at Hilton Head eight days later at the age of twenty. Fifield was employed as a nurse in the regimental hospital beginning on July 21, 1862. Hopkins, a lawyer, was promoted to lieutenant on July 1, 1862, and assumed command of his company on Pinckney Island but was hospitalized with malaria on August 10, 1862. *Photo courtesy of MOLLUS, Mass., U.S.A.M.H.I.*

Despite the flurry of opposition to Col. John D. Rust of the 8th Maine Infantry, his efforts and those of many others to enlist blacks were supported by Charles G. Halpine, an influential journalist who was serving as adjutant general on the staff of Gen. David Hunter. Halpine wrote the first order for recruiting blacks, and under the pseudonym "Miles O'Reilly," a fictional Irish soldier in the 47th New York Infantry, he penned a number of humorous articles and poems arguing that blacks had as much right as anyone else to join the army and be killed.

Halpine, a native of Ireland whose father was a noted Irish Protestant writer, had studied at Trinity College, and had then immigrated to the United States in 1851. He wrote advertisements and worked as a private secretary for Phineas T. Barnum and then was an editor and writer for several publications while publishing a volume of his poems. Active in politics, he served as a private secretary to Stephen A. Douglas and was a member of the general committee of Tammany Hall.

He enlisted in the 69th New York Infantry as a lieutenant in 1861 but soon joined Hunter's staff and came to South Carolina. The controversy surrounding his writing slowed his promotion, but he was breveted a lieutenant colonel in June 1864 and became a brigadier general after his resignation from the military a few months later. *Photo courtesy of National Archives*

CHARLES G. HALPINE
copy print

Lt. Charles P. Lord of Company F, 8th Maine Infantry, became embroiled in the controversy surrounding Col. John D. Rust, whom Lord derided as a political appointee. During April 1863 all but two of the twenty-nine line officers of the regiment submitted resignations, and court-martial charges were brought against Rust. An investigation ensued but he was not dismissed; instead, Lord was discharged at Hilton Head during December 1863. Lord later insisted that he was dismissed for refusing to answer objectionable questions, but official records indicate that he was cashiered for incompetence.

Lord, despite his derision, had no more military experience than Rust. A native of Maine, he was a machinist in Lowell, Massachusetts, before the Civil War. He was a member of a militia company that was enlisted into the 6th Massachusetts Infantry, and he ran the gauntlet as a member of that regiment in Baltimore during the riots in April 1861. After that company was mustered out during August 1861, he became a first lieutenant in Company F of the 8th Maine Infantry the following month. Service in South Carolina was difficult for him; his health was wrecked by his hard labors in charge of a crew of soldiers cutting a road through the tangled swamps near Hilton Head. *Photo courtesy of U.S.A.M.H.I.*

CHARLES P. LORD
copy print

153

J. Homer Edgerly
copy print

Sgt. J. Homer Edgerly was with Company K, 3rd New Hampshire Infantry, when it advanced on Pocotaligo in October 1862 as part of a large Union force sent to cut the Charleston and Savannah Railroad. After a clash with a smaller Confederate contingent, the Federals withdrew without damaging the line significantly.

Edgerly had recorded his occupation as "painter" when he enlisted in August 1861 at the age of seventeen as a private in Company K. His regiment came ashore at Port Royal in November 1861, and he was promoted to sergeant in May 1862, one month before his regiment participated in the ill-fated assault at Secessionville.

Seven months after Pocotaligo, he became a lieutenant in Company E of the same regiment. They landed on the southern end of Morris Island in July 1863 and then were among those repulsed at Battery Wagner on July 18 (Edgerly was the officer of the day, so he watched the attack from sandhills). Transferred to Company D in January 1864, Edgerly assumed command of that unit, though he was not promoted to captain until October 1864, after it had been ordered to Virginia. He became the assistant provost marshal for Wilmington, North Carolina, in early 1865 and was breveted a major for his efforts at Fort Fisher, where he captured a flag. He remained with the provost guard until discharged in the summer of 1865. *Photo courtesy of MOLLUS, Mass., U.S.A.M.H.I.*

M. ALBERTO BLAND
carte de visite
George S. Cook

The USS *Isaac P. Smith*, a steamer that mounted nine guns, was caught in artillery fire on the Stono River on January 30, 1863, and compelled to surrender. Cpl. M. Alberto Bland of Company A (Palmetto Guard), 18th Battalion of South Carolina Artillery, known as the South Carolina Siege Train, performed well in this triumph and applied for a commission. Despite endorsements from his commander, Maj. Edward M. Manigault, and the Confederate congressional delegation from North Carolina, where his father was an Episcopal minister, his application was denied.

Shortly after the war began, Bland had enlisted for six months in Company K of the 1st North Carolina Infantry. When that term expired, he moved south and joined the Palmetto Guard, which mustered in February 1862 at Pocotaligo as Company A. They served at Charleston, where Bland became a corporal in the fall.

He remained with his company after failing to become an officer. He was "slightly stunned" and suffered a concussion in the same rain of shells fired by Union gunboats that claimed the life of Pvt. William H. H. Ancrum (*pictured elsewhere*) at Legareville on Christmas Day, 1863. A native of Beaufort, South Carolina, Bland returned to North Carolina in September 1864 when he was hospitalized for three weeks at Charlotte. *Photo courtesy of University of South Carolina, Columbia*

USS *Commodore McDonough*
albumen print
Haas and Peale

This photograph shows the converted Staten Island ferry on the South Carolina coast during the summer of 1863. Purchased by the navy at the outset of the war, it had been modified to carry five guns and sent south.

The vessel was thought to be adequately armored, but on January 30, 1863, when the USS *Isaac P. Smith* was trapped under fire and ultimately forced to surrender, the *Commodore McDonough* proved unable to come to the stricken ship's rescue because it could not withstand the fire of the Confederates's rifled guns. Only by rapid manuevering did the *Commodore McDonough* escape the crossfire that compelled the *Isaac P. Smith* to surrender.

The captain of the *Commodore McDonough* did continue his bombardment of the Confederate positions until nightfall from a safe distance downstream, ending with a few shells thrown into the town of Legareville in the hope of setting it ablaze. During the following summer the *Commodore McDonough* carried troops to James Island, where they disembarked in an effort to distract Confederates from the impending landings on Morris Island to capture Battery Wagner. *Photo courtesy of Library of Congress, no. USZ62-49371*

USS *PASSAIC*
albumen print

Rear Adm. Samuel F. Du Pont had almost no confidence in the offensive power of his monitors, but under great pressure from Washington, he ordered them to challenge the guns of Fort Sumter on April 7, 1863. Second in the line of attack that day was the USS *Passaic,* captained by Percival Drayton. As the Federal fleet approached Sumter, the *Passaic*'s crew fired thirteen rounds from the twin guns in her turret. At the same time, the vessel was being struck by thirty-five shells that jammed its turret and shattered its pilot house. Du Pont suspended the action after a few hours, and did not again directly confront Sumter before he was relieved of command at his own request.

The *Passaic* was the first of its class: ten single-turret monitors with more armor and heavier ordnance (each had an 11-inch and a 15-inch Dahlgren gun) than the original. In addition to the *Passaic,* these vessels included the *Weehawken* (which led the attack on April 7, 1863), *Lehigh, Nahant, Patapsco, Montauk, Catskill,* and *Nantucket,* all of which served in South Carolina waters. They became the backbone of the Atlantic blockading squadrons, and as a class saw more service than any other type of monitor. This photograph was taken at Charleston during 1863, after the failed assault by the ironclads on Fort Sumter in April. *Photo courtesy of National Archives*

Chapter 5

Best-Protected City on the Coast: The Siege of Charleston, 1863–1865

After the disaster at Charleston on April 7, 1863, Gen. David Hunter, like Adm. Samuel F. Du Pont, was replaced, the former with Gen. Quincy A. Gillmore and the latter with Rear Adm. John A. Dahlgren. Gillmore had reduced Fort Pulaski at Savannah, and he was confident that he could do the same to Fort Sumter and thus open Charleston harbor for the Union fleet. The siege of Charleston, however, proved to be the longest campaign of the Civil War and technically ended in failure for the Federals. No Union force ever wrested the city from its defenders; the port fell into Federal hands only after its garrison left to confront Gen. William T. Sherman in North Carolina. Secretary of the navy Gideon Welles in his annual report for 1865 admitted that Charleston during the Civil War was the "most invulnerable and best protected city on the coast."[1]

Gillmore arrived in South Carolina with ten thousand reinforcements in June and began devising a plan for the capture of Charleston in concert with Dahlgren. Rather than asking the Union fleet to confront Fort Sumter unsupported, they decided to capture Battery Wagner, an earthwork on Morris Island, and thus secure the north, or harbor, end

of the sandspit. They would then be able to establish breaching batteries on Cummings Point to reduce Fort Sumter and run past it into the harbor when the time was right. The Federals were encouraged by the transfer of Confederates away from South Carolina. When Du Pont attacked in April 1863, there were about thirty thousand troops defending the state; three months later this number had decreased by half, and only about a fifth of those troops were posted around Charleston.

On July 10, 1863, Gillmore launched an overwhelming early morning attack against the tiny Confederate garrison on the southern tip of Morris Island. Following an artillery bombardment from the Union fleet and shore batteries on Folly Island, more than three thousand Federals disembarked under a cover fire on Morris Island. These troops, commanded by Gen. Truman Seymour, a veteran of the April 1861 bombardment of Fort Sumter, suffered relatively light casualties while killing, wounding, or capturing nearly half of the 650 defenders from the 1st South Carolina Artillery, Johnson Hagood's 1st South Carolina Infantry, and the 21st South Carolina Infantry. The unequal contest ended with an attack by the 6th Connecticut

Infantry, which swept through the rifle pits of the Southerners from the flank and rear.

After the capture of the south end of Morris Island by Gillmore, Confederate reinforcements—including detachments from the 1st (Hagood's), 7th, and 21st South Carolina Infantry, and the 1st South Carolina Artillery—were rushed to Battery Wagner, which bristled with twelve pieces of well-protected artillery and was ringed with rifle pits and mines. On July 11, a column composed of the 7th Connecticut Infantry, 76th Pennsylvania Infantry, and 9th Maine Infantry, attacked that position without artillery support. They fell back after losing more than three hundred casualties—including their commander, General Seymour, whose wound put him out of action for six months. The Confederate defenders lost only two killed and ten wounded.

The guns of Battery Wagner periodically fired upon the Federals during the next week, and their fire was intermittently returned. Suddenly, on July 18, the Union artillery began a concentrated bombardment of Wagner. For eleven hours the siege guns brought to reduce Fort Sumter were used against the smaller earthwork, hurling about nine thousand shells while naval batteries aboard nearby Union ships added their payload. Gillmore assumed the garrison had been eliminated or stunned, so as night approached, a Union assault column of two brigades, led by the black infantry of the 54th Massachusetts, charged the position. Gillmore's assumption proved to be tragically wrong. The defenders emerged from their bomb-proofs and poured a devastating fire into the attackers. Despite a valiant effort, and a brief occupation of the left bastion of Battery Wagner, the Federals retreated once again.

In the attempt to take Battery Wagner by storm, the Union army lost 1,515 men—one-third of those engaged—including Gen. George C. Strong and three colonels. Among the latter was Robert G. Shaw of the 54th Massachusetts Colored Infantry, the first regiment of freedmen raised in a northern state. A Confederate officer noted that his body was found on Wagner's parapet, next to the bodies of some of his soldiers and the regimental flag that his color bearer had planted. He was buried with the latter in a common grave in a deliberate, and futile, attempt to express contempt for him as a leader of black troops. In fact, after the unpleasant incident at Darien, Georgia, Shaw had lobbied for the transfer of his regiment from the brigade commanded by Colonel Montgomery to that led by Strong. When the latter was chosen to spearhead the assault on Battery Wagner, Strong asked that Shaw's troops be allowed to lead the way. In the attack the freedmen won a grisly measure of glory by suffering the greatest number of casualties of any regiment involved: 272, or 40 percent of their effectives. By comparison, Confederate losses totaled only 174. Fittingly, many of the wounded blacks from the 54th Massachusetts Colored Infantry were carried away from Morris Island by Robert Smalls, piloting the *Planter*, which had been refitted as a hospital ship.

The fighting at Charleston during the summer of 1863 forced the Confederates to confront a thorny problem. A number of the Union prisoners captured by Hagood were black soldiers from the 54th Massachusetts Colored Infantry. There was no consensus among Hagood's superiors regarding such captives, while the situation was complicated by the fact that Hunter had earlier ordered the internment of prominent South Carolinians in the jail at Beaufort as hostages for the proper treatment of black troops who became prisoners. Hunter had subsequently been replaced by Gillmore, but the Union position on the question was clear. The matter passed into Beauregard's hands with the transfer of these black prisoners to Charleston, and he responded to instructions from Richmond by surrendering them to Gov. Milledge L. Bonham. Four of the blacks who allegedly had been slaves were to be tried for insurrection, but the court refused to accept jurisdiction over them and they returned to the Charleston jail. White officers and soldiers were exchanged, but the blacks endured a year and a half in close confinement with poor rations. Finally, as the end of his term approached in December 1864, Bonham returned the captive blacks to the military. They were interned briefly in the prison camp at Florence, South Carolina—where several died of fever—then were shuttled from place to place until they were released near Goldsboro, North Carolina, at the end of the war.

Gillmore, frustrated in his attempts to take Battery Wagner by storm, undertook an extended siege of the position, during which shells from Union land and sea batteries fell almost constantly on Battery Wagner and Fort Sumter beyond it while engineers dug trenches toward the former. By early August, Federal works were within five hundred yards of Battery Wagner, but work had to be halted when it was reported that shells from Fort Sumter were making the Union entrenchments uninhabitable. Gillmore ordered a long-range precision bombardment of Sumter—supported at times by the guns of the Union fleet—begun on August 17 that destroyed most of the walls in that installation and silenced all but one of its cannons, an ineffective smoothbore 32-pounder used as a signal gun.

After the suppression of Fort Sumter, digging resumed on Morris Island; by the first week of September the Federals had dug to within fifty yards of Battery Wagner. The Union engineers were protected by a continuous artillery barrage whose intensity made it difficult, if not impossible, for the Confederates to handle their guns. In fact, the Federal bombardment, especially from the naval batteries, was so intense that the garrison of Battery Wagner had to be relieved every five days. Upon the advice of its commander, Col. Lawrence M. Keitt, Battery Wagner was abandoned during the night of September 6. The Confederates spiked their artillery, but they failed in their attempt to detonate the magazine.

Col. Alfred M. Rhett, the commander of Fort Sumter, declared after Union troops had established breaching batteries on Morris Island that they might silence his guns but he would "fight the fort low down." He proved true to his word; on August 24, 1863, Gillmore proudly reported that Sumter, which had been struck by 450 shells daily for a week, had been reduced to a "shapeless and harmless mass of ruins." The Confederates refused to evacuate the post, however. The same day that Gillmore was boasting of its destruction, Gen. Roswell S. Ripley, overall commander at Charleston, and his engineers visited Sumter. They determined to hold it at all costs. Most of the munitions were removed, and on September 4, 1863, Rhett's garrison of artillerists was replaced by infantry under the command of Maj. Stephen Elliott, Jr. The 1st South Carolina Artillery, having left Sumter, was assigned to other batteries around Charleston, and Rhett's efforts were recognized by his promotion to the command of all interior harbor defenses, which included the Fort Sumter garrison.[2]

The Union forces quickly discovered that the "shapeless" ruin of Fort Sumter was far from "harmless." After occupying Battery Wagner, the Federals renewed their bombardment of Sumter as well as Fort Moultrie and other posts on Sullivan's Island. Elliott refused a surrender demand from Dahlgren, who then sent a landing party of four hundred men in barges to Sumter at about one o'clock in the morning on September 9, hoping they would make their way into the fort through a breach that had been opened by artillery fire and catch the garrison in their beds. Elliott was ready for them; he waited until the Federals were within a few yards of the fort's walls before ordering a hail of gunfire, hand grenades, and chunks of masonry to commence. At the same time, batteries elsewhere in the harbor opened on the hapless raiders. More than a fourth of them were killed, wounded, or captured before they could flee out of range. The Confederates gleefully gathered five stands of colors, including a tattered national flag that they believed was the one lowered by Maj. Robert Anderson when he surrendered the fort in 1861.

The Federal fleet and batteries on Cummings

Point continued to pound Fort Sumter in October and November, sometimes firing more than 1,000 artillery shells a day into the post. Casualties among the Confederates working in the ruins were relatively light most of the time. On New Year's Eve, 1863, Elliott reported that 19,808 shells had struck Fort Sumter since August; during that time 38 men had been killed and 142 wounded. Most of those killed were lost to only 2 shells: a Parrott round collapsed a roof on a dozen members of the 25th South Carolina Infantry and a hapless Georgia soldier, burying them alive; another shot exploded a magazine, killing 11 men and igniting a fire that burned for a week. Despite such danger, by December 1863 the garrison had converted Sumter from a casemated fort with thick, brick walls into an almost impregnable earthwork mounting six large-caliber guns, including a battery mounting three cannon trained on the main channel into the harbor. Sandbags, palmetto logs, and chunks of masonry had been used to close breaches and build bombproofs for sheltering troops who, in the event of an assault, could be massed under cover for a counterattack.

Gillmore, with the capable assistance of Dahlgren, had secured Battery Wagner and reduced Fort Sumter, but the naval commander still hesitated to run into Charleston harbor. Sumter remained quite powerful, while its guns that had not been remounted had been transferred to other batteries elsewhere around the harbor. There was plenty of evidence to indicate what might happen to the Union fleet if they dared to engage the batteries at Charleston.

In September 1863 the USS *Weehawken*, the monitor that had led the attack on Fort Sumter in April, ran aground within range of the Confederate batteries on Sullivan's Island. Before it was freed the ship suffered tremendously from the fire of the guns on shore; this damage contributed to her sinking two months later. Another monitor, the USS *Lehigh*, was punished by Confederate guns at Fort Moultrie when it grounded near Cummings Point

during November 1863. After the summer of 1863, Union forces made no more attempts to take Charleston or close its harbor by a direct assault.

The Confederates were not content to wait for the Federal attack that never came. On the night of October 5, 1863, an attempt was made to sink the USS *New Ironsides*. A four-man crew piloted a "David," a small submerged steamer carrying an explosive charge on a boom, next to the ironclad ship. They detonated the charge against the side of their target, but its thick armor proved impervious to the amount of powder they had used. The geyser of water from the explosion swamped the Confederate vessel, which was also quickly riddled with small-arms fire. Two of the crew abandoned their stricken craft and were captured, but the two who remained managed to rekindle the fire beneath the boiler and navigate under fire through the Federal fleet to safety.

During the night of February 17, 1864, after several unsuccessful sorties, the crew of the Confederate submarine CSS *Hunley*, which had been built in Mobile and shipped to Charleston by rail, managed to sink the USS *Housatonic*, a sloop of war engaged in the blockade. Unfortunately, the Confederate vessel, which had departed from Battery Marshall on Sullivan's Island, was again lost with her entire crew when her victim settled on top of her. The "peripatetic coffin" had claimed the lives of her fourth, and last, crew at Charleston. She had claimed the lives of most of those who had volunteered to serve on her, including her designer and namesake, Horace L. Hunley.

Frustrated with the Confederates' persistence, Gillmore decided to bombard the city of Charleston itself in an effort to reduce morale and force an evacuation or negotiations. In August 1863, while the Federals were still attempting to reduce or capture Battery Wagner, their engineers built a platform in the marsh between Morris and James islands. In this emplacement they mounted an eight-inch Parrott rifle that could throw two-hundred-pound shells into Charleston. Gillmore demanded that Beauregard surrender the city; when Beauregard refused, the "Swamp Angel" commenced firing on the night of August 21. The giant cannon fired thirty-six rounds filled with Greek fire, an incendiary compound, before it burst on the second night of its bombardment of the city. Fifteen of its shells landed within the city, but damage was negligible.

Stray shells fell on Charleston during the next few months, but a systematic bombardment commenced in mid-November, after the Union occupation of batteries Wagner and Gregg. On Christmas Day, 150 rounds fell on the city; the daily total increased to 273 by the end of January. Astoundingly, only five civilians, including a slave, were killed, but thousands more fled as their homes were destroyed. Much of the city near the waterfront became a no man's land where grass grew in deserted streets that were trod only by those who had important, or nefarious, reasons to risk their lives. Gillmore departed for the front in Virginia at his own request during May 1864, but the shelling of Charleston was continued by Gen. John G. Foster, who succeeded Gillmore as commander of the Department of the South.

On June 13, 1864, in an attempt to convince Foster to suspend the bombardment of Charleston, Gen. Samuel Jones, who had replaced Beauregard as commander of Confederate troops in South Carolina during the previous April, reported that a number of Union officers were being held as prisoners of war in the city, in areas exposed to Federal fire. The breakdown of the exchange programs during the summer had filled regular prisoner-of-war camps in the South to overflowing. Makeshift stockades would be built—one of the most notorious of these was at Florence, South Carolina, where food and blankets were scarce and brush arbors served as hospitals—but in the meantime temporary accomodations had to be provided. In Charleston, Union officers were held in the Roper Hospital building and in private homes as space became scarce.

Foster angrily responded that not only was Charleston a military target that he would continue shelling, but also that he would expose an equal number of captive Confederate officers to Jones' artillery fire unless the Federal prisoners were moved to safety. In order to carry out this threat, Confederate prisoners of war were brought to Hilton Head from Fort Delaware, a prison camp in the North. Jones asked that these respective groups of prisoners be exchanged, and this was done. However, when Foster learned that Federals were still in Charleston, six hundred Confederate officers were transferred from Fort Delaware to a stockade on the beach on Morris Island. The "Immortal Six Hundred" remained in their Morris Island pen, exposed to daily shelling, until October 1864, when Jones informed Foster that the last Federal prisoners had been removed from Charleston. At that time a third of the Confederates detained on Morris Island were sent to Hilton Head, whence they were returned to Fort Delaware during March 1865.

The accommodations for Confederate prisoners at Hilton Head were not much better than those on Morris Island or those provided by Confederates for Union prisoners. The prison stockade on Hilton Head Island was about fifty yards square. Within it were two flimsy shacks for officers, fifteen tents for enlisted men, and a field kitchen. Within this tiny space more than a thousand men were crowded by the end of 1864, after the capture of Savannah. Among the prisoners who sojourned there as the war ground to its conclusion was George A. Trenholm, last secretary of the treasury for the Confederacy and a distinguished resident of Charleston. Much to the dismay of the newspaper correspondents on Hilton Head, Jefferson Davis, after his capture, spent a few hours on a ship off the island but was never placed in the stockade. That was just as well for him; the daily rations were a pint of poor quality meat and four ounces each of bread and onion pickles.

While the shelling and bickering continued at Charleston, Union troops continued to probe toward the Charleston and Savannah Railroad in an effort to sever that link between the port cities. A Union expedition landed on John's Island during early February 1864, intending to cut the rail line and thus divert Confederate attention from Truman Seymour's ill-fated Florida campaign. The Federals captured several pickets from Company F of the 6th South Carolina Cavalry before daylight on February 9. Informed of the loss, Capt. Moses B. Humphrey attacked the Union troops with three dozen of his troopers. The Federals greatly outnumbered their attackers, but the former were unsure of the actual number of Confederates in the predawn darkness and fog, and so they withdrew. When daylight and the dissipation of the fog revealed the truth, Humphrey's contingent was driven from the field. Not until the next day were the Confederates able, with a number of reinforcements, to compel the Federals to withdraw.

In July 1864, Foster coordinated an assault at several points on the South Carolina coast, intending again to cut the Charleston and Savannah Railroad. A contingent of five thousand infantry, supported by cavalry and artillery and led by Gen. John P. Hatch, landed on Seabrook Island with instructions to capture the ferry at the north end and, crossing to the mainland, destroy the rail line. At the same time, a brigade of Union troops under Gen. William Birney was put ashore at White Point to destroy the bridges over the South Edisto and Ashepoo rivers. To prevent the Confederates from reinforcing the defenders of the railroad, demonstrations were staged on James Island and against the harbor defenses at Charleston. All of these efforts failed, and the Union forces withdrew after suffering losses that totaled about 330, including the capture of 140 officers and men on July 3 at Fort Johnson on James Island. Total Confederate losses in this campaign were about the same. Frustrated with his debacle, Foster intensified the shelling of Fort Sumter; more than seven thousand rounds struck that post before the end of July.

Despite constant Federal raids along the South

Carolina coast and the unrelenting bombardment of Charleston, Confederate units were frequently ordered to Virginia to reinforce Robert E. Lee's hard-pressed army. In January 1864, Lee complained to President Davis about the large number of South Carolinians that were volunteering to serve in units in that state rather than be drafted to fight in Virginia or Georgia. He pointed out that it was becoming almost impossible to replenish the veteran South Carolina regiments, which had suffered heavy casualties, and suggested that either the men in the home defense regiments be assigned to older units or that these overenrolled regiments be sent to the front. Davis chose the latter, despite the anguished protests of Governor Bonham and the concerns of General Jones. In early May, General Jones sent his last infantry brigade, Johnson Hagood's, to Virginia. Desperate for troops, he told the mayor of Charleston to organize the fire brigades into home defense companies and asked the president of the South Carolina Railroad to muster his employees, who were exempt from conscription, for the defense of the city. A naval battalion was also created for land defense.

The dwindling number of adult males under arms in South Carolina also compelled Jones to call on the cadets at the Citadel once more, as well as on those attending the Arsenal Academy, a freshman preparatory school in Columbia. The legislature on January 28, 1861, had organized these students into the Battalion of State Cadets. The Cadet Corps at the Citadel comprised Company A, and those from the Arsenal were designated as Company B. Each group was commanded by their superintendents, James B. White and John P. Thomas, respectively. The cadets manned some of the guns that fired on the *Star of the West* in January 1861, and then had often been called into service to defend Charleston during the ensuing years. During June 1864 they returned to James Island, where they had been under fire two years earlier, and dug in once more to endure Union artillery shells.

Gen. William J. Hardee succeeded General Jones

as commander of the department on October 5, 1864. Jones remained as commander of the state of South Carolina, but Hardee inherited the greater strategic concern of manpower. The Federals were quick to test the new arrival. In late November 1864, Rear Adm. John A. Dahlgren led a party of sailors and marines, together with a battery of 12-pounders, ashore at Boyd's Landing on the Broad River under the protecting guns of six Union warships. Gen. John P. Hatch joined him there with fifty-five hundred soldiers, most of whom were black troops from Hilton Head. Their intention was familiar—to march inland and cut the Charleston and Savannah Railroad—but their motive was slightly different; they were to do so in order to facilitate William T. Sherman's investment of Savannah.

Hatch, despite Dahlgren's insistence that the railroad appeared to be unguarded, postponed his march inland until November 30, giving Hardee enough time to scrape together a defensive force. Hardee collected about fourteen hundred Georgia and South Carolina militia, Citadel and Arsenal cadets, and veterans of the 3rd South Carolina Cavalry and placed them under the command of an ailing Gen. Gustavus W. Smith to oppose the Federal advance. When Hatch casually moved inland toward Grahamville, his troops were hit hard by a few Confederate cavalry. The resulting chaos allowed Smith to bring up his infantry and occupy some trenches, dug at Lee's order years earlier, on a low ridge known as Honey Hill.

Hatch ordered a series of assaults that were foiled in part by the confusion initiated when the Confederates fired the tall grass in front of their works. The 35th United States Colored Troops and 55th Massachusetts Infantry valiantly charged but were punished by the Confederate artillery. Allegedly, the 55th Massachusetts, in its third charge, lost about 100 men killed and wounded in five minutes, including its colonel (wounded). The Union troops withdrew to Boyd's Landing late in the afternoon, having lost 746 men killed,

wounded, or missing. Smith lost only 8 killed and 42 wounded. More important to the Confederates: the railroad remained intact.

Hatch and Dahlgren tried to move inland again within a week. After a careful reconnaissance, troops departed on December 6, 1864, from Boyd's Landing aboard shallow-draft transports that made their way up the Tulifinny River, bypassing the Confederate troops entrenched at Grahamville and Coosawhatchie. Once ashore, the Federals encountered a makeshift defensive force that again included the cadets from the Citadel and Arsenal, as well as the Beaufort Volunteer Artillery. A determined attack by the 56th and 157th New York Infantry drove the South Carolinians back in confusion, but a counterattack spearheaded by the cadets on December 7 regained the ground they had lost the previous day. In all, the Federals lost about 300, while losses among the Confederate commands totaled only 52.

Hatch's Federals tried once more to push inland on December 9, with no success, and then his axmen cleared a field of fire through the thick trees and undergrowth for his artillery, which was trained carefully on the Charleston and Savannah Railroad, thus rendering it almost useless for the Confederates. A member of the South Carolina militia later recalled that the few trains that used the line crept through the area as quietly as possible while their crews cowered on the running boards on the side away from the Union batteries. Many of the Confederate units in the area were assigned elsewhere; the Cadet Battalion, for example, returned to its post on James Island.

Gen. William T. Sherman entered Savannah on December 21, 1864. The Confederates in South Carolina warily waited for the attack they knew would come. At Charleston, Capt. Thomas A. Huguenin, commander of Fort Sumter, had his men watch constantly for Union assault vessels, especially in the hours just before sunrise. On the morning of January 15, 1865, he was told that a monitor was moving toward his post. Ascending a watchtower, from where he communicated by speaking tube, Huguenin directed the officer in charge of the fort's battery to fire. When nothing happened, Huguenin repeated his order, then asked why his directions were not being followed. The battery commander replied that he could not see the target; when Huguenin scanned the water with a field glass, he discovered that he could not find the intruder either. Daylight and the falling tide revealed the truth: the USS *Patapsco*, a veteran of many engagements with Battery Wagner and Fort Sumter, had struck a submerged mine and had quietly sunk with sixty-two of her crew. Only the smokestack of the vessel stood clear of the water, indicating the site of her watery grave.

Shortly after the destruction of the *Patapsco* on January 21, Sherman boarded a steamer to visit Foster at Beaufort. Four days later, the "March from the Sea" began. On the night of February 17, Huguenin supervised the evacuation of Fort Sumter, making a final inspection of the post alone. Ironically, he had commanded the last detachment to leave Battery Wagner in September 1863 and now had to perform the distasteful duty of evacuating his post once more. His troops joined the rest of the Charleston garrison on its march to intercept Sherman's army in North Carolina. The next day, February 18, the commander of the Federal forces who had occupied Charleston was rowed to within forty yards of Sumter, where he met a boatload of Confederate musicians who had been left behind, and learned that the installation was abandoned. He directed a subordinate to enter the fort and raise the U. S. flag for the first time in nearly four years.

QUINCY A. GILLMORE
albumen print
Haas and Peale

The well-dressed officer in front of the tent is Gen. Quincy A. Gillmore on Morris Island in the summer of 1863. A graduate of West Point, where he ranked first in the class of 1849, he served in the engineers and as an instructor at his alma mater before the Civil War. After serving as chief engineer for the Port Royal expedition in November 1861, he directed the reduction of Fort Pulaski at Savannah, Georgia. He advanced to brigadier general and then to major general in July 1863, after he was ordered to South Carolina to assume command of the Department of the South.

Gillmore was confident that he could reduce the defenses of Charleston like he had Fort Pulaski. He directed operations on Morris Island that included the capture of Battery Wagner and Battery Gregg and the shelling of Charleston, but he was unable to secure the surrender of the port. At his own request he was transferred with the X Corps to Virginia, where they were bottled up with other units in the Bermuda Hundred campaign. Gillmore assumed command of two divisions of the XIX Corps during July 1864 in the Shenandoah Valley, but he was badly injured when his horse fell on him. He soon recovered and resumed command of the Department of the South in February 1865, when he was finally able to occupy Charleston after Confederates forces evacuated the city. *Photo courtesy of Library of Congress, no. B8178-87*

JOHN A. DAHLGREN
copy print

Appointed to command the South Atlantic Blockading Squadron in the summer of 1863 after the failure of Rear Adm. Samuel Du Pont to capture Charleston, Rear Adm. John A. Dahlgren stands next to a rifled gun of his own design aboard the USS *Pawnee* off the South Carolina coast. Dahlgren cooperated with General Gillmore and his successor, Gen. John G. Foster, and at last had the pleasure of tying his ships up at the Charleston wharves on February 18, 1865, after the city had been abandoned by its Confederate garrison.

The son of the Swedish consul at Philadelphia, Dahlgren was appointed a midshipman in the U. S. Navy in 1826 when he was seventeen years of age. He specialized in naval ordnance, inventing the popular cannon, with which he is pictured, as well as a boat howitzer with an iron carriage. He became a captain in July 1862 and assumed command of the Ordnance Bureau that same month. One year later he was commanding vessels engaged in the desperate and futile attempts to reduce the fortifications near Charleston, where he refused, unlike his predecessor, to allow his ships to challenge the batteries of Fort Sumter and other installations at close range. *Photo courtesy of Library of Congress, no. B8171-7149*

The Confederate garrison on the southern tip of Morris Island was caught napping when a Federal force landed on July 10, 1863, in a joint operation planned by Rear Adm. John A. Dahlgren and Gen. Quincy A. Gillmore. The surprise attack was accomplished despite earlier sparring over the wreck of the *Ruby*, a blockade runner that was chased ashore near Lighthouse Inlet one night during late June. Federal gunners, massing in preparation for the assault, eagerly ran their guns forward and began shelling the stranded vessel to prevent any Confederate salvagers from combing the site. However, when their fire was returned, the Union artillerymen quietly retired rather than jeopardize the impending landing. The Southerners jubilantly stripped the wreck of anything valuable and built a lookout on the ship's masthead, but they allowed their vigilance to lag. *Photo courtesy of MOLLUS, Mass., U.S.A.M.H.I.*

WRECK OF THE *RUBY*
albumen print

JOHN M. PARKER
copy print

More then 3,000 Federal infantry disembarked after an artillery bombardment on the southern tip of Morris Island on July 10, 1863, overwhelming the Confederate garrison of about 650 posted there. Among the triumphant Union soldiers who participated in this operation was Sgt. John M. Parker of Company I, 3rd New Hampshire Infantry.

A native of Kingston, New Hampshire, Parker was employed as a clerk at the time of his enlistment at Concord as a sergeant in August 1861. His regiment was engaged in fighting during 1862 on James Island, where they were among the Union units repulsed at Secessionville, and at Pocotaligo the following October. They swept forward from their victory on July 10 to the sandhills in front of Battery Wagner, where they were thrown back in a bloody assault a week later.

Parker received a furlough as a reward for his performance at Wagner and then became a lieutenant in Company C at the age of twenty-seven during November 1863, at which time he was still stationed on Morris Island. He transferred to Company A the following January when he was serving on Folly Island. Later hospitalized and then assigned to the ambulance service of the X Corps, he resigned from the army at Laurel Hill, Virginia, in October 1864. *Photo courtesy of MOLLUS, Mass., U.S.A.M.H.I.*

ALONZO T. DARGAN
copy print

Lt. Col. Alonzo T. Dargan of the 21st South Carolina escaped capture when portions of his regiment were overrun on the south tip of Morris Island on July 10, and he emerged unscathed from the desperate fighting at Battery Wagner the following day, when the remainder of his regiment played a prominent role in repelling a series of Federal assaults. Dargan and his troops remained on picket duty at Morris Island until Battery Wagner was evacuated in September 1863 and then went to Virginia eight months later. In the fighting at Walthall Junction they moved forward until they broke under a flanking fire, whereupon Dargan seized the regimental colors to rally his men. They did return, but not before he was shot and killed.

Born at Darlington in 1839, Dargan attended Wake Forest College and then studied law under his father and became a lawyer. He was elected as a lieutenant in Company B (Wild's Rifles) of the 21st South Carolina Infantry at Georgetown in December 1861, but he became lieutenant colonel the next month when the regiment was mustered into Confederate service. Until they were ordered to Virginia, his men served primarily, except for a brief trip to North Carolina, on James and Morris islands, where they conducted a reconnaissance on April 10, 1863, on Lighthouse Inlet, which the Federals crossed in July to land on Morris Island. *Photo courtesy of Confederate Relic Room, Columbia, South Carolina*

JAMES H. RION
carte de visite
Richard Wearn and William P. Hix

Maj. James H. Rion commanded the picket line at Battery Wagner during the Union attack on July 11, 1863, and then led a night raid three days later. His troops helped repulse the Federal assault on July 18 and often served in the post until its evacuation.

Born in Montreal, Canada, Rion spent much of his youth in South Carolina and graduated from South Carolina College in 1850. He practiced law in Winnsboro, where he raised the sixth infantry regiment authorized by the legislature in December 1860. He lost his commission when his troops entered Confederate service, so he enlisted Company B (Lyles Rifles) of the 7th Battalion, South Carolina Infantry, known as the Enfield Rifles, in November 1861. He served as their captain until April 1863, when he was promoted to major of the battalion, which merged with other units to form the 22nd South Carolina Infantry during the fall of 1863.

Rion's regiment went to Virginia in 1864 as part of Johnson Hagood's brigade. Just before the transfer, Rion endured a bout of typhoid fever, so he was absent when Col. Henry L. Benbow of the 23rd South Carolina Infantry chaired an investigation of disaffection among Rion's troops, despite Hagood's belief that these men were his best disciplined because of Rion's "zeal and ability." Rion was wounded twice near Petersburg, the first time when his troops exchanged volleys with the enemy at close range for ten minutes at Drewry's Bluff. In an assault on the Weldon Railroad on August 21, Rion's battalion had only 175 effectives, of whom 142 became casualties.

The remainder of his troops went to North Carolina in the fall. There Rion assumed command of a regiment comprised of all troops remaining in Hagood's brigade, a total of less than five hundred men. He was paroled with them at the war's end. *Photo courtesy of University of South Carolina, Columbia*

Confederates and Federals sparred on James Island during July 1863 in a mutual effort to distract attention from the struggle for Battery Wagner. Seventeen-year-old Pvt. Arthur M. Parker, Jr., of the Marion Artillery company in the South Carolina Light Artillery was with his unit when it took part in a reconnaissance on July 16 against the 54th Massachusetts Colored Infantry. This operation netted a number of prisoners, which ultimately proved a vexing problem for Confederate authorities.

Parker was photographed in 1862, when he had just enlisted in the Marion Artillery. He was initially stationed on the coast near Charleston at Adams Run, before he transferred in the summer of 1863 to James Island. Moving to Johns Island, they successfully engaged Federal batteries and infantry there during February and July 1864 while suffering only slight losses themselves. Parker had two horses shot from under him in these heated exchanges.

The final engagement of the Marion Artillery was against Federal landing parties north of Charleston during February 1865. They prevented the Union troops from establishing a beachhead until after the port city was evacuated and then marched to North Carolina, where the remnants of the Marion Artillery surrendered with Joseph E. Johnston's army at the end of the war. *Photo courtesy of University of South Carolina, Columbia*

ARTHUR M. PARKER, JR.
carte de visite
Quinby and Company

ROBERT GOULD SHAW
carte de visite

Col. Robert Gould Shaw arranged for his 54th Massachusetts Colored Infantry to lead the assault on Battery Wagner on July 18, 1863. When Gen. George C. Strong melodramatically asked who would carry the national standard if the color bearer fell, Colonel Shaw removed a cigar from his mouth and answered simply, "I will." Shaw stayed close to the color bearer while leading six hundred men in the evening attack on Wagner, which appeared to become a "mound of fire," and was killed on the parapet.[3]

Shaw was a member of a prominent Boston family. He attended Harvard for three years, but he left in 1859 to work in a New York accounting firm. In April 1861 he joined a three-month regiment and then in May accepted a commission as a lieutenant in the

2nd Massachusetts Infantry. He participated in many clashes while advancing to the rank of captain, and in the spring of 1863 became the colonel of the 54th Massachusetts Colored Infantry, the first black regiment from a free state. He married in May 1863 and then led his troops to South Carolina.

Shaw's troops had taken part in the raid on Darien, Georgia, and in the demonstration on James Island two days prior to the Battery Wagner assault. The Confederates buried him in a common grave along with the dead from his regiment. Gen. Quincy A. Gillmore offered to retrieve the body, but Shaw's father said it should remain where it was. *Photo courtesy of U.S.A.M.H.I.*

HIRAM AND
LEONIDAS M. JORDAN
copy print

Because Gen. Quincy A. Gillmore assumed that his preliminary artillery bombardment had eliminated any effective resistance by the Confederates within Battery Wagner, a number of white Union regiments were poised to follow the 54th Massachusetts Colored Infantry after that unit established itself within the parapets. Youthful Leonidas M. Jordan stood in the ranks of Company C of the 62nd Ohio Infantry, one of many privates who would not take the Confederate bastion that day, and who would then have to participate in a siege of almost two months.

The oldest son of Hiram Jordan, Leonidas was the principal supporter of his mother and six siblings due to the poor health of his father, who appears in this photograph with what appears to be a Bible in his hand. The younger Jordan enlisted at the outbreak of the war as a private in Company C. After the siege of Battery Wagner ended with a Confederate evacuation, he went home to Ohio, but he joined Company G of the 31st Ohio Infantry as a private in January 1864, four months before his father died.

While on a foraging detail in north Georgia during October of 1864, Jordan suddenly disappeared. His rifle, knapsack, and other equipment were found lying beside a tree, but he was not. Many assumed that he was captured or killed by "bushwhackers," and he was officially declared "missing." *Photo courtesy of U.S.A.M.H.I.*

ARLON S. ATHERTON
copy print

The jubilation of Cpl. Arlon S. Atherton and other members of the 3rd New Hampshire Infantry over their easy triumph on July 10 against the Confederates on the south end of Morris Island turned to bitter disappointment when they were among the regiments that failed to take Battery Wagner eight days later.

After enlisting as a private in Company G of the 3rd New Hampshire Infantry in August 1861, Atherton had arrived in South Carolina with his company during the invasion of Port Royal in November 1861. The defeat at Battery Wagner was not their first; Atherton was promoted to corporal after his regiment participated in the abortive assault on Secessionville during June 1862, when they approached to within forty yards of the Confederate works before being repulsed. His company also took part in the clash at Pocotaligo four months later.

Atherton was promoted to sergeant in September, after Wagner was abandoned. After his regiment was transferred to Virginia in 1864, Atherton was promoted to lieutenant in Company E and then was shot through the right side of his chest at Deep Run on August 8 and taken prisoner. He returned to duty and became captain of Company I, serving as an assistant provost marshal in charge of the city jail at Goldsboro, North Carolina, before his discharge at that city in July 1865. *Photo courtesy of U.S.A.M.H.I.*

176

A few persistent Federals did establish a toehold within Battery Wagner, and casualties were heavy among the Confederate units assigned to extricate them. Capt. John Ward Hopkins, a former shoemaker from Anderson, led Company D (Sumter Guards) of the 27th South Carolina Infantry during this operation. His company "suffered severely" (eight killed and twelve wounded) while repelling Union soldiers who had made their way into a "gun chamber."[4]

Originally a lieutenant in his company, which was assigned to the 1st (Charleston) Battalion of South Carolina Infantry, Hopkins became captain in June 1862 after he was wounded and his predecessor was killed in that month's fighting on James Island. He retained that rank after his unit merged with others to create the 27th South Carolina Infantry in the fall of 1862.

Posted in Fort Sumter after the evacuation of Battery Wagner in September 1863, Hopkins commanded all the troops on the sea-face parapet and gorge during the repulse of the Federal night attack that same month. Detachments under his command served at Charleston until April 1864, when they were sent to Virginia, where Hopkins had been born thirty-one years earlier. He was killed at Petersburg on June 16; his brigade commander, Johnson Hagood, recalled that "His loss was a calamity to the regiment." *Photo courtesy of University of South Carolina, Columbia*

JOHN WARD HOPKINS
carte de visite
George S. Cook

Hundreds of Federals, black and white, who charged at Battery Wagner on July 18, 1863, did not survive to taste the bitterness of defeat. Most of these soldiers were buried in common graves by their Confederate opponents who did not know the names of their foes and so recorded them simply as "unknowns." One such unfortunate was Pvt. Joseph W. White of Company A in the 7th New Hampshire Infantry.

White enrolled at the age of eighteen in October 1861 in Manchester, New Hampshire, where he worked in a cotton mill. He and his comrades landed at Port Royal in November 1861 and then disembarked on James Island in June 1862 after several months of operations along the South Carolina coast. They suffered heavy casualties in the assault on Secessionville that month, but were reinforced and put ashore on Morris Island the following summer. Repulsed in a bungled attack on Battery Wagner on July 11, when they advanced without supporting artillery fire, White and his companions took part in one last, and ultimately futile, attempt to take the earthwork by assault on July 18. *Photo courtesy of MOLLUS, Mass., U.S.A.M.H.I.*

JOSEPH W. WHITE
copy print

178

FULL SAP
albumen print
Haas and Peale

Having failed to take Battery Wagner by storm, Gen. Quincy A. Gillmore besieged the post, putting his troops to work digging trenches ever closer to the Confederate works. This reenactment of the operations on Morris Island during the summer of 1863 was staged by members of the 24th Massachusetts Infantry, on the left, and 1st New York Engineers, on the right, for photographers Haas and Peale. Large saps such as these protected most of the diggers from small-arms fire but did not shield them from well-placed mortar fire; fortunately for the Federals, the defenders of Battery Wagner had few of these. Those whom the saps failed to protect were either removed from the trenches or buried inside the trench walls themselves after the removal of bodies became too tedious.

On September 6, 1863, troops from the 24th Massachusetts Infantry and the 3rd New Hampshire Infantry stormed a ridge near Wagner, capturing sixty-seven Confederates who were afraid to leave their rifle pits because they did not know the disposition of mines placed nearby. The securing of this forward position permitted the construction of a fifth parallel. Within days of this close investment of Wagner by Union engineers and infantry shielded by saps, the Confederate garrison evacuated the post.
Photo courtesy of Library of Congress, no. B8178-17

BATTERY STEVENS
albumen print
Haas and Peale

Long-range shells fired by the gunners in Fort Sumter made work in the Federal trenches before Battery Wagner quite hazardous. Gen. Quincy A. Gillmore ordered the construction of batteries with siege guns to suppress the fire from Sumter. Digging for Battery Stevens and other such posts commenced on July 27, 1863. Heavy fire from Confederate positions forced the Union engineers to dig mostly at night. Work proceeded slowly, impeded by the high water table on Morris Island and the presence of numerous corpses. Many of these were the bodies of those killed in the earlier assaults on Wagner, but, allegedly, the island had also been used as a burial ground for quarantined persons who had died in antebellum Charleston.

Battery Stevens, which mounted a pair of 100-pounder Parrott rifled guns, was completed in time to take part in the saturation bombardment of Sumter, which began August 17. Detachments from Company C, 1st United States Artillery, and the 7th Connecticut Infantry served the guns, which soon destroyed many of the post's walls and silenced all of its cannons but one, a small smoothbore used as a signal gun. The Confederates removed their heavy artillery but reinforced Sumter as an infantry position, refusing to abandon the installation that had become a symbol of defiance. *Photo courtesy of Library of Congress, no. B8184-10001*

Two officers of the 1st United States Artillery, one of whom was involved in the siege of Battery Wagner, have been identified in this photograph. Capt. Loomis L. Langdon, who commanded two batteries on Morris Island during the summer of 1863, is leaning on the chair of an unidentified companion, while Lt. John S. Gibbs is seated at right.

Langdon, a native of New York, graduated from West Point in 1854 and was serving at Fort Pickens as a lieutenant in Battery A, 1st United States Artillery, when the war began. He endured the Confederate bombardment in the fall of 1861 and then in January 1862 was promoted to captain of Battery M, the remnants of which had been withdrawn from Texas

and were now stationed at Fort Jefferson in the Florida Keys. Battery M landed at Beaufort in June 1862 and then was engaged on October 22, 1862, at Pocotaligo, where one private was killed.

Gibbs was appointed a lieutenant in Battery B of the 1st United States Artillery in December 1861. The battery landed at Beaufort in June 1862, and shortly thereafter Gibbs transferred to Battery D, though he was assigned "special duty" with Battery M. He commanded that unit during Langdon's absence in the spring of 1863, and then he commanded his own battery when his captain left the following summer. *Photo courtesy of MOLLUS, Mass., U.S.A.M.H.I.*

LOOMIS L. LANGDON AND JOHN S. GIBBS
albumen print
Samuel A. Cooley

GEORGE D. RAMSAY, JR.
copy print

Second Lt. George D. Ramsay, Jr., had just graduated from West Point in 1863 when he was sent to Morris Island that summer as the acting ordnance officer. The son and namesake of the chief of ordnance for the Federal army, Ramsay was commissioned a second lieutenant in Battery D of the 1st United States Artillery (note the emblem on his cap), but he was not allowed to join his battery at Beaufort until the middle of August 1863. The quiet of that coastal town must have been a welcome respite after a long month of heat, sand, and almost constant combat. Ramsay remained in South Carolina only a few more months before he was promoted to lieutenant, transferred to the Ordnance Department, and assigned to the national arsenal in Washington. *Photo courtesy of U.S.A.M.H.I.*

The Federal batteries did murderous work within Battery Wagner. Capt. John H. Gary and Company A of the 15th Battalion, South Carolina Heavy Artillery (commanded by Maj. John J. Lucas, *pictured elsewhere*), were posted in Battery Wagner. Gary was mortally wounded when a lighted shell landed within his works; he seized it and threw it out, but it exploded while it was still too close to him. He died five days later, on August 17, 1863.

Gary, the younger brother of Gen. Martin W. Gary, was the captain of the cadet company at South Carolina College in 1861 when this portrait was made of him. Emily LeConte, the daughter of a professor at the college, recalled how Gary, standing upon a stage on the campus, "banner in hand spouted fire and fury and swore so many things about [the cadets'] flag."[5] He led his unit to Charleston, where they served on Sullivan's Island during the bombardment of Fort Sumter. They disbanded a few weeks later, but many, like Gary, found it difficult to return to their studies. He enlisted as a lieutenant in Company B of the 15th Battalion in June 1861, and on January 3, 1862, he was promoted to captain of Company A in the same organization. Only three weeks later, his 24-pounder rifled guns were the first to fire on the USS *Isaac P. Smith* in the Stono River. *Photo courtesy of Museum of the Confederacy, Richmond, Virginia*

JOHN H. GARY
carte de visite
Richard Wearn and William P. Hix

J. JULIUS ALSTON
carte de visite
Quinby and Company

Disease felled many of the Confederates who served in Battery Wagner during the summer of 1863, some of them long after that post was evacuated. Lt. J. Julius Alston of the 1st South Carolina Artillery served three times in Wagner and then died of typhoid fever contracted there after he returned to his home in Greeneville, South Carolina.

A South Carolina native educated at Cambridge College in Massachusetts, Alston practiced law until the Civil War began and then he and several associates outfitted a company at their own expense. Assigned to the 1st South Carolina Artillery, they served in Fort Sumter until they were posted on Morris Island at Lighthouse Inlet. During the Union assault on July 10, 1863, Alston was stunned when he was struck in the head by a piece of shell, but he recovered and led the remnants of his company to Wagner after their captain was killed. Alston commanded a gun during the repulse of the Federal attack on July 11 and then was sent to Sumter with his company to rest and recruit. He served twice more at his own request in Wagner, commanding a Columbiad in duels with Union monitors. According to his obituary, he was being considered for a promotion at the time of his death on September 20, 1863, two weeks after the Confederate evacuation of Wagner. *Photo courtesy of F. Bruce Kusrow*

FEDERAL SURGEONS, MORRIS ISLAND, 1863
albumen print
Haas and Peale

The casualties were almost as heavy among the Federal besiegers as they were among those inside Battery Wagner. This photograph of a medical operation being performed inside a tent that served as a Union field hospital was made on Morris Island in July 1863 during the siege of Wagner. The man in shirtsleeves with the hat and beard is Samuel A. Green, the chief medical officer of the island. Opposite Green, bending over the patient, is John J. Craven, medical director of the Department of the South.

The casual attire and lack of formal posing by the men within the tent suggest that this, unlike many other photographs taken by Haas and Peale, may be a genuine medical procedure and not a reenactment. There are no surgical instruments visible, but Green holds what appears to be a splint in his right hand as he bends over the table while the man by the patient's head is holding a white cloth that may be soaked in chloroform. The man on the table perhaps has a broken leg that requires the attention of the medical personnel. *Photo courtesy of MOLLUS, Mass., U.S.A.M.H.I.*

Devices such as these saw limited service with Union troops at Charleston. However, several Requia batteries were posted to protect Union gunners while they bombarded Battery Wagner prior to the Confederate evacuation, and they were also used to drive defenders from one of their last ridgetop positions obstructing the advance of the diggers behind the saps.

The Requia battery consisted of twenty-five rifle barrels, fixed side by side; cartridges were affixed to a strip of brass, inserted all at once, and fired by means of a single hammer. If properly handled, a Requia battery could fire 175 shots a minute and was allegedly effective at distances of more than a mile. This unit was photographed on Morris Island in 1863, the year in which companies of the 39th Illinois Infantry occupied Battery Wagner after the Confederates abandoned it in September. *Photo courtesy of Library of Congress, no. B8184-10619*

REQUIA BATTERY, 39TH ILLINOIS INFANTRY
albumen print

FORT SUMTER, 1863
albumen print
George S. Cook

The Federal fleet and shore batteries redoubled their efforts to reduce Fort Sumter after the Confederate evacuation of Battery Wagner during the night of September 6, 1863. George S. Cook, the noted Charleston photographer, visited the beleaguered post during the bombardment on September 8. Some of his equipment was carried away by Union shells when he climbed on the parapet to photograph the ironclads that were firing at Sumter, another round exploded in the parade ground as he exposed a plate, but he persisted and recorded some very compelling images of the post.

This photograph shows the eastern barracks of Fort Sumter. The upper deck and casemate are in ruins, while the parade ground is almost impassable due to rubble from exploding shells. The two Confederates are atop an oven used to heat solid shot during an engagement, an operation that had become anachronistic with the introduction of ironclads. It could also be used to bake bread for the soldiers housed in the barracks to the right. This barracks later collapsed when struck by a shell, killing many of the men who were sleeping inside. *Photo courtesy of Library of Congress, no. B8184-10448*

WILLIAM M. SMITH
carte de visite
Quinby and Company

JOHN O. CAMPBELL
carte de visite
F. Gutekunst, Philadelphia

On September 4, 1863, the Charleston Battalion was assigned to Fort Sumter as part of the 27th South Carolina Infantry. When Federals attacked in the early morning of September 9, William M. Smith hurled hand grenades and then, as adjutant of the post, accepted the surrender of 138 Union attackers.

This photograph of Smith was taken when he was a cadet at the Citadel, where he enrolled after attending King's Mountain Military Academy. He was eighteen years of age when he served on Morris Island with other cadets during the bombardment of Fort Sumter. Before graduating in 1863, he served as a drillmaster for recruits and tended to family property on the coast. In the summer of 1863 he was invited to join the staff of Gen. James J. Pettigrew, but Pettigrew was killed at Falling Waters. Smith then became quartermaster of the Charleston Battalion. He was buried in sand several times by artillery shells at Battery Wagner in August 1863, but he was not seriously injured.

After taking leave to cope with rheumatism, Smith resumed his duties as adjutant at Petersburg during May 1864. On June 3, he was shot through the groin at Cold Harbor. His mother tended him in the hospital and at the home of William P. Miles, but despite her ministrations, Smith died on August 19, 1864. *Photo courtesy of University of South Carolina, Columbia*

With the transfer of many Federal units from South Carolina to Virginia and the depletion of remaining organizations because of disease and battle casualties, recruitment became a top priority in the late summer and fall of 1863. Among the officers sent home to recruit was Capt. John O. Campbell of Pennsylvania.

During September 1861, Campbell had enlisted at the age of twenty-nine as a lieutenant in Company E of the 45th Pennsylvania Infantry at Spruce Creek. He was promoted to captain of his company two months later and commanded them in the spring and summer of 1862 along the South Carolina coast. He served as provost marshal while he was stationed on Hilton Head and then was sent home in the fall of 1863 to gather conscripts.

He returned in December 1863 to his regiment, which was sent to Virginia the following spring. He was shot during the Battle of the Wilderness on May 6, 1864, and died the next day from his wound. *Photo courtesy of MOLLUS, Mass., U.S.A.M.H.I.*

Gen. Pierre G. T. Beauregard enthusiastically supported the building of torpedo boats such as these, each of which was known as a "David" in honor of the first one built. Each craft was forty-eight feet in length and six feet in width, with a cabin squeezed between the boiler and the engine, which turned a single propeller. An explosive charge was carried on a pole protruding from the bow. In the water, almost nothing of a David could be seen except the smoke-stack and a few feet of deck, while a coat of blue-gray paint further reduced the steamer's visibility.

The first David was constructed near Charleston. A strike and the appropriation of the shipyard by the navy delayed its completion. Begun in November 1862,

the original *David* was not completed until September 1863. During the night of October 5, a crew of four maneuvered this vessel close to the USS *New Ironsides* and exploded a charge under their target, inflicting substantial damage. The Confederate craft was almost swamped in the explosion and two crewmen were retrieved from the water as prisoners, but the remaining pair navigated back to a Charleston wharf.

The original continued to operate in 1864, and several more like it were built. Nine were found in Charleston at the end of war; this is number four. Note the photographer's wagon beyond the bow. *Photo courtesy of National Archives*

A "David"
albumen print
S. R. Siebert

FORT SUMTER, DECEMBER 1863
albumen print
George S. Cook

Gen. Quincy A. Gillmore had a series of three
photographs taken of Fort Sumter during his reduction of that installation, which began on August 17,
1863. This final image was probably taken on
December 11, 1863. It is doubtful that George S. Cook
actually made this photograph, but he may well have
acquired a print that he could reproduce and offer for
sale to proud South Carolinians. At the end of the
month Maj. Stephen Elliott, Jr., commander of Fort
Sumter, reported that almost twenty thousand shells
had struck the post since August. While the installation was terribly battered, as Gillmore expected, casualties had been relatively light, and the Confederate
flag still flew defiantly over what was left of the walls,
which had been reinforced with sand, rubble, and
palmetto logs to create an almost impregnable earthwork. *Photo courtesy of University of South Carolina,
Columbia*

190

During the Federal siege of Battery Wagner in the summer of 1863, Company A (Palmetto Guards) of the 18th Battalion, South Carolina Artillery, manned their guns at Battery Haskell on James Island, near where they had fought with the USS *Pawnee* just four months earlier. After the evacuation of Wagner, they transferred to Charleston until December, when they again ventured forth in an attempt to destroy the USS *Marblehead* on Christmas Day.

One of the members of this itinerant company was James B. Keckeley, who had enlisted in February 1862 at Pocotaligo as a twenty-two-year-old private in Company A (Palmetto Guards), 18th Battalion of South Carolina Artillery, which was also known as Manigault's Battalion and the South Carolina Seige Train. He became a corporal and then a quartermaster sergeant in that unit in the summer of 1863. He traveled with them to north Florida in the spring of 1864 and then resumed picket duty at Charleston.

In December 1864 the company was issued antiquated Belgian muskets and posted under the command of their major, Edward M. Manigault, in rifle pits on James Island. More than a third of the Confederates were lost, including Manigault, when they were overrun by several Union regiments in February 1865, but Keckeley escaped and surrendered in North Carolina a few months later. *Photo courtesy of University of South Carolina, Columbia*

JAMES B. KECKELEY
carte de visite
Quinby and Company

WILLIAM H. H. ANCRUM
carte de visite
George S. Cook

Before daylight on December 24, 1863, Company A (Palmetto Guards) of the 18th Battalion of South Carolina Artillery quietly took their positions at Legareville on the Stono River, where masked batteries had been prepared for their guns. Among the privates was William H. H. Ancrum, who had enlisted in March 1863 at the age of eighteen in what became known as Manigault's Battalion after Maj. Edward M. Manigault took command a few months later, though some continued to refer to it as the South Carolina Siege Train.

Ancrum's company positioned their two 30-pounder Parrotts and then at sunrise began firing at the USS *Marblehead*. The reply from the Union gunboat and two others that came to its rescue was terribly accurate. When Ancrum brought forward a team of horses to drag his guns to safety, a shell tore off his leg and killed two of the horses. Ancrum died a few hours later, after the Confederates abandoned Legareville. Ironically, the *Marblehead* was struck twenty times but suffered almost no damage because the shells were faulty and failed to explode upon impact. *Photo courtesy of University of South Carolina, Columbia*

Federal forces were sent from South Carolina to Florida during February to conduct an offensive in the latter state. To prevent Confederates from dispatching reinforcements in a similar manner, the remaining Union regiments along the coast of South Carolina conducted a series of raids to divert the attention of the defenders near Charleston. Lt. Charles F. Bornemann of Company D, 41st New York Infantry, took part with his comrades in clashes with Confederate forces on John's and James islands in February, when a Union raid on the Charleston and Savannah Railroad was undertaken, and then returned to James Island in May.

A twenty-two-year-old "piano maker," Bornemann had joined Company D as a private in June 1861 at New York City. He became a corporal in March 1862 and a sergeant the following December. During March 1863 he became sergeant major of his regiment, which soon thereafter fought at Gettysburg. Eight months later, after his unit had been sent to Folly Island, he was appointed a lieutenant, with the commission backdated to the first day of battle at Gettysburg (where he apparently fought). He left the army during June 1864 because of a disability. *Photo courtesy of U.S.A.M.H.I.*

JOHN S. DUTART
copy print of ambrotype

In the early morning hours of February 9, 1864, about a thousand Federals advanced across Seabrook and Kiawah islands and captured a picket force from Company C of the 6th South Carolina Cavalry at Haulover Cut on John's Island. Many members of Company C were former cadets from the Citadel; their captain, Moses B. Humphrey, led about three dozen of them in a desperate attempt to stop the Union advance. In the predawn darkness and thick fog, Humphrey mistakenly assumed the Federals were withdrawing and ordered his men to charge. As Sgt. John S. Dutart approached the Union position, he was shot three times and instantly killed.

Dutart, a native of Charleston, was nineteen years of age when he joined thirty-five of his fellow cadets in leaving the Citadel during June 1862. They performed their duties that day and then after supper lined up and walked through the front gates, giving their names to and shaking hands with the cadet serving as officer of the day. The rebels formed an independent company, which was soon thereafter incorporated as Company C in the 6th South Carolina Cavalry and assigned to picket duty along the coast of their home state. *Photo courtesy of Citadel Archives, Charleston, South Carolina*

WILLIAM P. EMANUEL
copy print

Sixteen former students of the Citadel became prisoners of war; one of these was William P. Emanuel. He also endured the unhappy distinction of being the highest ranking South Carolinian among the "Immortal Six Hundred" confined under fire on Morris Island in September 1864 in retaliation for the quartering of captive Federals in Charleston while it was being bombarded. Emanuel and the others were placed in a stockade near Battery Wagner. There they were guarded by members of the 54th Massachusetts Colored Infantry, who presumably were not any happier than their charges at being between the contending guns. Miraculously, only a few prisoners were wounded during their forty-four days under fire.

A native of Marlboro County, Emanuel enlisted as a captain in Company C of the 12th Battalion, South Carolina Cavalry, and then became a major and retained that rank after his original command was consolidated with others in December 1862 to create the 4th South Carolina Cavalry. In 1862 he served on the coast of his home state, though for the latter half of that year he was under arrest by order of Gen. Pierre G. T. Beauregard, who held him responsible for misconduct by his men. Transferred to Virginia with the rest of his command, he fought at Haw's Shop in May 1864 and at Cold Harbor. He then was captured at Trevilian Station on June 11, 1864, and sent to Fort Delaware, whence he was transferred to Morris Island. *Photo courtesy of U.S.A.M.H.I.*

Conditions for Federal prisoners in South Carolina were certainly no better than those afforded the Confederates on Morris Island in the fall of 1864. The suspension of exchange programs during the last year and a half of the war forced the hasty creation of new prison pens. The most notorious of these was at Florence, where prisoners from Charleston were sent in the fall of 1864 along with the overflow from Andersonville in Georgia. Rations were meager and only a fourth of the prisoners had blankets, while trees left standing inside the stockade were quickly cut down for fuel and shelter. Brush arbors served as a hospital, where as many as fifty prisoners a day died from disease.

Thomas Silk, who recorded his occupation as shoemaker, enlisted as a private in Company D, 4th Massachusetts Cavalry, at Readville during January 1864, when he was eighteen years of age. He was captured at Gainesville, Florida, in August 1864 and sent to Florence. Arrangements were made for an exchange of five thousand invalid prisoners at Savannah in November 1864; when the lines of communication between that port and Florence were cut, Federal officials moved to Charleston to complete the exchange. Silk was among the Union prisoners repatriated at Charleston, but he did not return to active duty until May 1865. *Photo courtesy of U.S.A.M.H.I.*

THOMAS SILK
copy print

196

BENJAMIN DITCHER
albumen print
Haas and Peale

Discipline within the Federal army on the South Carolina coast was inexorable and often harsh. Benjamin Ditcher is the unhappy prisoner with his head shaved and his hands bound behind him, wearing a placard that explains to onlookers that he "Stole Money from a Wounded FRIEND." The musicians with him are playing the "Rogue's March," which along with the escort carrying reversed rifles was standard procedure for incidents such as this.

Ditcher was an eighteen-year-old freedman employed as a barber who enlisted as a private in Company F, 55th Massachusetts Colored Infantry, at Readville in June 1863. The court martial in August 1864 sentenced him to hard labor—with a log chained to his leg—in confinement for a month, during which on each Monday he would have his head shaved and be paraded with the placard. He also had a month's pay, sixteen dollars, deducted, though he stole only two dollars from the servant of an officer.

Discharged from custody, Ditcher was wounded in the charge of the 55th Massachusetts at Honey Hill on November 30, 1864. During March 1865 he deserted while his regiment was marching through Charleston and was returned under arrest; he was confined in Castle Pinckney for three months and fined another month's pay. After his release he was mustered out of the service in August 1865. *Photo courtesy of Library of Congress, no. B8184-4546*

197

JOHN P. HATCH
albumen print
George N. Barnard

Gen. John P. Hatch, a West Point graduate and veteran of the Mexican War, assumed command of the Federal troops at Hilton Head in June 1864. During the next six months he participated in a number of operations intended to cut the Charleston and Savannah Railroad, with little success. He was finally able to position field artillery batteries that made daylight travel on the line quite hazardous. At the end of the war he was commander of the District of Charleston, in which city this photograph was taken of the general at his headquarters.

The inclusion of a large magnolia blossom belies his martial abilities. He began the war as a captain in charge of commissary operations in New Mexico, but he commanded a cavalry brigade that fought in the Shenandoah Valley during 1862 and briefly commanded a division at Second Bull Run and South Mountain, where he was severely wounded in a performance that earned him a Medal of Honor. It was only after his convalescence and a stint of administrative duties that he came to South Carolina. *Photo courtesy of MOLLUS, Mass., U.S.A.M.H.I.*

The constant pressure of Union operations on the coast, along with the demands of Richmond authorities for units to fight in Virginia, drained South Carolina of manpower. In the summer of 1864 the Cadet Battalion, composed of students from the Citadel in Charleston and the Arsenal Academy in Columbia, was posted on James Island. During the following November many of the Cadets were rushed to Honey Hill, where they assisted in the repulse of Union troops trying once more to cut the Charleston and Savannah Railroad. The cadets' mettle was truly tested on December 7 when they faced Federals that had bypassed the Honey Hill positions and landed along the Tulifinny River. The Union veterans pushed the makeshift collection of defenders aside, but the cadets led a counter-attack that retook the lost ground. Despite such efforts, however, the Federals were able to position artillery to enfilade the railroad, making it useless.

Among the Cadets from the Citadel was Orderly Sgt. William H. Snowden of Company B, a native of Charleston. They returned to James Island and then marched out of Snowden's hometown when it was evacuated in February 1865 and were furloughed two months later. This cabinet print is a copy of a photograph taken of Snowden when he was a cadet during the war. *Photo courtesy of Citadel Archives, Charleston, South Carolina*

WILLIAM H. SNOWDEN
cabinet print
Liedloff's Studio, Charleston

Chapter 6

Staying Power: South Carolinians in the West

A captain in the 3rd South Carolina Infantry described the troops from his home state as "impetuous" and "reckless with mad fury during a charge," but he declared that "they lacked staying power."[1] The many South Carolinians who fought in the Army of Tennessee proved otherwise. They did not join that ill-fated organization until after the bloody fighting at Shiloh in 1862, but they stayed with it through the grinding Hundred Days before Atlanta and the disasterous final drive into Tennessee under the impetuous John Bell Hood. Refusing to quit after the debacle in the snow at Nashville in December 1864 and the heart-breaking retreat into Mississippi, the remnants of proud South Carolina regiments marched with others to face the troops of William T. Sherman once more in North Carolina before the Southerners laid down their arms for good.

After the Confederates lost a tremendous opportunity to destroy Gen. Ulysses S. Grant's Federals at Shiloh, Gen. Pierre G. T. Beauregard, given command of the Confederate forces in north Mississippi after the death of Albert Sidney Johnston, called for reinforcements from South Carolina. In response to his pleas, two regiments,

the 10th and 19th South Carolina Infantry, were sent to Corinth. There they were assigned to a brigade commanded by fellow South Carolinian James H. Trapier, a veteran of the U. S. Army who had supervised the construction of coastal defenses in his home state until he was transferred west.

The 10th South Carolina Infantry was commanded by an officer who became one of the most noted combat commanders in the Army of Tennessee: Arthur M. Manigault, who rose to the rank of brigadier general before a head wound he suffered at Franklin in November 1864 compelled his retirement. Of the ten South Carolina regiments authorized in December 1860, only Manigault's regiment was not sent to Virginia; instead, it had remained on the South Carolina coast until ordered west. While in his home state, Manigault had served in the bombardment of Fort Sumter and then had busied himself with the construction of coastal defenses. Now, he would get the chance to prove himself in battle.

It was not long before Manigault's ability was recognized. In May 1862, when Trapier was transferred to command a division, Manigault temporarily took charge of the brigade that later bore his name. He led it in the futile attempt to stop Gen. Henry W. Halleck's cautious advance, fighting with the Federal army at Farmington on May 28 shortly before Beauregard abandoned Corinth. Trapier, at his own request due to his health, was reassigned in the fall of 1862 to command the Fourth Military District in South Carolina. Manigault succeeded him in command of the brigade, in which capacity he had been serving through the summer, though in fact this shift in leadership was not officially sanctioned until April 1863.

Beauregard left on leave during June 1862 and soon returned to South Carolina, but Manigault remained in the west and led his brigade during Gen. Braxton Bragg's invasion of Kentucky in the late summer and fall of 1862. At Munfordville, on the Green River, the 10th South Carolina skirmished with the Union garrison for three days before the latter surrendered on September 17, delivering almost five thousand prisoners into the hands of the Confederates. Manigault's troops did not fight at Perryville, but they did serve in the rear guard during Bragg's retreat into Tennessee. Though many of the South Carolinians were clothed in rags and marched without shoes, they clashed sharply with the pursuing Federals on at least one occasion.

Following his defeat at Perryville, Bragg retreated to the vicinity of Murfreesboro and reorganized his command, which henceforth was known as the Army of Tennessee. In late December, informed that a Union army was moving south from Nashville to attack him, Bragg chose to meet them along the Stones River at Murfreesboro. Each side intended to attack with their left wing while holding fast with their right. When Bragg attacked first on December 31, 1862, and won the initiative, Manigault's brigade was among the last to go into action on the Confederate left. His troops were twice repulsed by enfilading fire, but the third time they swept the Federals back until the Confederates rallied on the Nashville Turnpike.

Manigault's losses on the first day at Murfreesboro were heavy: of about 2,200 effectives, approx-

imately 530 men and officers were killed and wounded, including the commander of the 19th South Carolina Infantry. In Manigault's original command, the 10th South Carolina Infantry, five out of seven captains were killed or wounded. The South Carolina regiments, however, had fought well. They took a battery of four guns that had inflicted heavy casualties on them, inscribed the cannon with the names of the men who died in the assault, and sent the guns to Charleston for a formal presentation to the government of South Carolina.

Manigault's weary South Carolinians were joined by others from their home state in 1863. In early May, Beauregard was asked to send reinforcements from Charleston to assist in the defense of Vicksburg. He responded by sending two infantry brigades. One of the brigades, under the command of Gen. States Rights Gist, included two South Carolina regiments, the 24th and the 16th, and a battery commanded by Thomas B. Ferguson, a Citadel graduate who had fired one of the guns trained on the *Star of the West* at Charleston in January 1861.

The 24th South Carolina Infantry, commanded by Lt. Col. Ellison Capers, arrived in Mississippi in time to take part in the fighting at Jackson when Grant's troops attacked on May 14, 1863. Assigned with other Confederate troops to defend a ridge on the road between Jackson and Clinton, Capers' regiment was assailed by an entire Union division, which advanced through a driving rainstorm. They managed to hold their position for four hours until they were forced to withdraw after fighting at close range with the Federals. Capers was himself wounded and lost 105 casualties; the Federals lost more than twice that number, but they occupied Jackson later that afternoon.

By mid-May, the situation in Mississippi had deteriorated enough that Nathan G. Evans' veteran brigade was ordered west from South Carolina, despite the protests of Beauregard and Gov. Francis W. Pickens. This brigade included six South Carolina regiments, but even these reinforcements did not provide Gen. Joseph E. Johnston, who had been given the responsibility for rescuing Vicksburg, with sufficient troops to break the Union grip on the besieged river port. The South Carolinians and other units under Johnston's command did little more than wait until the siege ended with the surrender of the Confederate garrison.

After the fall of Vicksburg, Gist's brigade was transferred to the Army of Tennessee when Bragg called for reinforcements. Gist's reunion with Manigault took place within the context of the greatest concentration of troops ever accomplished by the Confederacy. By the late summer of 1863, Bragg's army had been maneuvered out of the state of Tennessee. Reinforced with the newcomers from Mississippi and five brigades of Longstreet's corps from Virginia—among which were Joseph B. Kershaw's and Micah Jenkins' South Carolinians— Bragg resolved to strike back at his opponent, Gen. William S. Rosecrans, in the tangled woods along Chickamauga Creek.

None of the South Carolina troops were engaged on the first day at Chickamauga—September 19, 1863—but the following day was a different story. Gist arrived on the morning of the second day after an all-night march with part of his command, among which was Capers' 24th South Carolina Infantry. Kershaw assumed command of those parts of Lafayette McLaws' division that were on the field, including his own brigade, and took charge of Gen. John Bell Hood's three brigades after that officer suffered a wound that later necessitated the amputation of his leg. On the extreme left of the Confederate line was Manigault's brigade, which still included the 10th and 19th South Carolina Infantry.

Gist's small brigade, which numbered no more than 1,000 very tired men, was ordered at about eleven o'clock to advance into the woods to support several Confederate units whose assault on the Federal left had failed. The 24th South Carolina Infantry led the way, but they were repulsed after almost forty minutes of desperate fighting in which the regiment suffered 169 casualties. Despite such a rough beginning, however, they were reinforced and returned to the fighting to take part in the pursuit of routed Federals later in the day.

About midday, on the Confederate left, Kershaw threw the five brigades under his command across the Chattanooga road and drove the Union troops before him back to Snodgrass Hill, where they rallied under the direction of Gen. George H. Thomas. Kershaw was quickly reinforced, but the Federals easily repulsed a series of uncoordinated assaults by the Confederates. Nevertheless, the Confederates continued their attacks until darkness ended the fighting and allowed Thomas to withdraw his troops to safety, having saved the Union army from a complete rout.

Manigault's brigade also fought on the left of the Confederate line. His men attacked at about lunchtime, but were unable to carry the Union works in their front and were driven back when Federal troops flanked them on the left. Only the success of Kershaw and other Confederates forced the Union defenders to abandon their works in front of Manigault. Moving forward once more, Manigault's brigade flung themselves at the final line of defense formed by Thomas, pushing their Union opponents back in disorganized fighting among thick timber but not breaking their perimeter. In the confusion, the flag of the 10th South Carolina Infantry was captured, but it was just as swiftly regained by the regiment to which it belonged.

Chickamauga was a victory for the Confederates, but they suffered more casualties than the opponents whom they had driven from the field. In all, 1,196 South Carolinians were killed or wounded at Chickamauga. Kershaw lost 488 men from his brigade; Manigault's losses totaled at least 539, though some reports indicate that this number was actually greater. Manigault himself narrowly escaped serious injury. A bullet hit his horse, passing through under its saddle and then tearing through one of the general's pants legs and nearly cutting his sword in half.

After their victory at Chickamauga, Bragg's army beseiged the defeated Federals in the city of Chattanooga. The Confederates occupied Lookout Mountain and Missionary Ridge, preventing most supplies from reaching the Union forces by road or by riverboats, which could travel up the Tennessee River. Among the besiegers, command of Hood's division at this crucial juncture was given to Jenkins. At the same time, the leadership of Jenkins' brigade devolved upon Col. John Bratton. Longstreet, when ordered west to reinforce Bragg, had weakened his corps by dispatching two brigades to help defend Charleston, but had insisted upon retaining Jenkins' brigade, recognizing the South Carolinian's qualities as a fighter. Now the young Jenkins found himself in a position of great responsibility.

During the night of October 28, 1864, after Federal troops had crossed the Tennessee River and were preparing to assault the Confederate positions on Lookout Mountain, Longstreet ordered Jenkins to attack an isolated Union division. Bratton's South Carolina brigade attacked the Federal camp near Wauhatchie and drove the enemy back in confused fighting, but when two other Union divisions arrived he was told to withdraw rather than risk being overwhelmed by repeated Federal charges. In all, Bratton suffered 408 casualties, only a few less than his opponent, and failed to prevent the Union forces from opening a vital supply line to Chattanooga.

Realizing that he would not be able to take Chattanooga by siege, Bragg, at the suggestion of Jefferson Davis, turned his attention to pushing the Federals out of Knoxville. He sent Longstreet with two divisions, which included the South Carolina brigades of Jenkins and Kershaw, up the Tennessee Valley during November 1863. Jenkins' brigade was heavily engaged in the fighting that accompanied the advance on Knoxville in which the Confederates failed to prevent the Union troops from withdrawing into the well-prepared defenses surrounding the city. On November 18, Kershaw's troops drove the Union defenders from a section

of their advance positions, but a massed assault by elements of that brigade and others on November 29 against the Federal salient at Fort Sanders failed miserably. Longstreet, upon the approach of Union reinforcements, withdrew northeast and went into winter camp near Greeneville, Tennessee.

Longstreet's campaign in Tennessee precipitated a clash between two South Carolina generals that hindered both of their careers. Evander M. Law served in Hood's division at Gettysburg, taking charge after his superior was wounded. Jenkins, who like Law had studied at the Citadel, was not with Hood during that battle, but the return of his brigade from detached duty for the Tennessee campaign brought controversy, as Law was junior to him in rank. Hood resumed command to avoid a conflict, but his loss of a leg at Chickamauga forced Longstreet to choose a temporary successor for him. He chose Law, but Jenkins later led the division at Wauhatchie. Law, on detached duty with a brigade, was ordered by Longstreet to support Jenkins but failed to do so. Longstreet's later assault at Campbell's Station also miscarried because Law did not cooperate with Jenkins. Longstreet attempted to have Law removed from command, but he failed. Understandably, when Hood was given command of a corps, his division was not given to Law or to Longstreet's favorite, Jenkins, but to Charles W. Field.

Another controversy that involved Jenkins during the Tennessee campaign led to a promotion for another South Carolina general, Kershaw. On the morning of the attack at Fort Sanders, in which Jenkins' troops were to participate, he asked Lafayette McLaws, his senior in rank and the commander of the vanguard for the assault, whether it might not be prudent to have the men carry fascines with them, in order to fill the ditch in front of the Union parapet. McLaws refused the suggestion, and when Jenkins forwarded his misgivings to Longstreet, that commander also told him to forget about the fascines. When the Confederates charged on November 29, they became mired in the muddy, icy ditch. Many were killed; others surrendered rather than running the gauntlet of fire and returning to their own lines. Of the Confederate force, 813 were killed, wounded, or missing; Union losses were no more than 100. McLaws was subsequently relieved and never returned to Longstreet's corps; Kershaw took charge of his division.

While Jenkins' and Kershaw's troops were engaged in the futile campaign against Knoxville, four South Carolina regiments, in the brigades led by Manigault and Gist, were among the troops forced to withdraw from Missionary Ridge and thus abandon the southeast corner of Tennessee to the Federals. Manigault later remembered that he did not believe the Union attack up the ridge during the evening of November 25 could possibly succeed, but he did recall that many of his men were unusually agitated as they watched their opponents advance toward them. Taking advantage of the poor placement of many of the Confederate units, the Federals poured a withering fire into the defenders, forcing them to fall back and ultimately to leave the state altogether.

Many South Carolinians on Missionary Ridge stood their ground longer than most of the other Confederate units around them. Manigault's second line, those upon the top of the ridge, had a clear field of fire, and so they fought until the brigades on their right and left broke under the fire of Union attackers who took advantage of cover just in front of their positions. Two of Manigault's regiments, including the 10th South Carolina, tried to maintain their line, but the others gave way despite his order to his provost guard to shoot anyone who ran. Finally, Manigault ordered a retreat to a ridge five hundred yards to the rear and then fled through a hail of bullets to safety. About two-thirds of his panic-stricken men and officers—some of them stopped only by the threats of others to shoot them if they continued to run—rallied around him on the second ridge, where a check revealed that the brigade had lost 366 men.

During May 1864, Gen. William T. Sherman advanced south to Atlanta. He was opposed by the Army of Tennessee, now led by Joseph E. Johnston and which included two artillery batteries and four infantry regiments from South Carolina, brigaded under Gist and Manigault. A third South Carolina brigadier general, Clement H. Stevens, led an aggregation of Georgia regiments during the Hundred Days, as the Confederate defense of Atlanta came to be known. The South Carolina regiments were frequently engaged as Johnston maneuvered to remain between Sherman and Atlanta. The Confederate losses were less than half of those suffered by the Federals, but the former were not insignificant. Manigault's brigade lost almost 120 men and officers at Resaca to artillery fire while they waited in reserve in the second line of defense.

Johnston steadily retreated until he was replaced on the very outskirts of Atlanta by Hood in a change of command that most of the South Carolinians apparently opposed. Manigault had formed a negative opinion of Hood while serving in his corps during the fighting at Zion Church near Marietta, Georgia, on June 22, 1864. Hood ordered Manigault's brigade to take and hold a belt of woods occupied by Union troops on the right flank of the Confederate line, while other units swept forward to force the Federals to abandon their entrenchments elsewhere in the area. The South Carolinians did their job well, but the others were stopped by a deep boggy creek and withdrew after suffering heavy casualties. Manigault, whose men consequently had to spend a long night under incessant artillery and small arms fire in their exposed forward posts, never forgave Hood for this "miserable failure" that "cost us 1,500 or 2,000 men, to no purpose." He later wrote that the appointment of Hood was regarded as a "calamity" by the Army of Tennessee, and he bitterly added that it was "one of those hasty and ill-judged steps on the part of Mr. Davis" that "contributed materially to the downfall of the Confederacy, and possibly it caused it." After Hood replaced Johnston,

Manigault concluded, "From bad to worse we hurried to our ruin."[2]

Having assumed command of the Army of Tennessee, Hood soon bled it white in a series of futile assaults on Sherman's forces. The first was on July 20, while the Union army was astride Peachtree Creek to the north of Atlanta. In this engagement, the division of William H. T. Walker, to which was assigned Gist's brigade, suffered many casualties in a frontal attack on their opponents. At the same time, General Stevens, whom Manigault characterized as "one of the best officers in our army," was killed.[3] During Hood's second sortie on July 22, in which Walker lost his life, both Gist's and Manigault's South Carolinians fought in the front lines. Manigault's brigade led a Confederate assault along the railroad toward Decatur, losing 430 casualties but capturing a Federal battery.

Stephen D. Lee of South Carolina, who had returned to action after being captured at Vicksburg, took charge of Hood's corps on July 27. The following day, at Ezra Church, he directed a series of unsuccessful attacks on the Federal lines southwest of Atlanta. Manigault's troops, assured that they would encounter only light resistance, charged into well-entrenched Union lines, which had easily repulsed earlier assaults, and were thrown back with heavy casualties. Manigault, recalling that desperate effort, declared that "it was a sad sight to see the shattered remnant of this fine body of men as they withdrew from the contest, to think what had become of the rest of them, and how uselessly and foolishly they had been butchered."[4]

Having exhausted its offensive power, the Army of Tennessee settled into its trenches before Atlanta to await Sherman's next move. The Federals began to envelop the city, intending to cut its supply lines and either trap Hood or force him to evacuate. On August 31, 1864, Lee's corps and that of William J. Hardee—which included Manigault's and Gist's brigades—failed to push Sherman's army back from Jonesboro, which lay upon Hood's last railroad from Atlanta. Manigault's men, tired and dis-

couraged, were ordered to attack the main Federal lines, but he admitted that, despite his greatest efforts, they could not be induced to approach within eighty yards of the Union works.

With his last line of communication threatened, Hood decided to abandon Atlanta. When Lee retired northward from Jonesboro on September 1 to screen the Confederate evacuation, parts of five Union corps converged on Hardee at that essential point upon the southbound rail line. Gist's brigade formed the right flank of Hardee's thin line; the railroad cut itself was defended by the 24th South Carolina Infantry, which was supported by the 16th South Carolina Infantry and other units. The Federals captured an entire brigade in the center of Hardee's perimeter, but the South Carolinians repulsed their attackers, in part because of careful preparations that included erecting timber barricades and interlacing small trees to serve as abatis. Hardee himself rode over to congratulate the defenders of his right flank. Later, he withdrew his troops south to Lovejoy's Station, where he battled with pursuing Federals for several days until he was joined by the remaining two corps of Hood's army.

The number of South Carolinians who answered the roll calls south of Atlanta was only a fraction of those who had served in the Army of Tennessee prior to the Hundred Days. During the Atlanta campaign, Manigault estimated that he had about 2,100 troops in his brigade. Of these men, 1,250 were killed or wounded, 150 were captured or reported missing, and 75 became ill and were sent behind the lines to convalesce. By early September, after the fall of Atlanta, Manigault reported that he had about 625 effectives. Most of the casualties he attributed to Hood's rash actions after he assumed command at Atlanta.

After the Federals captured Atlanta, they settled in that city while Hood pondered his next move and reorganized his army near Palmetto, Georgia. By the last week of September 1864, Hood had decided to try luring Sherman north by marching into Tennessee. Gist's brigade and others were ordered to assault Dalton, but the Union garrison surrendered without a struggle. The 24th South Carolina Infantry was not so lucky a few days later: on October 16 they were ordered to hold Ship's Gap as a screen for the rest of the army. Ellison Capers, their colonel, placed two companies in advance of his main line and then reported to Gist that he could see at least seventeen regimental flags among the Federal host advancing toward him. Told to stand fast, Capers lost more than three dozen officers and men when his advance detachment was overwhelmed, but he managed to extricate the remainder of his regiment after a spirited exchange of fire.

Without further incident, the Confederates marched north and west into Alabama, where some of them received new clothing and shoes, and then continued into Tennessee, despite the misgivings of Hood's corps commanders, including Lee. Hood pursued the Union troops that withdrew before him to Franklin, where they settled in well-prepared fortifications to shield the crossing of their wagon train. On November 30, 1864, Hood unwisely ordered his troops to assault the main Union defensive line, across two miles of open ground and without a preliminary artillery bombardment. Despite their reservations, his officers formed their men into line and advanced toward the Union works.

The ensuing engagement was a disaster for the Confederates. Some of them reached the Federal emplacements, where they fought hand-to-hand trying to hold their position, but they suffered 6,252 casualties, which was almost one-fourth of those who were engaged and more than twice the number of Union casualties. Among the dead was Gist,

shot through the chest while leading his brigade forward after his horse was killed under him. Both Capers and Manigault, who did not lead his troops into the fight until late in the afternoon, were wounded. The former recovered and was able to return to duty, but the latter, shot in the head during the final Confederate charge, had to leave the service.

After their crushing victory at Franklin, the Federals marched to Nashville. Hood followed and, though his troops were too few for an assault, laid siege as best he could to the well-entrenched, more numerous Union force. Pressed by his superiors, the Federal commander at Nashville, Gen. George H. Thomas, attacked Hood on December 15 and 16, 1864, decisively beating Hood's weary men. During the fighting, Manigault's old brigade was moved from the center of the Confederate line to the left, where they took cover behind a stone wall, but the overwhelming number of Federals proved to be too much; the South Carolinians broke and ran.

Elsewhere on the first day, and again on the second, most of the thin Confederate line was repeatedly pushed back until, on the night of December 16, Hood decided to abandon Tennessee. Lee's corps undertook the grim task of serving as a rear guard for the retreat until the remnants of the Army of Tennessee arrived in Mississippi, where Hood resigned. Obedient to the last, the few South Carolinians who remained, as well as many others, marched east under the command of Lee and other officers in an effort to bolster the tiny army waiting in North Carolina under the command of Joseph E. Johnston. There they would fight Sherman's troops again before being allowed to return home.

JOHN B. VILLEPIGUE
albumen print

Most South Carolinians did not arrive in the west until after the battle at Shiloh, but a few professional soldiers from that state did serve with the western Confederate forces from the onset of the war. Among them was John B. Villepigue, a native of Camden who graduated from West Point in 1856 and then served five years in the dragoons on the western frontier before assuming command of the 36th Georgia Infantry during 1861.

Seriously wounded while commanding the defenders of Fort McRae at Pensacola during a Federal bombardment, Villepigue soon recovered and was appointed Chief of Engineers and Artillery for Gen. Braxton Bragg. Promoted to brigadier general, Villepigue assumed command of the garrison at Fort Pillow on the Mississippi River during the summer of 1862. He conducted a skillful defense until the more numerous Union forces compelled him to retire, whereupon he destroyed his works and led his troops to safety.

Villepigue commanded a brigade at Corinth in the late summer and fall of 1862 and then contracted a "long and serious illness." He died at the age of thirty-two on November 9, 1862. *Photo courtesy of University of South Carolina, Columbia*

BENJAMIN HUGER
carte de visite
E. and H. T. Anthony

The western theater, especially the Trans-Mississippi, frequently served as a professional graveyard for those officers who fell out of favor with the authorities in Richmond. Fortunately, not a few of these military exiles proved to have substantial talent. One such itinerant was Benjamin Huger (pronounced hu-GEE), a native of Charleston who bore the name of a well-known Huguenot family and whose grandfather and father fought in the Revolution and War of 1812, respectively. He graduated from West Point in 1825, at the age of nineteen, and earned three brevets as Chief of Ordnance during the Mexican War, one of only four officers so honored. He was in charge of the Federal arsenal in Charleston from November 1860 until after the fall of Fort Sumter and then resigned as a major and within six months became a major general for the Confederacy.

He commanded the Confederate forces at Norfolk, Virginia, but he abandoned the naval yard when Federal forces landed on the Peninsula. He then took charge of a division and was criticized for not pressing his attacks at Seven Pines and White Oak Swamp. He was given the title of inspector of ordnance and artillery and sent west to supervise manufacturing operations; then he was assigned to the Trans-Mississippi before the war ended. *Photo courtesy of University of South Carolina, Columbia*

NATHAN G. EVANS
cabinet print
John H. King, Baltimore, Maryland

Nathan G. Evans' career as a Confederate began well, but it was derailed after the Vicksburg campaign when he was tried and acquitted for drunkenness and disobedience but was nevertheless removed from command by Gen. Pierre G. T. Beauregard.

Born in Marion, Evans attended Randolph-Macon College and then graduated from West Point in 1848 and served on the frontier. The South Carolina legislature awarded him a sword for killing two Comanche chiefs. He married the sister of Martin W. Gary and then resigned his captaincy in February 1861. As a major in the South Carolina army, he commanded on James Island during the bombardment of Fort Sumter. As a captain in Confederate service he led a brigade at First Bull Run and then was promoted to colonel and commanded the Confederates at Ball's Bluff. For the latter victory he received a commendation from the Confederate Congress and a medal from the legislature

of South Carolina, and he was immortalized in a song entitled "The Southern Land of Canaan."

He became a brigadier general and assumed command of the Third District in South Carolina in time for the Federal attack at Secessionville in July 1862. Evans next led a South Carolina brigade at Second Bull Run, South Mountain, and Antietam. On December 13, Evans engaged eleven thousand Federals with two thousand of his own troops at Kinston, North Carolina. The Confederates were mauled and one-fifth were captured, but Evans refused to surrender.

After losing his brigade, Evans returned to duty in March 1864 at Charleston. Seriously injured in a fall from his horse, he went on leave and then served once more in the spring of 1865, when he accompanied Jefferson Davis to Cokesbury, South Carolina. *Photo courtesy of University of South Carolina, Columbia*

Among the regimental commanders who marched with Gen. Nathan G. Evans into Mississippi during the summer of 1863 was Col. Henry L. Benbow of the 23rd South Carolina Infantry. A veteran of the campaigns in Virginia who had already been wounded at Second Bull Run, Benbow emerged unscathed from the Vicksburg campaign and returned to Virginia.

A graduate of Cokesbury College and a native of Clarendon County, Benbow originally enlisted, at the age of thirty-one, as a private in Company C (Manning Guards) of Hampton's Legion. He became a lieutenant, but transferred to Company I, 23rd South Carolina Infantry, known as the "Coast Rangers," and was promoted to captain and then colonel of the regiment when it was reorganized during May 1862.

Benbow stayed with the brigade as it returned to Virginia and was placed under the command of Stephen Elliott, Jr., in 1864, the same year that Benbow began a three-year term as a South Carolina legislator. The 23rd South Carolina was one of three regiments led by Elliott in the desperate counterattack at the Crater on July 30, 1864. On the morning of April 1, 1865, Federals overwhelmed the Confederate defenders at Five Forks. Benbow was shot through both hips in this fight and captured. Confined in Lincoln General Hospital in Washington, he was not released until June 1865. *Photo courtesy of U.S.A.M.H.I.*

HENRY L. BENBOW
carte de visite

211

THOMAS B. FERGUSON
albumen print

Thomas B. Ferguson, a Charleston native, served as Chief of Artillery for Gen. Pierre G. T. Beauregard after the latter returned to South Carolina during the fall of 1862. In that same capacity for Gen. William H. T. Walker, he led his battery in the summer of 1863 to Mississippi, where he was shot through the right lung during the fighting at Jackson on July 14, 1863.

Ferguson had fired the Citadel cadets' third, and final, cannonshot at the *Star of the West*, but like the first gunner, he missed. After graduating from the Citadel in 1861, he served briefly as an adjutant for Maxcy Gregg's six-month regiment. He then mustered a battery of artillery, which was recruited from a number of Southern states and included Beauregard's son Rene as a lieutenant, and entered Confederate service during April 1862 at Charleston, whence he left for Mississippi about a year later. While he was recuperating, Ferguson commanded the arsenal in Charleston. He became a major after his recovery and served as an assistant inspector of artillery for the Department of South Carolina, Georgia, and Florida. At the end of the war he was in charge of the First Military District in South Carolina. *Photo courtesy of Citadel Archives, Charleston, South Carolina*

Pvt. Calvin Hill joined Company G of the 26th South Carolina Infantry on New Year's Day, 1863. He spent his first month as a soldier at home with the mumps, but during the summer of 1863 he accompanied his regiment when it marched to Mississippi in an effort to relieve Vicksburg. Hill and his comrades got no closer to the besieged city than the Big Black River before falling back into the entrenchments around Jackson, where they skirmished with Union troops. After the Federals took the river port, the 26th South Carolina returned to their home state.

Born in Timmonsville, South Carolina, on December 12, 1831, Hill was the youngest of five brothers who fought for the South. Of these five, two were killed and two, including Calvin, were captured. Only one was present for the surrender at Appomattox in April 1865.

The 26th South Carolina left their native state again in April 1864, traveling first to North Carolina and then to Virginia. They fought during the Bermuda Hundred campaign and then went into the trenches before Petersburg. Hill was promoted to corporal on January 18, 1865 and then was captured at Five Forks on April 1, 1865, and imprisoned at Point Lookout, Maryland, until the end of the war. *Photo courtesy of U.S.A.M.H.I.*

CALVIN HILL AND WIFE
copy print

THOMAS D. KEITH
copy print

Lt. Thomas D. Keith was serving in the 26th South Carolina Infantry during the summer of 1863 when they traveled west to Mississippi as part of Nathan G. Evans' brigade. Keith commanded his company while it fell back from the Big Black and fought with Federals at Jackson and then led them back to Charleston.

Keith, who had attended Furman University from 1854 to 1856, was a twenty-three-year-old merchant in Darlington when South Carolina seceded. He was originally the captain of a company in the 9th Battalion, South Carolina Infantry, but he lost that position when the unit was reorganized during the spring of 1862 after the conscription act was passed. Following the merger of his battalion with another to create the 26th South Carolina Infantry in the fall of 1862, Keith was elected a lieutenant in his old company, which he commanded in the absence of a captain.

His military career was interrupted after his regiment returned to South Carolina from Mississippi because he was late in rejoining his company at Charleston after a furlough in January 1864. He was arrested, tried, and dismissed from the service by a court-martial in March, but he apparently later joined a cavalry unit and then served with the Pee Dee Battery until the end of the war, when he surrendered in North Carolina with Joseph E. Johnston's army.
Photo courtesy of Darlington County Historical Society, Darlington, South Carolina

CHARLES E. THOMAS
carte de visite

A graduate of the Citadel, Charles E. Thomas, a younger brother of another cadet, Edward Thomas (pictured elsewhere), joined Company C of the 16th South Carolina Infantry (Greeneville Regiment) during March 1863 as a sergeant. The regiment was ordered west from its camp at Adams Run, South Carolina, in May 1863 and traveled as far as Yazoo City in Mississippi before it was recalled to Chattanooga.

During the Vicksburg campaign, Thomas was demoted to private by Gen. States Rights Gist for an unspecified offense. While his regiment was in north Georgia, Thomas became ill in September and was confined to a hospital in Atlanta. He returned home and was discharged from Confederate service in the fall of 1863.

Prior to his unpleasant experiences in the west, Thomas had done well in military-related endeavours. A native of Fairfield County, he attended King's Mountain Military Academy and then left the Citadel in early 1861 when he was just seventeen years of age. He served as a drillmaster for the 6th South Carolina Reserves before he enlisted in the 16th South Carolina Infantry. After being dismissed from Confederate service, he resumed his duties as a lieutenant and drillmaster for the state militia in January 1864. *Photo courtesy of University of South Carolina, Columbia*

THOMAS G. CLEMSON
copy print of *carte de visite*
Alexander Gardner

Federal operations along the Mississippi River during 1863, which climaxed with the capture of Vicksburg and the splitting of the Confederacy during July, isolated the Confederate Department of the Trans-Mississippi. Authorities in Richmond had to scramble to create a new administrative structure to sustain resistance in the far west. Among those assigned across the river was Thomas G. Clemson, whose expertise in mining made him an obvious choice to be the supervisor of the Confederate Nitre and Mining Bureau for the Trans-Mississippi.

A Pennsylvanian by birth but educated in France, Clemson had married Anna Marie Calhoun, the daughter of John C. Calhoun, during 1838 and settled into South Carolina society. In 1844 he began a seven-year term as the United States chargé d'affaires in Belgium, and in 1860 he was appointed as the superintendent of agriculture, a position in which he served two months before resigning. Well known for his technical knowledge, he received both the Belgian Order of Leopold and the French Legion of Honor during his lifetime.

His appointment in 1863 brought with it another distinction: it provided him with the military rank of first lieutenant in the Confederate army. He served in the Trans-Mississippi until the war ended. *Photo courtesy of Clemson University*

216

JOHN CALHOUN CLEMSON
copy print

A grandson of John C. Calhoun and the son of Thomas G. Clemson, John Calhoun Clemson followed his father west after the latter was appointed superintendent of the Confederate Nitre and Mining Bureau for the Trans-Mississippi. During September 1863, the younger Clemson, who held the rank of lieutenant, was captured on the east bank of the Mississippi River while in command of a payroll escort. He remained a prisoner at Johnson's Island in Ohio until June 1865.

Clemson had enlisted at the age of twenty as a private in Company B, 1st South Carolina Rifles, during July 1861 and then in December joined Company H of the 1st South Carolina Artillery and was elected to be second lieutenant the following month. His company served in harbor batteries at Charleston, principally in Fort Sumter and Castle Pinckney. When his father was assigned to the Trans-Mississippi, the younger Clemson was serving at Castle Pinckney but resigned his command to accompany him. *Photo courtesy of Clemson University*

217

DONALD J. AULD AND VENETIA HAMMET AULD
carte de visite
Quinby and Company

By the time that Sgt. Donald J. Auld and the other members of the Infantry Battalion of Hampton's Legion marched to Tennessee as part of James Longstreet's corps in the late summer of 1863, they were already battle-hardened veterans of some of the most bloody battles in the east. In Tennessee, they fought in the confused night engagement at Wauhatchie, then participated in the campaign to recapture Knoxville.

Auld had enlisted at Columbia during June 1861 at the age of twenty-one as a sergeant in Company H (South Carolina Zouave Volunteers) of the Infantry Battalion of Hampton's Legion. They fought at First and Second Bull Run, Seven Pines (where they suffered 37 percent casualties), Gaines' Mill, and in Maryland.

After he returned to Virginia, his unit was reorganized as mounted infantry and remained through the end of the war with the Army of Northern Virginia. Auld surrendered at Appomattox as a private, having been demoted for an unspecified offense the previous fall.
Photo courtesy of University of South Carolina, Columbia

JAMES R. DAVIS
quarter-plate ambrotype

Pvt. James R. Davis of the 6th South Carolina Infantry was wounded at Antietam in September 1862, but he recuperated while his regiment was in southern Virginia and North Carolina during the summer of 1863. When they went to Tennessee as part of James Longstreet's corps, Davis was in the ranks.

He enlisted as a private in the 6th South Carolina Infantry in June 1861 at Darlington and then after a bout of mumps reenlisted at Louisa Courthouse in Virginia during April 1862. He emerged unscathed from the horrific engagements on the Peninsula, but his regiment suffered 52 percent casualties at Seven Pines, where two of his brothers-in-law were killed. A hundred more were lost at Gaines' Mill and Frayser's

Farm. He was again not harmed at Second Bull Run, where more than a hundred of his comrades were killed or wounded, but his luck ran out at Antietam.

Davis' regiment fought at Wauhatchie and Knoxville and then rejoined the Army of Northern Virginia for the bloody campaigns of 1864. On May 2, he wrote to his wife, "if i come out Safe this time i shal Begin to think that i will live to sea the ware end," but he confessed in a letter less than three weeks later that "we have So much to do now it is hard to Stand up to it."[5] Wounded again and captured on the North Anna River, he died at Point Lookout, Maryland, in September. *Photo courtesy of Darlington County Historical Society, Darlington, South Carolina*

219

JOSEPH B. KERSHAW
carte de visite
E. and H. T. Anthony

During the second day of the battle along Chickamauga Creek in September 1863, Brig. Gen. Joseph B. Kershaw ordered the five brigades that were temporarily under his command to charge the Union positions in his front. His troops swept the Federals back until the latter rallied on Snodgrass Hill. Despite several subsequent attacks, Kershaw was unable to dislodge his stubborn foe, who retreated after nightfall.

The son of a U. S. congressman, Kershaw practiced law and politics in his hometown, Camden. After the Mexican War, in which he became a lieutenant for a South Carolina regiment, he was elected three times to the legislature and was a delegate to the secession convention. He commanded the 2nd South Carolina Infantry at Fort Sumter and First Bull Run and then was promoted to brigadier general during February 1862 to replace the commander of his brigade, Milledge L. Bonham, after Bonham resigned.

Kershaw's South Carolina brigade fought in the Seven Days and at Antietam, Fredericksburg, Chancellorsville, Gettysburg, Chickamauga, Knoxville, the Wilderness, Spotsylvania, and Cold Harbor. Promoted to major general, Kershaw served under Gen. Jubal Early in the Shenandoah Valley. Kershaw was captured at Sayler's Creek on April 6, 1865, with a remnant of his command. *Photo courtesy of University of South Carolina, Columbia*

Among the members of Gen. Joseph B. Kershaw's staff in the fall of 1863 in Tennessee was Capt. William M. Dwight, who served as the adjutant and inspector general for the brigade. After hard fighting at Chickamauga and Knoxville, Dwight and the other troops in James Longstreet's corps returned to Virginia in early 1864.

Born in 1839, Dwight graduated from the Citadel and, when the war began, enlisted as a private in Company A of the 2nd South Carolina Infantry (Palmetto Regiment), then commanded by Kershaw. Dwight was wounded at First Bull Run and then became a second lieutenant on Kershaw's staff in time to serve during the Seven Days. After being injured in a fall, he was captured at Maryland Heights in September 1862.

He returned to his home in Winnsboro on parole but rejoined Kershaw's staff as his adjutant and inspector general before the battle of Fredericksburg. Serving with Kershaw at Gettysburg and Chickamauga, Dwight became a captain during the fall of 1863. He was captured again at Spotsylvania on May 12, 1864, confined at Fort Delaware, and then went home during February 1865 to await an exchange. He reported on April 3 that he was willing to return to duty whenever he was exchanged, but that never happened. This photograph was taken when he was a prisoner at Fort Delaware. *Photo courtesy of University of South Carolina, Columbia*

WILLIAM M. DWIGHT
albumen print

WILLIAM P. DuBose
copy print

William P. DuBose became the chaplain for Joseph B. Kershaw's brigade in December 1863, while that unit was campaigning in east Tennessee, and surrendered with it in North Carolina at the end of the war. Allegedly, during the war he carried a weapon only once, though he was seriously wounded several times.

A native of Fairfield County, DuBose had graduated from the Citadel in 1855, earned a master of arts from the University of Virginia, and attended the Episcopal seminary at Camden from 1859 to 1860. He enlisted as adjutant of the Holcombe Legion in 1861. Two-thirds of that unit were killed or wounded at Second Bull Run; DuBose was shot while rallying his comrades with the regimental flag in his hands. The remainder of the Legion was reorganized into three companies, which were led by DuBose until he was captured at South Mountain. Exchanged, he led his troops at Kinston, North Carolina, where he was disabled by a gunshot. He commanded the Legion during the Vicksburg campaign and then in the fall of 1863 returned with them to South Carolina, where he was ordained as an Episcopal deacon.

DuBose crossed the mountains to join Kershaw's brigade in Tennessee and then accompanied it in the battles near Petersburg. Sent to defend Charleston from Gen. William T. Sherman, the brigade marched to North Carolina after that city's evacuation. *Photo courtesy of Citadel Archives, Charleston, South Carolina*

WILLIAM A. COURTENAY
carte de visite
Quinby and Company

Lt. William A. Courtenay of Company B in the 8th South Carolina Infantry, assigned to Joseph B. Kershaw's brigade in James Longstreet's corps, emerged unscathed from the assault made by that unit at Chickamauga, just as he had from the bloody fighting at First Bull Run, Fredericksburg, and Gettysburg. After his return to Virginia, however, Courtenay was captured along Opequon Creek near Winchester during Gen. Jubal Early's campaign in the Shenandoah Valley. He was still a prisoner at Johnson's Island when the war ended.

Not yet thirty years of age when South Carolina left the Union, Courtenay, a member of the Washington Light Infantry who worked in his brother's Charleston publishing house, enlisted as a private in Company B of the 8th South Carolina Infantry. By doing this, he left most of his compatriots behind; most of the members of the Washington Light Infantry were eventually mustered into the 25th South Carolina Infantry and did not leave their home state until 1864. *Photo courtesy of University of South Carolina, Columbia*

Lt. Col. Axalla John Hoole of the 8th South Carolina Infantry, assigned to Joseph B. Kershaw's brigade, was not as fortunate as Lt. William A. Courtenay of Company B in his regiment. The latter survived the charge that drove the Federals to Snodgrass Hill at Chickamauga in September 1863, but Hoole was killed in the repeated assaults ordered by Kershaw.

A slaveholder committed to secession, Hoole resided in Darlington, his hometown, at the outset of the war, though he had briefly resided in Kansas during the late 1850s in an attempt to help establish slavery in that territory. He was elected probate judge of Douglas County, Kansas, but returned home in December 1857 and resumed his place as captain of the Darlington Guards, a position he had held for many years. He wears his militia uniform in this photograph.

Hoole mustered the Darlington Guards as Company A of the 8th South Carolina Infantry in April 1861. He led them during First Bull Run and then became lieutenant colonel of his regiment in May 1862, serving in that capacity during the engagements at Maryland Heights, Antietam (where he led 45 effectives onto the field and lost 23), and Fredericksburg. Hospitalized during May 1863 for pneumonia, he returned to active duty in time to fight at Gettysburg. He was forty years of age when he was killed. *Photo courtesy of University of South Carolina, Columbia*

When Johnson Hagood's 1st South Carolina Infantry was ordered to Tennessee as part of Joseph B. Kershaw's brigade, Lt. James Nott Moore of Company H was serving as an assistant quartermaster for the regiment. Moore was not among the forty-five casualties lost by his regiment during the confused night engagement at Wauhatchie, but he was badly wounded at Campbell's Station on November 16, 1863, during Gen. James Longstreet's futile campaign to take Knoxville.

Moore's regiment had originally mustered in December 1860. When it was reorganized at Charleston in the spring of 1862, he was serving as a lieutenant in Company H. During the summer of 1862, the regiment was sent to Virginia, where it participated in the battles of South Mountain, Antietam, and Fredericksburg.

Moore recovered from his wound and rejoined his unit in time to take part in the grinding battles of 1864 around Petersburg. He was paroled with the remnant of his brigade, under the command of Gen. John Bratton, at Appomattox. Apparently, Moore intended this photograph for a friend; he wrote on the back, "Put me where I will not be kicked too badly." *Photo courtesy of University of North Carolina, Chapel Hill*

JAMES NOTT MOORE
carte de visite
Quinby and Company

ALBERT N. STONE
copy print of ambrotype

Pvt. Albert N. Stone, a member of Company K in the 4th South Carolina Infantry, was wounded at Antietam in bitter fighting that led to the consolidation of his regiment with the infantry battalion in Hampton's Legion. Stone recovered from his injury and was in the ranks when the reconstituted Legion found itself engaged at close range with Union troops in the night clash at Wauhatchie on the Tennessee River in October 1863.

This photograph of Private Stone was probably taken during the fall of 1861, when he was furloughed to return to his home in Anderson County after an attack of typhoid fever in Virginia. During December 1861 he rejoined Company K, in which he had enlisted after joining the South Carolina militia in February 1861 and with which he had fought at First Bull Run under the command of Nathan G. Evans. Consolidated into a small battalion in April 1862, the 4th South Carolina fought during the Seven Days, at Second Bull Run, and in Maryland. It was then reduced once more, to two companies, and merged into Hampton's Legion.

Stone remained with the Legion, which was reorganized as mounted infantry upon its return to Virginia, through the end of the war. Under the command of Martin W. Gary, it was one of the last units to leave Richmond in April 1865. *Photo courtesy of Mrs. James B. Harris*

226

Among the casualties at Campbell's Station in November 1863 was Pvt. Moses E. McDonald of Company E in the 6th South Carolina Infantry. His regiment had participated earlier in the fighting at Wauhatchie, when James Longstreet's troops had futilely tried to block the Federal movement across the Tennessee River below Chattanooga and then marched toward Knoxville in what proved to be an equally ineffective effort to capture that city.

McDonald had originally enlisted at the age of eighteen as a private in Company F of the 9th South Carolina Infantry at Sumter in July 1861. Sent to Virginia during the fall of 1861, he, along with many other members of his company, joined Company E of the 6th South Carolina Infantry, commanded by John Bratton, after the passage of the conscription act in the spring of 1862.

He was with his unit when it fought on the Peninsula as well as at Boonsboro and Antietam. His regiment stayed in Virginia during the Gettysburg campaign, at which time he was furloughed to travel to his home in Sumter, South Carolina, but he returned in time to march into Tennessee under Longstreet's command.

After his regiment returned to Virginia, McDonald was wounded once more on September 30, 1864, when his regiment took part in the assault by Bratton's brigade on Fort Harrison at Petersburg. He recovered and then surrendered at Appomattox. *Photo courtesy of University of South Carolina, Columbia*

MOSES E. MCDONALD
quarter-plate ambrotype

WILLIAM M. GIST
carte de visite
Richard Wearn and William P. Hix

Maj. William M. Gist of the 15th South Carolina Infantry was shot and killed instantly at Knoxville on November 18, 1863, while he was preparing to lead his regiment in a charge. The attack failed to prevent the consolidation of Federal forces within their entrenchments at Knoxville, and so Gen. James Longstreet initiated a siege of that city that ended only after another disastrous Confederate assault on November 29.

A little more than two years earlier, at the age of twenty, Gist had mustered a company in Union County for the 15th South Carolina Infantry. He remained the captain of Company B for only a few months because in October 1861 he was promoted to major. The regiment initially served on James Island, but in 1862 it was assigned to Longstreet's corps of the Army of Northern Virginia.

Gist went home on furlough after participating in Second Bull Run and Antietam, where his regiment lost 110 casualties while standing fast as most of Gen. Thomas F. Drayton's command gave way on the Confederate right. He rejoined his unit, though, in time for the summer operations of 1863, in which it lost 137 of the 448 men engaged at Gettysburg, and then marched to Tennessee that fall. Ironically, Gist was one of only three members of his regiment killed at Knoxville. *Photo courtesy of Museum of the Confederacy, Richmond, Virginia*

JOHN W. JENNINGS
copy print of ambrotype

After James Longstreet ordered his corps away from Knoxville in early December 1863, they settled into winter camp in nearby Greeneville. The Tennessee campaign was not quite over, however, as Sgt. John W. Jennings of Hampton's Legion soon learned. While fighting in east Tennessee he was wounded at Dandridge in January 1864 and his left leg had to be amputated at the thigh.

Jennings, a sergeant in Company B of the Infantry Battalion in Hampton's Legion, originally enlisted as a private at Columbia in June 1861, but he was promoted the following month. Since that time he had fought in many battles—First and Second Bull Run, Seven Pines, Gaines' Mill, and in Maryland—with only one brief furlough in the summer of 1863.

He was assigned to the Invalid Corps, but in October of that year he applied for an artificial limb. After an examination, he was "retired" on October 18, 1864, and returned home to Abbeville County. *Photo courtesy of George Esker*

JOHN S. PALMER AND
ALICE ANN GAILLARD PALMER
copy print of ambrotype

Gen. William T. Sherman marched for Atlanta in the spring of 1864. The Confederates who opposed him during the Hundred Days, as this campaign became known, were initially commanded by Joseph E. Johnston, but John Bell Hood took his place at Atlanta and ordered a series of futile attacks. Among the casualties was Capt. John S. Palmer, who was killed at the age of twenty-eight on July 28 during the sortie at Ezra Church.

Palmer was a prosperous slaveholder who still lived with his father, an even wealthier planter, in 1860. The younger Palmer enlisted as a lieutenant in Company K of the 10th South Carolina Infantry during September 1861 at Charleston. After a miserable time on Cat Island off the South Carolina coast, where many of the members of the regiment suffered from disease, the unit was sent to Mississippi in March 1862.

He became captain of his company in May 1862 and led it in the Kentucky campaign that fall. He was wounded at Murfreesboro on December 31, 1862, four months after his brother was killed at Second Bull Run, but he returned to duty in a month. His company was only slightly involved at Chickamauga, but they were among those driven from Missionary Ridge.

Palmer poses here with his wife, whom he married during the war and who was three years younger than he. *Photo courtesy of University of South Carolina, Columbia*

STATES RIGHTS GIST
carte de visite
Quinby and Company

Five Confederate generals were killed on November 30, 1864, at Franklin; one was States Rights Gist. Leading his brigade on foot after his horse was shot, he was mortally wounded by a minié ball that ripped through his right lung. He died a few hours later, asking only to be taken to his wife whom he had married more than a year earlier, but with whom he had spent little time. Gist had attended South Carolina College and was one of three Confederate generals who studied law at Harvard College. He practiced law in Unionville and became a brigadier general in the militia, serving as an aide to Governors James H. Adams and William H. Gist, his brother. He resigned from the militia in April 1860 but was Gist's envoy to other Southern governors that fall, pleading for unity in the cause of secession.

In January 1861, Gist became adjutant general of his state. He served on Gen. Pierre G. T. Beauregard's staff at First Bull Run, where he was wounded while leading an Alabama regiment, and then resumed his duties at home. Appointed a brigadier general of the Confederacy during March 1862, Gist served at Charleston until May 1863, when he led a brigade to Mississippi in the ill-fated attempt to relieve the garrison of Vicksburg.

Sent to north Georgia, his brigade suffered heavy casualties at Chickamauga. It then stood fast during the debacle at Missionary Ridge and served in the rear guard for the Confederate withdrawal. Constantly engaged during the Hundred Days, Gist won renown and, at Atlanta in July 1864, briefly assumed command of his division after the commanding general was killed. *Photo courtesy of University of South Carolina, Columbia*

231

ELLISON CAPERS
carte de visite

Col. Ellison Capers of the 24th South Carolina Infantry was wounded for the third time at Franklin, but he was promoted to brigadier general in place of States Rights Gist, in whose brigade he had served since leaving South Carolina in May 1863. He surrendered in North Carolina during May 1865.

This portrait of Capers wearing the uniform of the Citadel, where he was an assistant professor, was made in 1861. A native of Charleston, he had graduated from the Citadel in 1857 and then had worked as the principal of Mount Zion School in Winnsboro before returning to his alma mater. In December 1860 he became a major in the 1st Regiment of Rifles, South Carolina Militia, in which he served during the bombardment of Fort Sumter. Promoted to lieutenant colonel, he retained his rank when the unit became the 24th South Carolina Infantry.

He directed the first attack against the 100th Pennsylvania Infantry on James Island on June 3, 1862. Thirteen days later, he commanded a battery that greatly assisted in repulsing the Union assault at Secessionville. After his regiment was ordered to Mississippi as part of Gist's brigade, Capers was wounded in the leg at Jackson on May 14, 1863, while temporarily in command of his regiment. Returning to duty, he was wounded again at Chickamauga before he was promoted to colonel in December 1863. *Photo courtesy of University of South Carolina, Columbia*

Undeterred by the bloodletting at Franklin, Gen. John Bell Hood followed the retreating Federal detachments to Nashville. He settled near the city, even though his troops were far fewer in number than their opponents. When the Union army attacked on December 15, 1864, Hood's troops were easily defeated.

Among the casualties at Nashville was Peter T. Hollis, who posed for this photograph when he was just eighteen years of age. Enlisted before his eighteenth birthday as a private in Company H, 24th South Carolina Infantry, at Chester in March 1862, he quickly advanced to lieutenant. His regiment initially served on James Island and in North Carolina, but in May 1863 it hurried west to Mississippi in States Rights Gist's brigade.

Hollis and his comrades participated in the fighting at Jackson that summer. Transferred to Chattanooga, they fought at Chickamauga and then stood guard on Missionary Ridge until withdrawn on the night of November 25, 1863. Retreating before Gen. William T. Sherman's Federals during the Hundred Days, Hollis's regiment turned and attacked at Peachtree Creek and then, after the fall of Atlanta, marched again into Tennessee.

Hollis had been wounded in the shoulder in August 1864 at Atlanta, but he was with his regiment at Nashville, where he was captured. He remained at Johnson's Island until the war ended. *Photo courtesy of University of South Carolina, Columbia*

PETER T. HOLLIS
carte de visite

233

As the Army of Tennessee retreated after the rout at Nashville, Gen. Stephen D. Lee suffered his first wound while his corps served as the rear guard. His career in the west had been quite distinguished but often unpleasant—when Vicksburg surrendered, Lee was paroled there as the commander of a brigade, having been promoted and sent west after his performance at Antietam.

A Charleston native and a graduate of West Point, he appears here in the uniform of a major after joining the staff of Gen. Pierre G. T. Beauregard at Charleston in March 1861. He later commanded the artillery of Hampton's Legion and won promotion to brigadier general. At Vicksburg, he led infantry and artillery in the repulse of the Federal attack at Chickasaw Bayou and the Confederate defeat at Champion's Hill. Exchanged, he commanded cavalry in the west and in the summer of 1864 became a lieutenant general, the youngest at that rank, in charge of John Bell Hood's corps. When they went to North Carolina in 1865, Lee remained in Georgia to convalesce and muster a brigade, which also marched to join Joseph E. Johnston. Mary Boykin Chesnut, who saw them at Chester, South Carolina, was amazed that they were singing and wrote, "There they go, the gay and gallant few, doomed, the last flowers of Southern pride, to be killed, or worse, to a prison." *Photo courtesy of University of South Carolina, Columbia*

STEPHEN D. LEE
copy print of *carte de visite*
Quinby and Company

234

Maj. John T. O'Brien was one of the few South Carolinians who surrendered with the Confederate Army of the Trans-Mississippi. When the war began he was within a few months of graduating from the U. S. Military Academy. He originally enlisted in a company attached to the 1st South Carolina Artillery, but during April 1862 he was appointed a captain in the Confederate army and assigned to the staff of Gen. Charles S. Winder, with whom he served in the Shenandoah Valley and during the Seven Days. The next fall he joined the staff of Gen. Pierre G. T. Beauregard at Charleston, and in March 1863 he became a major.

Ordered to the Trans-Mississippi in November 1863, he left after purchasing a "French Pistol Revolving" with cartridges, a gunbelt, and a haversack from the arsenal at Charleston. During January 1864, though, he reported that he could not cross the Mississippi River. Ironically, his request to be temporarily posted on the east bank was approved on the same day, February 13, that O'Brien was captured on the west bank of the river.

He was imprisoned at New Orleans, whence he was exchanged in July 1864. Returning to duty, he served as inspector general in Arkansas and then as assistant inspector for the Department of the Trans-Mississippi. He was paroled in June 1865 at Shreveport. *Photo courtesy of University of North Carolina, Chapel Hill*

JOHN T. O'BRIEN
carte de visite
Quinby and Company

Chimney Stacks without Houses: Sherman's March through South Carolina

Gen. Judson Kilpatrick, the flamboyant commander of Gen. William T. Sherman's cavalry during his campaign through Georgia and the Carolinas, gave a party for his subordinates on the evening of January 27, 1865. Gathering his officers around him, he delivered a fiery speech in which he declared, "In after years, when travellers passing through South Carolina shall see chimney-stacks without houses, and the country desolate, and shall ask, Who did this? some Yankee will answer, Kilpatrick's cavalry."[1] Georgia and North Carolina certainly suffered from the incursion of Sherman's army, but the damage done in those two states paled in comparison with what was done in South Carolina. Sherman's troops blamed South Carolinians for the war, and they wreaked terrible havoc while marching through the state.

Sherman carefully prepared for his invasion of South Carolina. He divided his army of approximately sixty thousand men into two columns and ordered the commanders, Generals Henry W. Slocum and Oliver O. Howard, to feint toward Augusta and Charleston, respectively. In fact, their primary objective was Columbia. Sherman selected an inland route, away from Charleston, because an advance on that city would be impeded by deep rivers and swamps. Marching through the uplands would avoid a number of these impediments once his men were away from the coast. At the same time, his troops could destroy the railroads that linked South Carolina to the remainder of the Confederacy.

Sherman's ultimate intention was to establish communications with Union forces operating from the coastline of North Carolina and trap the Confederates in the area for a final showdown. Although he did not anticipate encountering substantial resistance south of the Cape Fear River, he realized his plan was not without some risk. As he wrote to his wife, "I think chances of getting killed on this trip are about even."[2] He had little but contempt for Gen. Pierre G. T. Beauregard, still the darling of many South Carolinians and the officer whom the Union general expected to confront, but he had tremendous respect for Gen. Joseph E. Johnston, whom he had last faced at Atlanta and who was rumored to be assuming command in the Carolinas.

Sherman's march through South Carolina began during early January 1865. Howard had one of his corps transported to Beaufort and by mid-January reunited his two corps on the Charleston and Savannah Railroad near Pocotaligo. Sherman joined Howard and waited for Slocum's slower-moving column. In the meantime, Kilpatrick's troopers filled their pockets with matches and fanned out through several counties, serving as a vanguard for Slocum's infantry. Kilpatrick himself hosted a dance while Barnwell burned.

Slocum's two corps crossed the Savannah River into South Carolina and laboriously moved up the rail line to rendezvous with Howard. As each of Slocum's regiments crossed the river, they cheered, eager to be campaigning in the state they held most accountable for the war. However, their entry into South Carolina proved to be anything but cheery. They marched through the thickest swamps along the coast, discovering these to be at best miserable and at worst almost impassable. The discovery of buried torpedoes in the road, which killed and wounded several soldiers, reinforced the Federals' resolve to punish the state, and incessant rain did nothing to improve their mood. Some slept in trees to avoid standing water, and sentries patrolled one camp in canoes. For at least one officer, the memory of South Carolina was "indelibly printed as a stubborn wrestle with the elements, in which the murky and dripping skies were so mingled with the earth and water below as to make the whole a fit type of 'chaos come again'. . . ."[3]

The Confederates scrambled to slow the advance of Sherman's men. The remnant of the Army of Tennessee was ordered from Mississippi to the east coast, and Beauregard came with them. In response to his demands, Gen. Wade Hampton was also sent to South Carolina with a cavalry division commanded by Matthew C. Butler. In his home state, Hampton was joined by Gen. Joseph Wheeler, whose troopers were beginning to wear down under the incessant pressure of Sherman's advance. Other troops sent from Virginia included Joseph B.

Kershaw's old brigade, which was led by John D. Kennedy in place of James Conner, whose wound at Fisher's Hill in October 1864 had necessitated the amputation of a leg. Beauregard met with Generals William J. Hardee, Daniel H. Hill, and Gustavus W. Smith near Augusta to discuss the situation. After determining that even with these reinforcements they had fewer than thirty-four thousand men to oppose Sherman, they realized it was impossible to do more than impede his march through South Carolina as much as possible.

While Slocum's troops were sloshing through the swamps, Howard's column was the first to encounter Confederate opposition. Hardee entrenched about ten thousand troops and a number of cannon along the Salkehatchie River to block Howard's passage through the marshes along the many channels of the waterway. During the first week of February 1865, the Union troops pushed the Confederates aside, often by attacking through water that reached their shoulders, but not before a number of Federals fell victim to concealed artillery. Many of the wounded had to prop themselves against trees to avoid drowning while they waited through the night to be rescued by their more fortunate comrades.

The Southerners had little time to gloat; Howard's men crossed the Salkehatchie, a feat that astounded the Confederates, and moved inland toward the Charleston and Augusta Railroad. The western-born Federals under Howard, like those led by Slocum, coped resourcefully with adverse elements, often at the expense of the communities through which they passed. Soldiers seeking material to build dry shelters destroyed houses, churches, and other buildings. In the morning, before they moved on, what remained of each settlement was frequently burned. Movement was accomplished by corduroying roads—chopping trees and laboriously laying them side by side in the roadbed. Sometimes the logs had to be laid several layers deep as the first disappeared into the muck. An officer with Howard's wing claimed that "mules and wagons actually [sank] out of sight" in the mud.[4] Deep waterways were bridged with pontoons and other ad hoc devices.

The columns led by Howard and Slocum reunited beyond the swamps on the Charleston and Augusta Railroad, a long section of which they soon destroyed. With his infantry consolidated once more, Sherman urged them forward to Columbia while ordering Kilpatrick to make a feint toward Augusta. Wheeler prepared an ambush for the Federals at Aiken on February 11, 1865, but nervous troopers fired too soon and the ambuscade dissolved into a melee in the streets of the little town. However, many Union troops were killed or captured; Kilpatrick himself almost became a prisoner and was unable to rally his men until they had been driven out of town.

As Sherman marched inland, Union forces near Charleston were once more placed under the command of Gen. Quincy A. Gillmore, who raided along the coast to divert Confederate troops from the main operation. The largest demonstrations were at Charleston, where on February 10, after a shelling by gunboats, two regiments and two companies of Federals attacked a line of rifle pits held by 131 Confederates under the command of Maj. Edward M. Manigault of the South Carolina Siege Train. Manigault fought for four hours, losing a third of his tiny force, and then ordered a retreat in which he was captured. A Union demonstration also took place during February at Bull's Bay, north of Charleston. There the Marion Artillery and two companies of infantry, all under the command of Capt. Edward L. Parker, dissuaded a large Union contingent from landing until after Columbia and the port city were occupied.

The Confederates confronting Sherman's main columns slowly fell back, futilely attempting to defend bridges and fords against his inexorable advance. A small force of home guards and regulars stood behind breastworks at Orangeburg to buy time for residents who wished to flee. The Federal XVII Corps easily pushed them aside and then burned and looted most of the town in retaliation. Union officers later insisted that an irate local merchant, not their troops, had burned the town, but such claims rang hollow. Locals did not forget, though, that Sherman visited an orphanage in Orangeburg while the town burned. There he found about three hundred children who had been moved from Charleston in an effort to keep them out of the path of his army. He posted a guard and left provisions before moving on to Columbia.

Howard's column reached Columbia in sixteen days of marching. On February 16, Sherman had his gunners lob a few shells into the city to disperse looters and endorsed the firing of a half-dozen rounds at the unfinished capitol building, perhaps in retaliation for Confederate artillery fire that killed several Federals the previous night. The Union XV Corps entered Columbia on February 17, the same day that Hampton became a lieutenant general and took charge of all cavalry in the Carolinas. Hampton blustered, urging Columbians to burn their city as the Russians in Moscow had done upon the approach of Napoleon, but when the blue-clad columns moved into the capital he told his troopers to withdraw. Among the retreating riders was Beauregard, mortified at his inability to defend the city.

Howard's troops departed from Columbia on February 20, leaving behind a "community overwhelmed with its losses, almost stupefied by the terrible change a few days had wrought, and only saved from starvation by the store of food which the National commander took from his army supplies to give them."[5] Before entering the city, Sherman had ordered that all private homes, libraries, and charitable institutions should not be destroyed, but that public buildings with military value should be burned. The first night, though, fire raged out of control, destroying almost fourteen hundred homes and stores, as well as other buildings. Howard later declared that he "never expected to leave such a wild desert . . . covered with blackened debris, smoldering embers and lone chimneys."[6] The city was left in ruins to its women, children, and old men, many of whom were still defiant enough to hiss and boo as the blue columns trudged out.

In years to come Union officers would try to blame Hampton's troopers for the conflagration that devastated Columbia. Several of Sherman's officers insisted that the Confederates looted the city before they fled and left bales of cotton burning in the streets. The Federals, they insisted, tried to extinguish the smoldering piles, but sparks from these ignited nearby buildings after nightfall and flames spread with the assistance of strong winds. The supreme irony for them was that wounded Confederate soldiers died when flames consumed several buildings at South Carolina College, which had been converted into a makeshift hospital.

Many observers, Northern and Southern, pointed out that there was another reason that the fire spread so quickly through Columbia. Drunken soldiers, unleashed in the "home of thousands of those wicked instigators to treason who have made this state so hated and despised," wreaked havoc with the torch.[7] The discovery of Camp Sorghum, a prisoner-of-war camp outside of Columbia, and the grim tales borne by the few inmates who had escaped from their guards at the approach of the Federals further angered Sherman's troops. Sherman and his subordinates labored to restrain their soldiers and restrict the spread of the flames. Howard deployed a line of skirmishers that swept through the city; 2 Federals were killed and 30 wounded, while 370 were arrested. Sherman himself saw one of his staff shoot a Union soldier for resisting arrest. The patrols could not be everywhere, though, and the result was ruin.

Sherman was "sincerely grieved" at the damage done to Columbia, and provided food for those who had been rendered homeless by ordering Howard to leave behind cattle, medications, and rations for the stricken people of the city.[8] When he learned that the Ursuline Convent had been burned, Sherman also assigned the looted mansion of John S. Preston, Hampton's brother-in-law who commanded the Confederate Bureau of Conscription, to the mother superior and her young female charges. The Federal commander never apologized, though, for the burning of Columbia; instead, he insisted it was just another step, perhaps well deserved, that hastened the end of the war. As Slocum later wrote, "A drunken soldier with a musket in one hand and a match in the other is not a pleasant visitor to have about the house on a dark, windy night, particularly when for a series of years you have urged him to come, so that you might have an opportunity of performing a surgical operation on him."[9]

The scorching of the South Carolina countryside continued after Slocum's column, which bypassed Columbia, rejoined Howard's wing on the far side of the capital. Federals fanned out, destroying the rail lines for twenty miles in all directions from the city. In Winnsboro, Union foragers dug up a recently interred coffin, tore the lid from it, and propped it up so the occupant faced the burning town. After Gen. John W. Geary arrested a number of looters, others took their vengeance on civilians. Sherman ordered a search of his army's baggage trains after Winnsboro, the first search since leaving Columbia, that uncovered five tons of loot in the wagons of one division alone. This material was burned, but subsequent searches revealed comparable booty.

From Winnsboro, the main Federal columns trudged toward Cheraw through torrential rains that swelled intervening streams to many times their usual width. A detachment from the XV Corps veered to enter Camden on February 24. They burned two railroad depots and a flour mill, as well as warehouses filled with cotton and food, before moving on. Wheeler's cavalry, however, scattered Kilpatrick's rear guard in Lancaster before they could burn the town—only the courthouse and jail were burned—while Butler's cavalry routed a Union detachment sent to cut the railroad at Florence, between Charleston and Cheraw.

Howard's occupation of Cheraw eliminated what little comfort the Confederate commanders could derive from their small victories. Believing that Sherman would march to Charlotte, North Carolina, after he left Columbia, the Confederates stashed many military supplies at Cheraw, including powder, cannons, and other valuable stores from Charleston. Likewise, many refugees streamed into Cheraw expecting to be bypassed by the invader. When Sherman swung toward the sea, he captured a rich bounty at Cheraw. The tragedy for South Carolinians was compounded when three tons of gunpowder were accidentally ignited by Union troops in Cheraw, killing several civilians as well as six soldiers.

Having taken Cheraw, three of Sherman's corps crossed the Pee Dee River and marched into North Carolina by March 8, leaving a swath of devastation in their wake. In addition to the burning and pillaging of homes, public and commercial buildings, and military and civilian stores, the Union troops also undercut the social and economic infrastructure that South Carolinians needed to recover from such losses. Thousands of freed blacks followed the Federal army into North Carolina, while many more sought to define their new freedom by striking out on their own. Two hundred miles of railroads were also destroyed, including most of the main line of the South Carolina Railroad. On April 19 almost all of the remaining rolling stock of that company was destroyed by Union raiders above Camden, leaving the company with only seventeen miles of usable rails.

The destruction wrought by Sherman's troops in South Carolina made them the target of bitter retaliations. Confederate cavalry were merciless to foragers, in part because reports of rape by Federals, of both white and black women, were commonplace. James Chesnut told his wife, Mary Boykin Chesnut, about a girl who died after seven Union soldiers raped her. The attackers were run to ground and killed by some of Wheeler's troopers. Such attacks by Confederates multiplied; Slocum reported finding the bodies of twenty-one of his soldiers dumped into a ditch, while

Kilpatrick lost eighteen in one day. When Sherman angrily told his generals to execute a Confederate prisoner for every Federal corpse found, Hampton informed the Union commander in writing that two Federals would be killed for every Confederate. Neither threat ended the bloody series of reprisals on both sides.

Sherman's troops destroyed much of South Carolina's ability to wage war, but the residents of that state were not ready to admit defeat in March 1865. Lily Logan, a Charlestonian refugee amid the ruins of Columbia, wrote to her brother, Gen. Thomas M. Logan, after Sherman left the capital that she was still certain of a Southern victory. The South Carolinians in the field were heartened by the appointment of Johnston, whom even Sherman respected, to lead them. Beauregard had resumed command of all units in South Carolina in February 1865, but shortly thereafter, Johnston took charge of all the troops in that state, Tennessee, Georgia, and Florida, thus superceding Beauregard, who became his second-in-command. Johnston, as Sherman feared, quickly began reorganizing his troops and discussing plans for an attack.

Among the South Carolinians who joined Johnston were those who had defended Charleston. When Gov. Andrew G. Magrath learned of plans to evacuate the city, he protested that "the retreat from Charleston will be the dead march of the Confederation."[10] When Sherman occupied Columbia, however, the garrison, which included Kershaw's veteran brigade, now led by Conner, abandoned the port. Mayor Charles Macbeth surrendered Charleston on February 18, 1865, to Adm. John A. Dahlgren and Gen. John G. Foster, who had been at Fort Sumter in April 1861. While Charleston burned behind them, ignited by the destruction of Confederate munitions and gunboats, the garrison marched north without rations or pay. Equipped mostly with antiquated arms, "large numbers of men were constantly deserting" due to concern for their families.[11] Only a hard core reached North Carolina, but they were ready to fight.

Johnston's forces also included the remnants of Johnson Hagood's South Carolina brigade. Sent south after more than six months in Virginia, detachments of two of Hagood's regiments, the 21st and 25th South Carolina Infantry, were captured when Fort Fisher fell on January 15, 1865. The remainder of his brigade fought around Wilmington and then served in the rear guard when the Confederates marched for the interior. Col. Charles H. Simonton of the 25th South Carolina Infantry, who had little combat experience, commanded the brigade at Town Creek. Hagood realized that his troops would be overrun and sent his aide, William E. Stoney, to tell Simonton to withdraw, but Stoney arrived just in time to see much of the brigade, including Simonton, become prisoners. In all, the brigade lost 461 that day. Hagood wrote that Simonton's errors "certainly leaned to virtue's side,"[12] but he regretted that the reinforcements he brought to Johnston were so meager at such a crucial time.

South Carolina cavalry struck the first hard blow at Sherman's army in North Carolina. Hampton had routed Kilpatrick's command in Virginia during March 1864, and one year later he got a chance to do so again. The Union general scattered his three brigades in an attempt to capture the Confederate troopers and then camped with one of the three near Solomon's Grove. On the evening of March 9, Moses B. Humphrey's company of the 6th South Carolina Cavalry led the way as both Butler's and Wheeler's divisions approached the Union camp. Humphrey and Butler were discussing the situation when a Federal detachment of about thirty troopers blundered into the Confederates and were captured. Kilpatrick was not among the prisoners, but hopes were high among the South Carolinians that he would not be so lucky in the morning, when they would attack the overconfident general's slumbering camp.

Butler's and Wheeler's divisions swept into Kilpatrick's camp as planned during the early morning hours of March 10, stampeding the surprised Federals and capturing 350 prisoners as well as wagons, artillery, and Kilpatrick's own headquarters. The Union commander, clad only in his nightshirt, fled to a nearby swamp. The grey-clad attackers, who actually were fewer in number than their victims, were compelled to withdraw when Federal troopers, reinforced by an infantry brigade, rallied and punished the Southerners with rapid fire from their Spencer carbines. About sixty South Carolina troopers, pinned by a deep bog, were killed by vengeful Federals. Such excesses could not eradicate the fact that Hampton had caught Kilpatrick napping again, capturing more than 500 prisoners and freeing 150 captive Confederates.

Kilpatrick's troopers were eager to restore their reputation in the field against Hampton, but a clash with the general himself, renowned as one of the best hand-to-hand combatants on either side, actually added to the growing legends about Hampton. On March 11, 1865, an advance party of about seventy Union riders swept boldly into Fayetteville, North Carolina. Warned about the Federal incursion by a scout, Hampton and five troopers charged the startled blue-clad riders, killing thirteen and taking twelve others prisoner. When a Union infantry column occupied the town a few hours later, Hampton was gone.

Sherman expected to unite his troops with others marching inland from the North Carolina coast. When John M. Schofield led his Federals west from Wilmington, he was met at Kinston on March 7 by a Confederate force that included the remainder of Hagood's South Carolina brigade, the brigade formerly commanded by Arthur M. Manigault, and Stephen D. Lee's corps, led by Daniel H. Hill while its commander was on leave. In a three-day battle the Southerners were pushed back and finally compelled to withdraw, marching to join the balance of Johnston's army in central North Carolina while Schofield followed.

Neither of the contingents from the coast arrived in time to take part in Sherman's first general engagement with Johnston's army. While skirmishing on March 15 along the road from Fayetteville to Raleigh, Kilpatrick's troopers encountered Hardee's rear guard. When Hardee told Col. Alfred M. Rhett's garrison troops from Charleston to stand fast, it became clear that the Confederates intended to fight. Federal infantry from Slocum's column arrived to meet a series of Confederate attacks that were halted only by nightfall. During the confused fighting, Rhett was captured, but his troops and others camped on the battlefield that night near Averasboro, planning to attack again the next day.

The Confederates resumed their assaults the next day until their lines dissolved due to clever maneuvering by the more experienced Federals. When the Union lines rushed forward, they found that the Charleston artillerymen, inexperienced at infantry fighting, had "almost literally been shot to pieces."[13] Most of the horses were dead, so three cannon fell into Federal hands along with many prisoners. The Union advance overran a second Confederate line, behind which the remnants of Rhett's brigade and others had rallied with another makeshift brigade from Charleston led by Stephen Elliott, Jr., but the Federals stalled before a third defensive perimeter. A Union officer recalled that Averasboro was a wretched place to fight—most of the field was ankle deep in water—but the South Carolinians were stubborn fighters and refused to give way until compelled to do so by greater numbers. Hardee withdrew in the night, having suffered 865 casualties, about 200 more than his opponent.

The fighting at Averasboro separated the two wings of Sherman's advancing army. Hoping to crush Slocum's column before Sherman could reconcentrate his forces, Johnston, reinforced with the troops marching inland from Kinston, attacked

Slocum a few days after the engagement at Averasboro. Hampton chose a site near Bentonville for battle and directed the initial assaults on March 19, 1865. Hagood's diminished brigade, in the front line, drove the Federals from their front, while the brigades formerly led by Manigault and States Rights Gist did the same. In the meantime, Kershaw's brigade, commanded by Conner, held their ground against a strong Union attack. Only Elliott's Charleston garrison troops were repulsed, while Rhett's brigade was withdrawn after three successive charges. Despite the South Carolinian's efforts, the more numerous Union troops quickly reformed their lines before darkness ended the fighting. In all, the Confederates lost 2,606 casualties, over 1,000 more than their opponents.

Little happened on March 20, but the next day, Sherman, who had most of his army in position, attacked at Bentonville. Johnston held his position, but that night he retreated to Raleigh and on to Greensboro. The South Carolinians, especially the brigades formerly commanded by Kershaw and Manigault, fought as well as any other Confederate units in these last battles, but the truth could not be ignored: to continue fighting would be senseless in the face of such overwhelming odds. After learning of Gen. Robert E. Lee's surrender, Johnston, in April 1865, reluctantly decided to ask Sherman for terms. Hampton and Logan were among the South Carolina generals who accompanied him to the meetings. By the first week of May the last significant Confederate force in the Carolinas had been disarmed and paroled, and thousands of South Carolinian soldiers began considering the monumental task of rebuilding in the wake of Sherman's destructive march.

WILLIAM T. SHERMAN AND ASSOCIATES
copy print

As commander of all Union troops in the western theater, Gen. William T. Sherman, after taking Atlanta, initiated a strategy of total war in Georgia that he brought to South Carolina in January 1865. He poses here with the subordinates who helped him carry out this task in the Carolinas. Left to right are Oliver O. Howard, John A. Logan, William B. Hazen, Sherman, Jefferson C. Davis, Henry W. Slocum, and Joseph A. Mower.

Howard and Slocum commanded the two wings into which Sherman divided his army. Howard, a West Point graduate and career army officer, lost his right arm on the Peninsula and then was sent with his corps to Sherman's command after Gettysburg.

Slocum was also a West Pointer and regular army veteran, and he accompanied Howard with his own corps to join Sherman in the fall of 1863.

Logan, a former congressman who had won a reputation as a capable combat officer, commanded the XV Corps in South Carolina. The 2nd Division in Logan's corps was commanded by Hazen, a West Point graduate who served on the frontier before the war. Davis, a veteran of the Fort Sumter bombardment in 1861, led the XIV Corps during Sherman's march, while Mower, who was the only one of the group who had participated in the Red River expedition, was in charge of the XX Corps. *Photo courtesy of National Archives*

244

JUDSON KILPATRICK
copy print

While Gen. William T. Sherman admitted that Gen. Judson Kilpatrick was a "hell of a damned fool," he declared that he wanted just such a man to lead his cavalry through Georgia and the Carolinas.[14] Kilpatrick was sent south in April 1864 to lead a division in Sherman's army. Badly wounded at Resaca, Georgia, he soon returned to duty and earned the respect of his commander, though the controversial general infuriated South Carolinians by refusing to restrain his licentious troopers, who demonstrated a penchant for looting and arson. He added scandal to outrage by taking the beautiful and free-spirited Marie Boozer of Columbia as his mistress during his march through the Carolinas. Kilpatrick had graduated from West Point in May 1861 and immediately accepted a commission as captain in the 5th New York Infantry. He was serving with that regiment at Big Bethel the next month when he received the dubious distinction of being the first officer from the regular army wounded in the Civil War. In September 1861 he transferred to the cavalry and quickly advanced in rank as a commander of volunteers while participating in almost every important engagement of that branch of service in the eastern theater. In Virginia as in the Carolinas, however, his nemesis proved to be Wade Hampton's cavalry, which routed him in March 1864 and again a year later. *Photo courtesy of Library of Congress, no. B8171-340*

Much of Gen. William T. Sherman's march through South Carolina was done in freezing rain that soaked his men. Such conditions did little to improve the morale of soldiers such as Cpl. Charles H. Holstead of Company A in the 52nd Illinois Infantry. On the eve of his departure from Savannah, Holstead's company was ordered to attack a Confederate outpost. Several Federals, including Holstead, stumbled into a ditch full of water in the nighttime operation, and the chilly December breeze made him quite ill. He recovered, though, and was discharged from the hospital at about the same time that he became a corporal in January 1865.

Holstead, on the right, enlisted as a private at Kaneville during October 1861, a month before his nineteenth birthday. In December 1861 a surgeon who was attending Holstead during a bout with the measles reported that he was blind in his right eye due to a childhood injury, but Holstead stayed in the army. He again endured several months in the hospital at Corinth, Mississippi, during the summer of 1862, after his regiment fought at Shiloh, and then returned to duty. He and his comrades served in the Hundred Days before Atlanta and then marched to Savannah. They fought along the Salkehatchie River in February, but then did not encounter strong resistance again until they arrived in North Carolina, where they took part in the fighting at Averasboro and Bentonville.
Photo courtesy of Library of Congress, no. B8184-10476

Capt. William L. Waddell of Company K in the 20th Ohio Infantry probably did not have many pleasant memories of South Carolina, because he was in constant pain by the time he entered the state as one of the XVII Corps in Gen. William T. Sherman's army. Waddell, a Pennsylvanian, had contracted rheumatism in the wet climate at Savannah. At the same time, his horse fell on him during the preparations to march out of that city, inflicting a painful hernia that the captain refused to report, preferring instead to purchase a truss and treat himself with medicine obtained from the regimental surgeon.

A salesman, the stubborn Waddell had been twenty-four years of age when he enlisted at Mt. Vernon, Ohio, in September 1861 as a private in Company E of the 20th Ohio Infantry. Soon promoted to sergeant, he became a lieutenant and transferred to Company I during February 1862, when his regiment was at Fort Donelson. In December of that same year he was assigned to Company K. He took command of Company K in May 1863 during the Vicksburg campaign, but he was not promoted to captain until one year later, at the outset of the Hundred Days. In January 1865, while his regiment was at Pocotaligo, he was assigned as a provost marshal to Third Division headquarters, in which capacity he served until mustered out at Louisville, Kentucky, during July 1865. *Photo courtesy of U.S.A.M.H.I.*

WILLIAM L. WADDELL
carte de visite

On January 26, 1865, Harrison Wilson, a decorated combat veteran, was appointed a lieutenant colonel and took command of the 20th Ohio Infantry, which was waiting at Pocotaligo, South Carolina, for the next phase of Gen. William T. Sherman's invasion to commence. Although he was only twenty-four years of age, Wilson led his regiment through the Carolinas and then mustered out at Louisville, Kentucky, in July 1865.

A teacher when the war began, Wilson enlisted during June 1861 at Columbus as a private in Company I of the 25th Ohio Infantry. He was discharged as a corporal in February 1862 at Fort Donelson so that he could be commissioned as a lieutenant in Company I of the 20th Ohio Infantry. He became the captain of Company E (and later Company F) of the 20th Ohio Infantry at Milliken's Bend in April 1863 and was subsequently awarded the XVII Corps Medal of Honor, in silver, for directing the regimental skirmishers at Raymond, Mississippi, in May 1863.

After fighting in the Hundred Days and marching to Savannah, Wilson's troops traveled by steamer to Beaufort. They waded in icy, waist-deep water to attack at Orangeburg in February and then were among the Federals who occupied Columbia. They destroyed the railroad tracks leading to Winnsboro and then continued into North Carolina, where they arrived late on the second day at Bentonville. *Photo courtesy of U.S.A.M.H.I.*

248

ROGER B. KELLOGG
copy print

The advance of Gen. Oliver O. Howard's column toward the Charleston and Savannah Railroad, where he was to join with the troops led by Gen. Henry W. Slocum, during January 1865 was not unopposed. Capt. Roger B. Kellogg of Company A in the 15th Iowa Infantry was shot in the abdomen and mortally wounded on January 14 in a skirmish near Pocotaligo. He died two days later at Beaufort, at the age of twenty-seven, and was buried there as he had no family to claim his body.

A native of Canada who resided in Vermont until the war began, Kellogg enlisted at Keokuk as a sergeant in Company A in February 1862. He was promoted to lieutenant during April 1862, after his regiment fought at Shiloh; in the fall of that year he was in command of his company when it fought at Corinth, but he was not promoted to captain until December 1864, after they had already endured both the Vicksburg campaign and the Hundred Days. They disembarked at Beaufort in South Carolina as part of the XVII Corps in Howard's wing and then moved inland to Pocotaligo. *Photo courtesy of U.S.A.M.H.I.*

Confederate authorities struggled to assemble a force to oppose Gen. William T. Sherman's march through South Carolina. A number of veteran regiments from the Army of Northern Virginia were transferred to their home state, including those assigned to the brigade formerly commanded by Joseph B. Kershaw, which was now led by John D. Kennedy. These men settled in Charleston, which must have provided an opportunity for a few bittersweet reunions to Cpl. James P. Boswell of Company G in the 3rd (Palmetto) Battalion, South Carolina Light Artillery.

Boswell had orginally enlisted at Camden in January 1861, at the age of twenty-seven, as a corporal in Company E of the 2nd South Carolina Infantry (Palmetto Regiment), which was then led by Kershaw. He remained with that regiment in Virginia—through the Seven Days, at Second Bull Run, and at Antietam—until the fall of 1862, when he mustered as a private in Company G of the 3rd (Palmetto) Battalion. Promoted to corporal in June 1863, he served on the South Carolina coast until Charleston was evacuated during February 1865, at which time most of the garrison troops marched to join Joseph E. Johnston's tiny army in North Carolina. After successive defeats at Averasboro and Bentonville, Boswell was paroled at Greensboro on May 1, 1865. *Photo courtesy of U.S.A.M.H.I.*

JAMES P. BOSWELL
copy print

250

JOHN R. MEW, WILLIAM W. GREGG,
WILLIAM F. MCKEWN, AND GEORGE A. MCDOWELL
albumen print

Gen. William J. Hardee's small force opposed Gen. Oliver O. Howard's column as it moved inland. The Federals pushed their way through the swamps, but not before both sides had suffered substantial casualties. Pvt. John R. Mew of the Beaufort Volunteer Artillery was captured on the Coosawhatchie River in late January 1865. An 1862 graduate of the Citadel who served on Morris Island during the siege of Fort Sumter in 1861, Mew had only recently rejoined his unit after serving with the engineers building fortifications and repairing railroads along the coast.

All three of Mew's Citadel classmates with whom he posed in this photograph were already dead by the time he was captured. William W. Gregg was killed at Gaines' Mill in May 1862. William F. McKewn worked for a few months after his April 1862 graduation as a teacher at a military academy in Alabama and then enlisted as a sergeant in the Palmetto Sharpshooters. He was wounded at Second Bull Run and, after South Mountain and Antietam, was promoted to sergeant major. He was mortally wounded at Fredericksburg on December 13, 1862. George A. McDowell joined the company of the 6th South Carolina Cavalry led by former cadet Moses B. Humphrey in June 1862. He became a corporal before he was killed along Haulover Cut on John's Island on February 9, 1864, at the age of twenty-one. *Photo courtesy of Citadel Archives, Charleston, South Carolina*

ALEXANDER MACBETH
carte de visite
George S. Cook

Gen. Quincy A. Gillmore attacked along the coast to provide a diversion while Gen. William T. Sherman's columns reunited and marched inland. On February 10, 1865, elements of four regiments charged a line of rifle pits on James Island, which were defended by only about 140 Confederates. Among the latter was Cpl. Alexander MacBeth of Company A (Palmetto Guards), 18th Battalion, South Carolina Artillery (South Carolina Siege Train), who had enlisted in February 1862 at the age of seventeen.

After several hours of shelling by Federal gunboats lying offshore, more than a thousand Union troops surged forward. The Confederates, commanded by Maj. Edward M. Manigault of the Siege Train, held

their position as long as they could and then were told by Manigault to retreat to a second line, where two companies of reinforcements waited. In the withdrawal, Manigault was seriously wounded; MacBeth stopped to help but was urged by the major to go on without him. After giving his commander a drink from his canteen, MacBeth continued his flight.

Manigault was captured but recovered, while MacBeth's jaw was shattered in March 1865 by a kick from a horse after James Island had been evacuated. Because he was hospitalized at the end of the war, he was not paroled until late in the summer of 1865. *Photo courtesy of University of South Carolina, Columbia*

Some of these men survived to march into South Carolina as part of the XVII Corps during January 1865. On February 3 they were engaged in the fighting along the Salkehatchie River, during which Federal soldiers waded through shoulder-deep water and persistent artillery fire to push aside Confederate defenders. Eight days later they skirmished again, this time with a small detachment of regulars and home guards at Orangeburg who made a stand behind rudimentary earthworks to win time for those who wished to flee. Like so many other South Carolina towns, Orangeburg was burned by the Federals.

Gen. William T. Sherman "casually mentioned" on February 15, 1865, that he would "appreciate the men who first made a lodgement in Columbia."[15] Challenged, quite a few detachments of his army made haste to raise their flags in the capital city. Many of these were pulled down by the official vanguard, which arrived about midday on February 16, but the late arrivals could not remove the flag of the 32nd Illinois Infantry from the flagpole over city hall because the Midwesterners had locked their color guard in the belltower with their banner. The members of the color guard were later arrested when they became inebriated and amused themselves by taking potshots into crowds of people milling in the streets of the fallen city. *Photo courtesy of U.S.A.M.H.I.*

Company C, 32nd Illinois Infantry
copy print

253

URSULINE CONVENT
albumen print
Richard Wearn

The inferno that gutted Columbia during the night of February 16, 1865, spared almost no one. On the day that the Federals entered the city, an officer visited the Ursuline Convent and offered to help protect it, but the mother superior, Baptista Lynch, refused his offer because she had been assured by Gen. William T. Sherman, whose daughter was once a pupil of hers, that the property would be safe. Sister Lynch steadfastly ignored the advice of friends through the day and kept her female students in the convent.

The officer returned with a guard detail, but they were not able to prevent a tragedy that night. When reports came that the city was burning, the nuns removed their sacred vessels from the altar of the chapel. Soon afterward, drunken soldiers battered down the chapel door and spilled inside. The chaplain, with a crucifix held high over his head, led the frightened nuns and female students out of the convent as it began to burn, ignited by soldiers who applied torches to the roof.

The women stumbled into St. Peter's Catholic Church, whence they were flushed a few hours later by troops who yelled that the building was about to be destroyed so that the troops might steal the bundles that their victims carried. The frightened students spent the rest of the night among the tombstones in the churchyard. *Photo courtesy of University of South Carolina, Columbia*

JAMES G. GILFILLIN
carte de visite
Quinby and Company

After Gen. William T. Sherman's troops occupied Columbia, Pvt. James G. Gilfillin marched out of Charleston in February 1865 with the rest of Company A (Palmetto Guards) of the 18th Battalion, South Carolina Artillery (South Carolina Siege Train). They had exchanged their artillery for Belgian muskets, described by one of them as "probably the most antiquated and worthless guns ever put in a modern soldier's hands." Only a few of them got Enfields before the clash at Averasboro with Sherman's well-armed troops.

Gilfillin was just eighteen years of age in February 1862 when he was mustered as a private in the Palmetto Guard. The following May his company was posted on Battery Island at the mouth of the Stono River, but they were withdrawn under Federal artillery fire to James Island and later settled in Charleston, where they manned breastworks constructed near Magnolia Cemetery. In January 1863 the Palmetto Guards took part in the capture of the USS *Isaac P. Smith* on the Stono River and then engaged the USS *Pawnee* at James Island in March and the USS *Marblehead* in December 1863. After a few months in Florida they were assigned to a picket line on James Island, where they stayed until Charleston was evacuated. *Photo courtesy of University of South Carolina, Columbia*

256

EDWARD THOMAS
carte de visite

Born at Valley Grove in Fairfield County, near Ridgeway, Edward Thomas was a senior at the Citadel during February 1865, when the academy was abandoned in the evacuation of Charleston. Hugh S. Thompson's company of the Cadet Battalion, in which Thomas served as a lieutenant, joined Stephen Elliott, Jr.'s, makeshift brigade and remained in the rear guard of the garrison as it marched to North Carolina.

The students from the Citadel, however, remained in South Carolina. They were joined at Spartanburg by the cadets from the Arsenal Academy, an affiliated school directed by Edward Thomas's cousin, John P. Thomas, who was determined that none of his charges would be captured. Most of the Citadel cadets were sent home during April, but the remainder fought alongside the Arsenal students in the last engagement of the Civil War in South Carolina, a brief firefight at Williamston on May 1, 1865, in which one cadet was wounded. A few weeks later, Thomas furloughed the last of his cadets at Newberry upon the advice of Gov. Andrew G. Magrath. Like the majority of the Citadel cadets, who were furloughed in April 1865, Thomas's stubborn remnant simply went home and never formally surrendered. *Photo courtesy of University of South Carolina, Columbia*

257

JOHN E. BOINEST
quarter-plate ambrotype

Cpl. John E. Boinest of Company B in the Cadet Battalion may well have been among the Citadel students who did not go home in April 1865. Unlike most of them, he did sign a formal parole at Augusta, Georgia, in May 1865, indicating that he remained in active service until the bitter end.

He had first enlisted at the age of sixteen as a private in Hatch's Battalion of Coast Rangers at Charleston during September 1861, but was discharged three months later, after that unit was reorganized as the 23rd South Carolina Infantry. He enrolled at the Citadel the next year and became a corporal in the Battalion.

The Citadel cadets served on James Island during the summer of 1862 and again in 1863 and then fought a brief engagement on the South Carolina coast at Tulifinny River in December 1864 before encamping for the last time on James Island later that month. When Charleston was evacuated in February 1865, the Citadel was closed, not to reopen for seventeen years. Boinest and his fellow cadets marched for North Carolina with the Confederate rear guard, but most of the Citadel students remained in their home state and were furloughed to return home in April 1865. *Photo courtesy of Citadel Archives, Charleston, South Carolina*

NEWTON BINGHAM
carte de visite

When the 48th Indiana Infantry marched into South Carolina during the winter of 1865, it was commanded by Capt. Newton Bingham. Bingham's troops, who had rejoined the XV Corps at Savannah after guarding supply lines, fought along the Salkehatchie and North Edisto rivers and then occupied Columbia. After leaving the capital, they were engaged once more in a skirmish, at West's Cross Roads on February 25, and then continued into North Carolina.

A twenty-year-old salesman in 1861, Bingham had enlisted at Mishawaka, Indiana, as a sergeant in Company F. He transferred to Company G as a second lieutenant in July 1862, and he was promoted to command that company in November 1863 while he was absent on a furlough due to his declining health. Several physicians told him that he had tuberculosis, but he insisted that he contracted chronic malaria while campaigning in Mississippi during the summer of 1863.

Healthy or not, Bingham was promoted to major in April 1865 and then lieutenant colonel the next month. He mustered out with his troops at Louisville, Kentucky, during July 1865. *Photo courtesy of Indiana State Library*

GEORGE A. BRADLEY
copy print

When the 5th Connecticut Infantry skirmished with Confederates along Thompson's Creek near Cheraw, South Carolina, on March 2 and 3, 1865, Pvt. George A. Bradley fought as a member of Company A. After the regiment entered North Carolina, it took part in the fighting at Averasboro and Bentonville, where Bradley was captured and again held in Libby Prison, as he had been in 1862. The collapsing Confederate government, however, paroled him a few weeks later.

A sixteen-year-old from Danbury who reported his occupation variously as either farmer or carpenter, Bradley had enlisted at Hartford as a private in Company A, 5th Connecticut Infantry, in July 1861. He suffered a saber cut to the head and was captured at Cedar Mountain, Virginia, in August 1862. Confined at Libby Prison in Richmond, he was exchanged the following month and rejoined his regiment in time to fight at Chancellorsville and Gettysburg, after which they were transferred west and fought in the Hundred Days before Atlanta as part of the XX Corps.

After his second imprisonment, Bradley did not again rejoin his regiment. He was assigned to the parolee's battalion in Maryland, but the end of the war made such a unit superfluous, and so he was discharged in June 1865 at Annapolis, Maryland. *Photo courtesy of U.S.A.M.H.I.*

Gen. William T. Sherman's veterans left little of use behind them as they marched out of South Carolina in March 1865. Much of that which had any military value became the responsibility of Maj. Julian Mitchell, who was appointed Chief Commissary of the state on April 3, 1865. The remaining military supplies were sent to Chester, where a depot had been established.

This photograph of Mitchell was taken in 1862, when he was promoted to major and given charge of the commissary for Gen. Roswell S. Ripley's brigade, which fought during the Seven Days. After Ripley was reassigned, Mitchell remained in charge of the commissary for the brigade and as such marched into Pennsylvania in the summer of 1863. He was captured at Smithburg on July 4, 1863, and confined at Fort Delaware, whence he was forwarded to Johnson's Island. In the later summer of 1864 he escaped briefly while being transferred to Elmira, New York. He then was taken to Fort Columbus in New York, where he was exchanged and returned to Charleston in October of that year.

By the time Mitchell was released, the brigade to which he was originally assigned no longer existed. Mitchell in January 1865 was sent to Columbia, South Carolina, and placed in charge of the supplies stored there. The destruction of that city left him without an assignment. *Photo courtesy of Clemson University*

JULIAN MITCHELL
carte de visite
Quinby and Company

THOMAS L. YARBOROUGH
AND MARTHA HARRELL
YARBOROUGH
copy print

Gen. Joseph E. Johnston expected to receive reinforcements from the Wilmington area, but the South Carolina units that had fought there in January and February 1865 were severely reduced. Pvt. Thomas L. Yarborough of Company B, 21st South Carolina Infantry, was among the members of Johnson Hagood's brigade that were ordered south from Virginia to reinforce Fort Fisher on January 15, 1865. By the time that brigade joined Johnston's small army, Yarborough was a prisoner of war.

He was a twenty-eight-year-old farmer with two children in Darlington County when the war began; his wife was twenty-one at the time. He enlisted as a private in Company B in May 1862, after the passage of the conscription act, but was absent on sick leave through the rest of the summer. He joined his company in November and survived unscathed the grueling campaigns during the summer of 1863 on Morris Island and the summer and fall of 1864 at Petersburg, where his regiment suffered heavy casualties. He was taken prisoner, however, when Fort Fisher fell only hours after his arrival. He died of pneumonia in the prison camp at Elmira, New York, on April 28, 1865. *Photo courtesy of Darlington County Historical Society, Darlington, South Carolina*

Pvt. William R. Greer of Company B of the 25th South Carolina Infantry was also among those from Johnson Hagood's brigade who were taken prisoner at Fort Fisher. After their arrival, Greer and several hundred others were told to run to the post over a mile of open ground under artillery fire. Stunned and buried in sand by a shell, with only one foot showing, Greer was rescued but became a prisoner when Fort Fisher fell to a Union assault.

Greer was about seventeen years old in 1861 when this image was taken after he enlisted as a private in the Washington Light Infantry, which became Company B of the 11th Battalion of South Carolina Infantry. The battalion, in July 1863, merged with others to create the 25th South Carolina Infantry (Eutaw Regiment). They served on James Island during the siege of Battery Wagner, and then Greer accompanied his regiment in April 1864 to Virginia, where he fought at Walthall Junction and Drewry's Bluff and along the Weldon Railroad before he was assigned to work in the brigade infirmary at Petersburg in the fall.

About the run that nearly cost Greer his life, Col. William Lamb, Confederate commander of Fort Fisher, recalled that most of the men arrived demoralized. He declared that "Never was there a more stupid blunder committed by a commanding general." *Photo courtesy of University of South Carolina, Columbia*

WILLIAM R. GREER
cabinet print of *carte de visite*
Quinby and Company

WASHINGTON LIGHT INFANTRY
albumen print

Johnson Hagood's brigade lost 461 casualties at Town Creek after Wilmington was evacuated. Col. Charles H. Simonton, who was captured while in temporary command of the brigade that day, appears here as the captain of the Washington Light Infantry on Sullivan's Island. From left to right are Pvt. A. Wallace Masters, Pvt. Octavius Wilkie, Pvt. Frederick Copes, Lt. Edward W. Lloyd, Simonton, and Pvt. Gibbs Blackwood.

Simonton, a Charleston attorney and legislator, led his company until it was merged into the 11th (Eutaw) Battalion and then became a major in charge of that battalion. After it joined with other units in June 1862 to become the 25th South Carolina Infantry (Eutaw Regiment), he commanded the regiment at Secessionville and during the siege of Battery Wagner. He was hospitalized for chronic dysentery at Petersburg in July 1864 and then in September was assigned to the defenses at Wilmington.

Lloyd, a Charleston carriage maker, commanded Company B of the 11th Battalion and the 25th South Carolina Infantry until he resigned on August 22, 1864. Wilkie and Copes served in Lloyd's company until they were detailed to the commissary department and the South Carolina Railroad, respectively, where they remained when their regiment left for Virginia. Masters and Blackwood enlisted in Company A; the latter was captured at Fort Fisher in January 1865.
Photo courtesy of MOLLUS, Mass., U.S.A.M.H.I.

ELIJAH A. DORN
copy print

Among the depleted units from the Wilmington area that rejoined Joseph E. Johnston's army was the 2nd South Carolina Cavalry, which had received a few reinforcements in its home state before being assigned to the coast. Some of these recruits illustrated how the conscription acts had pulled a lot of unlikely soldiers into the Confederate army. Elijah A. Dorn, a thirty-five-year-old farmer with eight children from Edgefield County, enlisted on James Island in March 1863 as a private in Company K of the 2nd South

Carolina Artillery. This unit was assigned to the defense of Charleston, and it was frequently engaged during the campaigns on Morris Island in the summer of 1863. Dorn was "exchanged" on August 15, 1864, at James Island for another private then serving in Company I of the 2nd South Carolina Cavalry. His new regiment remained on the coast of South Carolina until December 1864, when it was sent to North Carolina. *Photo courtesy of U.S.A.M.H.I.*

MATTHEW C. BUTLER
carte de visite

Gen. Matthew C. Butler became somewhat of a legend on March 9, 1865, when he and a small body of his troopers captured a picket outpost of Judson Kilpatrick's division. The following day his troops and others rode over the sleeping Federal camp, scattering Kilpatrick's men until they rallied with the aid of infantry.

Butler boasted impeccable credentials. He was descended from a military line: his great-grandfather was killed during the Revolution, his grandfather was a major general in the U. S. Army, his father was a surgeon in the U. S. Navy, and his mother was the daughter of Commodore Matthew C. Perry. He graduated from South Carolina College, practiced law, and married the daughter of Francis W. Pickens.

He served in the legislature until he resigned to be captain of the Edgefield Hussars in the cavalry battalion of Hampton's Legion. After First Bull Run he became a major in charge of all cavalry in the Legion; in August 1862 his troops became the core of the new 2nd South Carolina Cavalry.

Colonel Butler commanded his regiment at Antietam and Fredericksburg while carrying only a silver-trimmed riding crop. He lost his right foot at Brandy Station in June 1863 but was fitted with a cork foot and given command of a brigade when he returned; two of his brothers served on his staff. He became a major general in 1864 and led his men to North Carolina. *Photograph courtesy of Library of Congress, Biographical File*

266

MOSES B. HUMPHREY
copy print

Capt. Moses B. Humphrey was mortally wounded at Solomon's Grove. During the morning attack on Kilpatrick's camp, Humphrey noticed that a Union lieutenant was attempting to fire a cannon. Humphrey and two men charged the Federal, who fired canister and shattered the captain's arm. One Confederate was unharmed, and he shot the Union officer dead. Humphrey refused to allow an amputation, so he died on April 30 and was allegedly buried with his horse, Yago, in the same grave.

Humphrey had entered the Citadel in 1859 and served on the crew of the first gun that fired at the *Star of the West*. When three dozen cadets left the Citadel in July 1862 and joined the 16th Battalion of South Carolina Partisan Rangers, they chose him as

their captain. In September, they and other recruits became Company F, 6th South Carolina Cavalry, with Humphrey as captain.

On February 9, 1864, Humphrey led them in a wild attack at Haulover Cut on John's Island. Nine of his troopers were killed, wounded, or captured; Humphrey himself was shot twice in the leg and his horse was killed. Five months later in Virginia, Gen. Wade Hampton led them in a charge at Trevilian Station. Humphrey encouraged his men by telling them that they could not die while their women at home were praying for them, but he was again shot in the leg. He recovered to lead his men back to South Carolina. *Photo courtesy of Citadel Archives, Charleston, South Carolina*

ALFRED M. RHETT
carte de visite
Quinby and Company

Col. Alfred M. Rhett, the son of Robert B. Rhett, commanded a makeshift brigade of garrison troops that fought at Averasboro in March 1865. His men did well, though they were driven back by the more numerous and experienced Federals, but Rhett was taken prisoner. Still angry when he was presented to Gen. Judson Kilpatrick, Rhett assured him that fifty thousand men waited in South Carolina to defeat the Northern armies. Kilpatrick was probably amused and provoked his captive further by declaring that he was willing to search every swamp to find the "damned cowards" about which Rhett spoke.

Rhett had commanded a gun crew in Fort Moultrie during the bombardment of Fort Sumter in April 1861 and then had enlisted as the captain of Company B in the 1st Battalion of South Carolina Artillery. He became a major when that unit became a regiment in the spring of 1862. He then assumed command after killing his colonel, William R. Calhoun, in a duel on September 5, 1862. His gunners successfully defended Fort Sumter against the Union naval assault in April 1863 and then endured the Federal bombardment until an infantry garrison took their place in September 1863. He temporarily commanded the military district at Charleston, but his request for a promotion to brigadier general was denied. *Photo courtesy of F. Bruce Kusrow*

268

HILLIARD TODD
copy print

Pvt. Hilliard Todd joined Company K of the 1st South Carolina Artillery in July 1864, when that regiment was serving in the garrison at Charleston. They marched out of the city as part of the brigade assigned to their regimental commander, Alfred M. Rhett, and fought under his direction at Averasboro. Todd and his comrades were forced back, but they rallied along with other Confederates, including another brigade of garrison troops from Charleston commanded by the invalided Stephen Elliott, Jr., to establish a second and finally a third defensive line. Emerging unscathed from that engagement and a series of three charges at Bentonville, Todd was paroled at Durham Station, North Carolina, in April 1865.

Todd was more fortunate than his siblings: he had four brothers who served in the Confederate army, of whom three died of disease and the fourth was killed in combat. A native of Conway, he first enlisted at the age of eighteen in April 1862 at Columbia as a private in Company B of the 18th Battalion, South Carolina Artillery, also known as Manigault's Battalion and the South Carolina Siege Train. He left this company five months later, after he was wounded. *Photo courtesy of University of South Carolina, Columbia*

Pvt. Andrew Crawford enlisted in Company K of the 1st South Carolina Artillery at Columbia in July 1864, the same month that Hilliard Todd joined. Although Crawford was only sixteen years of age, he served with Todd and the others in Fort Johnson on James Island until Charleston was evacuated and then marched with them into North Carolina. Crawford and Todd fought together at Averasboro, where the inexperienced artillerymen refused to give ground until they had suffered heavy casualties and were driven from the field by veteran Union infantry, who attacked through ankle-deep water. They also survived three desperate attacks before being withdrawn at Bentonville. Crawford, who was apparently never wounded, was paroled near Greensboro on April 29, 1865. *Photo courtesy of University of South Carolina, Columbia*

ANDREW CRAWFORD
albumen print

270

THOMAS L. OGIER
carte de visite
George S. Cook

The garrison troops from Charleston, inexperienced at fighting in the field, suffered horrendous casualties at Averasboro in March 1865. Among the physicians present to tend the many wounded was Thomas L. Ogier, who had served since the beginning of the war as district surgeon in charge of the military hospitals in and near Charleston. When the Confederates evacuated the port city, he accompanied them to the carnage at Averasboro and Bentonville.

Born in Charleston, Ogier was sent as a boy to study in England. Upon his return he entered the South Carolina Medical College, whence he graduated in 1830 at the age of twenty. He immediately traveled to Paris, where he arrived in time to tend many of the civilians wounded in the fighting that accompanied the revolution of that year in France. Despite his rude welcome, Ogier remained in France for three years to further his medical education and then returned once more to the city of his birth to practice medicine.

His two sons and two sons-in-law had accepted Confederate commissions as well. When South Carolinians were ordered to Mississippi in May 1863, one of his sons had accompanied them as a surgeon, caught typhoid fever, and died. *Photo courtesy of University of South Carolina, Columbia*

271

Pvt. Ira Fish enlisted at the age of twenty-two as a private in Company A, 150th New York Infantry (Duchess County Regiment), at Amenia in August 1862. He became a corporal within a few months and then was promoted to sergeant in June 1863. Wounded at Gettysburg, he rejoined his regiment in the fall of 1863, when they were sent west. After fighting in the Hundred Days, he marched into South Carolina in January 1865 as a sergeant in Henry W. Slocum's XX Corps. Fish emerged from that state unscathed, but he was wounded again at Averasboro, North Carolina, on March 16, 1865, giving at least one South Carolinian at Averasboro a measure of retribution for the devastation of his state by the Federals. He mustered out in June 1865. *Photo courtesy of Library of Congress, no. B8184-10483*

IRA FISH
carte de visite
J. H. Young, Baltimore, Maryland

JOHN J. LUCAS
copy print of *carte de visite*

Of 224 alumni of the Citadel alive in 1861, 209 served in Confederate forces. Three dozen were killed or died of wounds, while 94 suffered nonfatal wounds in service. Among the latter was John J. Lucas, who led his artillery battalion north out of Charleston as part of Col. Alfred M. Rhett's brigade in February 1865 and then was wounded twice, at Averasboro and at Bentonville. He gave this *carte de visite* of himself to a niece, endorsing it "to Hattie from Uncle Lucas."

Lucas had graduated from the Citadel in 1851 and had become a Charleston businessman and legislator. He served as commander of the 15th Heavy Artillery Battalion, which was organized during the summer of 1861 with two companies and was later increased to five. This organization was headquartered at Fort Pemberton on James Island, which anchored the right end of the Confederate defensive line, in the summer of 1862, but detachments served in many other defensive installations around Charleston, where they often engaged Union troops until the port city was evacuated. Lucas and his troops were paroled with the remnant of Joseph E. Johnston's army. *Photo courtesy of Darlington County Historical Society, Darlington, South Carolina*

JAMES H. TAYLOR
copy print of ambrotype

The 3rd South Carolina Infantry was among those South Carolina regiments, assembled from almost every theater of the war, which fought together at Bentonville for the first and last time. Its ranks were severely reduced by hard fighting in Virginia during the long bloody summer of 1864. They fought in the Wilderness and at Spotsylvania and then withdrew further south and fought at Cold Harbor. Among the many replacements hurried northward was young James H. Taylor, who enlisted as a private in Company G of the 3rd South Carolina Infantry during October 1864, the month in which he celebrated his sixteenth birthday.

He remained with the company when it was sent to Charleston along with the other depleted regiments of Joseph B. Kershaw's old brigade. He then marched into North Carolina after the port city was evacuated. At Bentonville on March 19, 1865, the members of his brigade stood their ground, as did the majority of the South Carolinians, but it became clear that to continue fighting would be suicidal. After Joseph E. Johnston surrendered to William T. Sherman in April, Taylor was paroled at Grahamville. *Photo courtesy of Confederate Relic Room, Columbia, South Carolina*

When Matthew C. Butler was promoted to major general and given a division, he insisted upon Thomas M. Logan taking his place as commander of his brigade. Logan's promotion in February 1865 made him the youngest brigadier general in the Confederate army, but he scarcely had time to reflect on it. He accompanied Butler to North Carolina, where Logan led what was allegedly the last cavalry charge of the war while commanding the rear guard near Raleigh in April 1865. Logan then accompanied Joseph E. Johnston to negotiate terms with William T. Sherman on April 18. At that time, Logan was not yet twenty-five years of age.

Logan graduated from South Carolina College in 1860 at the head of his class and then enlisted as a lieutenant in Company A of the Infantry Battalion of Hampton's Legion the following year. Promoted to captain after First Bull Run, he led his company during the Seven Days; he was badly wounded in the foot, but accompanied his troops in an ambulance and led them at Second Bull Run. He became a major for his performance at Antietam and in Tennessee commanded all the infantry of Hampton's Legion, which often served as skirmishers for James Longstreet's corps. Returning to Virginia, Logan was painfully wounded at Riddle's Shop on June 13, 1864, but he was back in action by the fall. *Photo courtesy of University of South Carolina, Columbia*

Thomas M. Logan
carte de visite
Quinby and Company

Chapter 8

Flowers Have No Memory: South Carolina during Reconstruction

Much of South Carolina lay in ruins by the end of the Civil War. Gen. Carl Schurz, who visited the state in July 1865, reported that "No part of the South . . . had indeed suffered so much from the ravage of war as South Carolina." Federals and Confederates had stolen, burned, or otherwise destroyed property worth millions of dollars, while more than 18 percent of the state's adult white males had died in Confederate service. Rebuilding had to begin at once, but many felt like Carolina Gilman, the widow of a Unitarian minister who resided in Charleston. She wrote after the war ended in 1865: "I could not help thinking yesterday, as I saw the flowers look up and smile when the superincumbent weight and decay and ruin were removed, that they set us a good example politically. But then, flowers have no memory." Because they were human, most white South Carolinians resented the destruction and insisted upon having their customary leaders, many of whom were Confederate officers, to direct their reconstruction. These men would lose their grip on the state only a generation after the war, but they left an indelible stamp on South Carolina.[1]

On April 14, 1865, Robert Anderson raised the same flag over Fort Sumter that he had lowered four years earlier, but many residents of the state did not consider the war to be over. Some sheltered the first lady of the Confederacy, Varina H. Davis, during her desperate flight to safety. She and her children accompanied the train that brought the Confederate treasury to Camden, where she dined with old friends such as John S. Preston and James and Mary Chesnut. Because the railroad had been destroyed, the funds were transferred to wagons for the trip to Newberry, where the refugees and their cargo once more boarded a train on April 16. The tracks ended at Abbeville; Mrs. Davis stayed with an old family friend for a few days, then, parting company with the treasury escort, she continued on her way to Georgia.

Mrs. Davis traveled without knowing where her husband was, or if he was safe. The president entered South Carolina on April 26 with two thousand troopers and five Cabinet secretaries, including Secretary of the Treasury George A. Trenholm, a Charleston businessman. It was not Jefferson Davis's first wartime visit; he had inspected the lines on James Island in November 1863. Circumstances had certainly changed for the worse, but cheering crowds still lined the roads and he responded with words of encouragement. He spent his first night in South Carolina at a home near Fort Mill. The next day Trenholm resigned and left for Columbia, where he was arrested by Federals a few weeks later, but Davis reached Abbeville on May 2. He held a council of war in the same home where his wife had taken shelter. Told by the young generals present that they could not win the war, though they would defend him, a shaken Davis had to be led from the room. At midnight on May 3, Davis left Abbeville with the treasury wagons, which had joined his party.

Davis crossed the Savannah River into Georgia before daybreak on May 3, 1865. A number of South Carolinians, including Gen. Martin W. Gary, rode with him, but most stayed behind to face the fact that the war was over. Gov. Andrew G. Magrath issued a last proclamation on May 22. In it, he suspended the functions of his office and asked the people of South Carolina to accept the situation. Arrested three days later, after the 25th Ohio Infantry arrived in Columbia, he was imprisoned for seven months at Fort Pulaski with Trenholm. Pres. Andrew Johnson began his program of reconstruction by issuing an amnesty proclamation and appointing seven provisional governors on May 29. After meeting with a South Carolina delegation, he appointed Benjamin F. Perry to be their provisional governor.

After consulting with Johnson, Perry called for a constitutional convention, which met in September 1865. The delegates included former Confederate congressman James L. Orr, twelve members of the secession convention, former Confederate governor Francis W. Pickens and more than two dozen Confederate officers. The officers were led by Wade Hampton, who had reluctantly given his parole in April 1865 after being persuaded by his wife to abandon his plans to continue fighting. Following Johnson's directions, these men repealed the ordinance of secession and acknowledged the end of slavery through resolutions introduced by Pickens, who urged his comrades to "pour in the oil of peace . . . even if it means that in so doing we go backwards."[2] However, they did not repudiate the right to secede or the state debt incurred during the war. At the same time, their constitution, which was adopted without a referendum, did not allow blacks to vote, as Perry had advised in spite of the support of Hampton and others for black suffrage.

Hampton publicly declared he did not want to be governor, and so he narrowly lost the race to Orr, whose candidacy was endorsed by the convention. Orr, who took office during late November 1865, endured a stormy term as governor. While the legislature adopted laws to prevent the collection of war debts, which met with much approval, the legislators also enacted a Black Code whose terms and inequities were reminiscent of slavery. Gen. Daniel E. Sickles, military commander of the state, eventually suspended the payment of the war debt, but he nullified the Black Code on January 1, 1866. Under protest, South Carolinians amended their Code. Ignoring such rumblings, Johnson declared the rebellion at an end in the South on April 2, 1866. The number of Federal troops in South Carolina quickly dwindled until, by November 1866, there were fewer than three thousand, about a third of those assigned there eleven months earlier.

South Carolinians, having irritated many Northerners by refusing to repudiate their war debt or surrender many of the mannerisms of slavery, infuriated a larger proportion by supporting Johnson, who fought with Radical Republicans for control of Reconstruction beginning in December 1865. Perry, after leaving the governor's office, left for Washington to claim his seat in the Senate, but his credentials, like most of those held by Southern congressmen, were rejected. Perry joined Orr in organizing the National Union Party in South Carolina; in the summer of 1866, the state's delegates led by Orr, entered the national convention at Philadelphia arm in arm with delegates from Massachusetts. The assembly made clear their support for the embattled president, ignoring the tide of public reaction against him that was rising in the North.

Johnson's racial policies inflamed the Radicals in Congress and their supporters, and South Carolina leaders added fuel to the fire after they returned from Philadelphia. The National Union Convention adopted resolutions endorsing black rights, but Orr opposed the Fourteenth Amendment, which extended citizenship to blacks and provided for the guarantee of equal rights to them. The South Carolina legislature almost unanimously rejected the proposal, as did all the Southern legislatures except that of Tennessee. The bitter fight between the Radicals in Congress and President Johnson ended with a victory for the former when they secured a two-thirds majority in both houses during the elections of 1866. The following March, Congress divided the South into five military districts, in each of which a military commander was assigned to supervise the creation of proper civil governments.

Sickles continued in command of South Carolina until August 1867, when he was replaced with Edward R. S. Canby. The latter removed many state officials from office, prevented the legislature from meeting, and supervised the registration of approximately 148,000 loyal voters, more than half of whom were black. Conservative Democrats voiced their protest through a convention at Columbia chaired by James Chesnut; among the eight vice-presidents were Hampton and Perry, who urged whites not to vote in the impending election for delegates to a new constitutional convention because military rule was preferable to a civilian regime based on black suffrage.

Despite the conservatives' protests against the elections, 124 delegates were elected to the constitutional convention that met at Charleston in January 1868. Many South Carolinians resented the fact that only 48 of the delegates were white, while 76 were black; at the same time, less than half of the former were native Southerners, while two-thirds of the latter had been slaves. In spite of their inexperience, however, these delegates enacted a progressive constitution authorizing universal male suffrage and eliminating all property qualifications for office holding. Many previously appointed state officials would henceforth be elected. Debt imprisonment was ended, the war debt was repudiated, divorce was legalized, and both the schools and the militia were opened to members of both races. Approved by a two-to-one vote, this constitution remained in force until 1894.

The Republican administration of South Carolina accomplished many important objectives, not the least of which was the ratification of the Fourteenth Amendment and the readmission of the state into the Union, but it was plagued by resentment from the outset. The conservative Democrats found a number of issues which they could use to build a coalition to oust the Republicans. The state debt grew from $5.4 million in 1868 to more than $25 million by late 1873, and talk of repudiating all or part of this amount became common. Many resented the number of blacks in the legislature: in 1868, 10 of 31 senators and 78 of 124 representatives were black, and blacks remained a majority until 1874. Allegations of corruption, some of them unfortunately true, circulated freely. Gov. Robert K. Scott, the former commander of the Freedmen's Bureau in South Carolina, was honest but apparently blind to the baser impulses of many associates. His successor, Franklin J. Moses, Jr., who had served as a private secretary to Pickens at the outset of the Civil War and then became a Republican legislator, was reputed to be "immoral, extravagant, and without principle."[3]

The election of delegates to the national Democratic convention in 1868 became the first step in the conservative counterattack against the Republican hegemony. South Carolina Democrats met at Columbia in April. There they condemned the new constitution, which had not yet been adopted, endorsed limited black suffrage, and chose Wade Hampton to chair an executive committee and serve as a delegate to the national convention along with James Chesnut, Benjamin Perry, Martin W. Gary, and Robert Barnwell Rhett. As leader of the delegation, Hampton pushed for sectional reconciliation with home rule for the South under a Democratic president.

Former Democrats organized the Union Reform Party at a convention in Columbia in June 1870. About 150 delegates, representing two-thirds of South Carolina's thirty-one counties, attended; among them were approximately two dozen blacks. The delegates endorsed the Fifteenth Amendment and the existing laws of the state in an effort to woo both conservative white voters and moderate black voters. Richard B. Carpenter, a Republican attorney from Kentucky, was nominated for governor, but Matthew C. Butler, who had lost a foot while serving as a Confederate general, was chosen to run for lieutenant governor. The conservative press endorsed them, though Butler was chastised for urging racial unity.

Carpenter and Butler conducted a thorough grassroots campaign—the former spoke in all but one county, while the latter missed four—but they lost the race. The campaign was marked by bitter political divisions; former governor Orr, for example, opposed the Union Reform Party and called for continued support of the Republicans. Violence also marred the contest when open combat erupted between the Ku Klux Klan and black militia units in the upland counties. Clashes continued after Scott was reelected, ending only after about a thousand Federal troops were sent into the upland region to suppress the Klan.

Disunity among the Republicans encouraged the Democrats to keep pressing to regain control of the state. The Republicans split in 1872 when a substantial minority of the party, led by Orr and including black leaders such as Robert Smalls, refused to support the nomination of Moses. Moses won primarily because the Union Reform Party

had disbanded, preventing conservative Democrats from taking advantage of this opportunity. Two years later the Republican rift widened even as they elected Gov. Daniel H. Chamberlain, the former colonel of the 5th Massachusetts Colored Cavalry who had attended the 1868 constitutional convention and had served as attorney general under Scott. Realizing the danger, Chamberlain tried to reduce corruption and financial waste, but many fellow party members in the legislature ignored him.

Democrats understood that 1876 might be their year but disagreed on how to proceed. "Fusionists" wanted to support Chamberlain, believing the Democrats could not overcome the Republican hold on the black vote, but "Straightouts" wanted to defeat their divided foes. The latter won control of the Democratic Party in South Carolina after the rioting in Hamburg, Edgefield County, left one white and seven blacks dead. Gary, chairman of the Democrats in Edgefield County, and Butler, hailed as the "hero of Hamburg" for his role in that event, arranged the nomination of Hampton, whom Alexander C. Haskell, chairman of the state executive committee, endorsed as a "reform man . . . who would be able to unite the two races better than anyone else in the state."[4] Hampton was escorted to the convention in August by a Straightout torchlight procession. Fusionist James H. Rion nominated fellow Fusionist John Bratton, a member of the state executive committee, but he declined in favor of Hampton. Former governor John L. Manning also declined; then Hampton was nominated by acclamation.

All of the nominees on Hampton's ticket in 1876 were Confederate officers, and the campaign took on the appearance of a military operation. Many were former Fusionists like Johnson Hagood, the chairman of the Barnwell County Democratic executive committee who became comptroller general and succeeded Hampton as governor. Hampton asked for the votes of both races, promising there would be no "vindicative discriminations," but Gary believed in the "Mississippi Plan" of coercion.

He and Butler organized the "Red Shirts," armed Democratic clubs that used threats to persuade many voters, especially blacks, to avoid Republican rallies. Despite Hampton's opposition, violent clashes claimed the lives of six or seven whites and over a hundred blacks. Ordered by Pres. Ulysses S. Grant to disband, the Red Shirts in South Carolina adopted sarcastic names such as the "Hampton and Tilden Musical Club," formerly the "Columbia Flying Artillery," which referred to their field pieces as "twelve four-pounder flutes."[5] Once more, Federal reinforcements arrived to restore order.

Thanks to tactics that he did not officially endorse, Hampton won a narrow victory in 1876. On election day Gary put on his old uniform and ordered about eight hundred Red Shirts to occupy the Edgefield County Courthouse during the balloting. He arranged to have local blacks vote at a nearby schoolhouse, and he defied a Federal officer who tried to change his arrangements. When the ballots were counted, the Democrats had won a solid majority of the 9,374 votes cast in Edgefield County; however, this total exceeded by 2,256 the number of adult males residing in that county during the previous year.

Methods such as those employed by Gary prompted the Republicans to refuse to relinquish their control over the state government. Two state houses of representatives, one dominated by Republicans and the other by Democrats, met at Columbia in December 1876. The latter, with 65 members, including five Republicans, claimed to be a quorum; after the state supreme court declared them to be the legal house of representatives, they inaugurated Hampton on December 14. These actions were ignored by the 59 Republican representatives who had inaugurated Chamberlain nine days earlier. Tensions previously had almost reached a breaking point when both factions occupied the house chamber for four days, but the Democrats had withdrawn when the arrival of armed civilians and Federal troops made a violent clash appear imminent. Hampton and Chamberlain visited Pres. Rutherford B. Hayes in March 1877. Anxious to reduce the controversy that surrounded his election, Hayes on April 3 ordered the withdrawal of all Federal troops from South Carolina. The soldiers left on April 10; the next day, at noon, Hampton took possession of the governor's office.

Once back in power, the Democrats enjoyed only a few short years of harmony before divisions within their ranks brought an end to the dominance of ex-Confederates. The Republicans had a majority of one in the state senate in 1876, but the Democrats eliminated this by impeachment. The legislature created a one-man railroad commission in 1878 and gave the job to Milledge L. Bonham. The reduction of the state debt, which declined to $6.5 million five years after Hampton became governor, led to even greater rewards for the former general. Legislator Samuel McGowan nominated him for the U. S. Senate in 1878; the nomination was seconded by Charles H. Simonton. At that time Hampton was having his leg amputated after a hunting accident, but he recovered and joined Butler, his old cavalry subordinate, in the Senate.

The division that split the Democrats and ended Confederate rule was a bitter disagreement over racial policy. Conservatives such as Hampton were "tolerant white supremacists"; although no black won a statewide campaign for office after 1876, the legislature refused to enact Jim Crow legislation and shared the meager funds for public education. Hampton insisted on equal rights for all and was supported by Hagood and others, but they were opposed by Gary, an outspoken racist who supported the continuing violence against blacks. When Hampton left for Washington to take his seat in the Senate, his influence began to wane, but he still blocked Gary's bid for the governor's office, which went to Hagood. Gary died an angry man in 1881, but those who shared his racist views did not abandon their cause.

Benjamin R. Tillman, a one-eyed "farmer reared in the tradition of General Gary," beat the conservative candidate for governor, Alexander C. Haskell, by a margin of almost four to one in 1890. Tillman's rough manner and ardent racism—he had been a Red Shirt—appealed to many white farmers in South Carolina, who also believed that the conservatives ignored the needs of the common man. After taking office, Tillman supported the unseating of Senator Hampton and the redistricting of the legislature to end the dominance of the lowland counties. In 1894, Tillman beat Butler in a campaign for his seat in the U. S. Senate.

Many former Confederates remained active in state government, but an era had ended. Under Tillman's direction, a constitutional convention in 1895 enacted suffrage restrictions. Smalls, who had represented South Carolina in Congress for several terms in the Hampton years, was one of only six black Republicans who attended the convention; their protest was ignored by the 154 white Democratic delegates. Jim Crow laws, including segregated education, were later adopted and tacitly or actively endorsed by most surviving Confederates. After all, it was their dismantling of Republican government that had quashed any realistic hopes for reform, and their paternalism that had provided a foundation for Jim Crow legislation. Their direct control over the state had finally ended, but their influence would be felt for generations to come.

CHARLESTON, MARCH 1865
copy print
George N. Barnard

Many of South Carolina's communities lay in ruins at the end of the Civil War. Charleston in 1861 was a city of sixty-six thousand people—more than half of whom were slaves—which served as the economic, political, and social locus of the state, a lofty status that was apparent in the prosperous appearance of the businesses and homes that lined many streets. In 1865, journalist John T. Trowbridge found a ruined city. He noted that "above the monotonous gloom of the ordinary ruins rise the churches—the stone tower and roofless walls of the Catholic cathedral, deserted and solitary, a roost for buzzards; the burned-out shell of the Circular Church with its dismantled columns still standing, like those of an antique temple."[6]

In this photograph, black children pose against a column that formerly supported the portico of the Circular Church. All around them can be seen the devastation wrought during the war. A great fire swept through the city in December 1861, reducing an eighth of its buildings to charred ruins. More buildings fell victim to the persistent Federal bombardment that began in August 1863 and continued through the end of the war. Finally, a fire at the northwest depot during the Confederate evacuation sparked an explosion that killed hundreds of people and destroyed a large amount of property. *Photo courtesy of National Archives*

COLUMBIA, 1865
albumen print
Richard Wearn

These views of the business district of the state capital
focus on Main Street. One was taken looking up the
thoroughfare at the capitol; the other was apparently
made on the steps of the capitol itself. Journalist
John T. Trowbridge visited the city in 1865 and
recalled, "the entire heart of the city is a wilderness
of crumbling walls, naked chimneys and trees killed
by flames."[7] Emily LeConte, the seventeen-year-old
daughter of a professor at South Carolina College, was
far more graphic in the description she recorded in

COLUMBIA, 1865
albumen print
Richard Wearn

her diary. She wrote, "Standing in the center of town, as far as the eye can reach, nothing is to be seen but heaps of rubbish, tall dreary chimneys and shattered brick walls." Along Main Street, "The wind moans among the bleak chimneys and whistles through the gaping windows." Near the town market, which was in ruins, was "the old bell—'Secessia'—that had rung out every state as it seceded, lying half-buried in the earth."[8] *Photos courtesy of University of South Carolina, Columbia*

FORT SUMTER, APRIL 1865
albumen print
H. G. Foster, Charleston

At noon on April 14, 1865, four years to the day after Robert Anderson had departed from Fort Sumter, he raised the same flag he had lowered in 1861 over the battered post. The gathering was especially festive due to the arrival the previous evening of the news of Gen. Robert E. Lee's surrender.

Adm. John A. Dahlgren began the celebration by ordering twenty-one-gun salutes from every ship in the harbor. Rev. Matthias Harris, who had helped to raise the flag over Sumter four years earlier, delivered an invocation from the speaker's platform, which was thickly carpeted with "myrtle, mock orange and evergreen."[9] Columns rising from each of the four corners supported arches overhead, and a golden eagle crowned the main arch. Henry Ward Beecher, who had referred to Anderson as a saint four years earlier and had helped care for the women and children sent to New York from Sumter in February 1861, gave the keynote address calling for sectional reconciliation. Among the distinguished guests present were Gustavus V. Fox and William L. Garrison; allegedly, very few South Carolinians attended. Abraham Lincoln could not attend, but John G. Nicolay, his personal secretary, represented the president, who was assassinated only hours after the ceremony ended at Sumter. *Photo courtesy of University of North Carolina, Chapel Hill*

286

William M. Parker
half-plate ambrotype

The celebration at Fort Sumter in April 1865 meant little to many South Carolinians; for them, the war was far from over. Most of the Citadel cadets who were called into active service during the last months of the war were sent home on furlough in April 1865. Among them was William M. Parker, who ironically became one of the last South Carolinians killed in the Civil War. On May 9, 1865, Parker and other young men from Anderson County confronted a Union patrol. Parker ordered one of the Federals to surrender; when he refused to do so, the cadet leveled his gun and pulled the trigger twice. After the weapon misfired both times, the Union trooper shot Parker, who died in a few minutes. Although Parker apparently was not a senior in 1865, and his name does not appear on the muster rolls of the Cadet Battalion, he was honored in 1886 with the posthumous award of a diploma, along with those who should have graduated in 1865. *Photo courtesy of Citadel Archives, Charleston, South Carolina*

Henry Timrod
daguerrotype

The difficult circumstances in which many South Carolinians found themselves after the war proved more than some could bear. South Carolina author William Gilmore Simms wrote to an associate that poet Henry Timrod was "the very prince of Dolefuls, and swallowed up in distresses." Timrod himself complained in 1866 to fellow poet Paul H. Hayne, "You ask me to tell my story for the last year. I can embody it all in a few words. *Beggary, starvation, death, bitter grief, utter want of hope!*"[10] Timrod's home had been burned by Union troops and his infant son had died within the year, and he himself succumbed to tuberculosis in April 1866.

Born in 1828 at Charleston, he attended Franklin College, later renamed the University of Georgia, and then became a tutor so that he could devote more time to writing. Prior to the Civil War he published verses in a number of periodicals, including *Russell's Magazine*, in which he was a partner. A volume of his poetry was printed in 1860.

He volunteered as a private in Company B of the 20th South Carolina Infantry in March 1862 at Charleston but was detailed as a clerk and in December was discharged due to his tuberculosis. He wrote fervent war poems while working as a correspondent for the Charleston *Mercury* and other papers; for the last two years of his life he was an editor for the Columbia *South Carolinian. Photo courtesy of University of South Carolina, Columbia*

HENRY R. MILLETT
copy print

Some Union regiments were not allowed to leave the army when the war ended; not a few were sent to South Carolina as a garrison. Among these was the 29th Maine Infantry in which Henry R. Millett served as captain of Company E. A veteran of many engagements—including two campaigns in the Shenandoah Valley, the Antietam campaign, and the Red River campaign—Millett disembarked in June 1865 at Georgetown. His troops camped in the sand there until July, when they marched inland to Florence, where the sight of the former Confederate prison pen probably did nothing to improve their attitude. Soon afterward they settled at the regimental headquarters in Darlington for the remainder of their nine-month tour of duty in South Carolina.

A native of Norway, Maine, where he worked as a clerk for his father in a post office when the war began, Millett must have exchanged his heavy wool uniform for a linen suit and a straw hat like most of the members of his regiment did to cope with the unfamiliar heat. He had suffered from malaria while serving in Louisiana during 1864, so it is probable that he was among the company commanders who drilled their troops rarely, if at all, and eschewed the rigors of military discipline. Unlike others, though, Millett's sojourn in South Carolina was not interrupted by any personal scandal before he mustered out in March 1866 at Hilton Head. *Photo courtesy of U.S.A.M.H.I.*

The 29th Maine Infantry did not endear themselves to the people of Darlington County. Capt. William P. Jordan's Company C endured searing heat, sand, and scanty rations for two weeks at Georgetown in June 1865 before taking a steamer up the Pee Dee River. Their initial station was Marion, where Jordan "created a great deal of hard feeling and indignation among the residents by doing about as he pleased and disregarding their kind advice!"[11] A provost court was established at Darlington, where all matters that involved slaves were adjudicated. A regimental historian noted that the county jail was soon filled with young black males who were only too happy to draw rations and not have to work for their former masters.

The men of the 29th Maine Infantry were not predisposed to maintain military discipline, and Jordan was probably preoccupied as well. Widowed in 1861 at the age of thirty, he was left alone to care for his four-year-old daughter. He was severely injured during July 1864 when his hand was crushed between a wagon wheel and a metal bar with which he and others were trying to extricate a vehicle from a rut. A veteran of hard-fought battles in Virginia, Maryland, and Louisiana who had been breveted a major in March 1865, he must have been looking forward to leaving the army, which he did at Charleston in March 1866. *Photo courtesy of U.S.A.M.H.I.*

WILLIAM P. JORDAN
copy print

290

As much as many white South Carolinians despised the white Federal troops, they hated the blacks in blue uniforms even more. Black soldiers singing "John Brown's Body" led the way into Charleston in February 1865; close behind them came the 33rd United States Colored Troops, which was originally mustered as the 1st South Carolina Colored Infantry.

Enrolled at Beaufort, where this photograph was taken, in January 1863 after the ranks had been filled out with blacks from Florida, the regiment was commanded by Thomas W. Higginson, who previously had served in the 51st Massachusetts Infantry. They skirmished with Confederates in 1863 along the St. Mary's River between Georgia and Florida and around Jacksonville. Returning to Beaufort, members of the regiment, led by Higginson, rescued the crew of the USS *George Washington* after that vessel was sunk on April 9, 1863. A sortie up the Edisto River the next July was repulsed with heavy casualties, including the severe wounding of Higginson that forced his resignation a year later. After he left, his former command captured a battery on James Island and fought at Honey Hill. Sent to Georgia in March 1865, they returned to Charleston after a clash at Hamburg, South Carolina, in which bushwhackers killed several members of the regiment. They remained near Charleston until February 1866, when they mustered out. *Photo courtesy of National Archives*

1ST SOUTH CAROLINA COLORED INFANTRY
copy print

After the Federal occupation of Port Royal, thousands of blacks fled to Union lines. After South Carolina was organized with Georgia and Florida into the Department of the South in July 1862, aid came from both private organizations and the Treasury Department. Edward L. Pierce, a Harvard graduate, became the superintendent general of the "Port Royal project." He directed the blacks at work on the abandoned plantations, paid them wages, and provided for their education.

By the summer of 1862 about nine thousand blacks were cultivating twelve thousand acres of cotton on 189 plantations. Many blacks were later permitted by the Freedmen's Bureau to lease plots for their own use, but few managed to buy land before it was returned to its former owners after the war ended. The blacks sorting cotton were photographed at Fish Hall, the family home of Confederate general Thomas F. Drayton and U. S. commander Percival Drayton. Those planting sweet potatoes lived on the plantation of James Hopkinson. Note that several of the latter are wearing Union uniforms; many who joined the Federal regiment that mustered and disbanded in the summer of 1862 simply kept their uniforms. *Photos courtesy of MOLLUS, Mass., U.S.A.M.H.I.*

On May 2, 1865, Gen. Rufus Saxton, Jr., told a black audience at Charleston: "I wish every colored man, every head of a family in this department, to acquire a freehold, a little home that he can call his own."[12] Appointed the assistant commissioner of the Freedmen's Bureau in South Carolina, Saxton, following the orders of Gen. William T. Sherman, provided temporary titles for over 312,000 acres to 40,000 freedmen in 1865. Within three years, however, almost all of this land had been returned to its former owners after they received pardons from Andrew Johnson.

Saxton, a Massachusetts native and graduate of West Point, first arrived in South Carolina during the Port Royal expedition in 1861. On July 1, 1862, he took charge of the government-owned plantations on the sea islands. Described by Whitelaw Reid as "narrow, but intense; not very profound in seeing the right, but energetic in doing it when seen," Saxton found his postwar duties to be overwhelming.[13] He and his successors, Robert K. Scott and John R. Edie, could not overcome white opposition or a lack of funds and personnel. These obstacles led to the suspension of effective operations by 1869, but they did provide medical care to about 175,000 patients, issued no fewer than 3,000,000 rations, taught approximately 100,000 students, and negotiated labor contracts for about 300,000 blacks. *Photo courtesy of National Archives*

RUFUS SAXTON, JR.
albumen print
Hubbard and Mix

LAURA M. TOWNE
carte de visite

The Freedmen's Bureau supervised a number of schools in South Carolina, most of which were funded by private organizations in the North. Among the teachers who came to South Carolina was Laura M. Towne, a native of Pittsburgh. A few months after her thirty-seventh birthday in 1862, she conducted her first classes as director of Penn School Number One on St. Helena Island, which was sponsored by the Pennsylvania Branch of the Freedman's Union Commission. Interestingly, she allowed no corporal punishment, preferring instead to encourage her students with honors and rewards or to punish with detention and writing. Her students received instruction in mathematics, reading, writing, geography, civics, and American history.

The postwar period proved to be as difficult as wartime, but she taught for thirty-eight years on St. Helena Island, where she died in 1901. Referring to this early 1866 picture of herself and three "pets," Towne wrote that Dick Washington was "my right-hand man, who is full of importance, but has traveled and feels as if he has seen the world." Amoretta, who wears a kerchief on her head in the style of candidates for baptism, was "bright and sharp as a needle," while the other girl, Maria Wyne, was "very bright in arithmetic . . ."[14]
Photo courtesy of University of North Carolina, Chapel Hill

BENJAMIN F. PERRY
carte de visite
Frederick A. Wenderoth, William Taylor,
and J. Henry Brown of Philadelphia

Benjamin F. Perry, a Unionist who participated in the Confederate government, served as provisional governor of South Carolina in 1865. An opponent of both universal black suffrage and Federal intervention in state affairs, he became an outspoken opponent of Congressional Reconstruction in South Carolina.

Born in the upland county of Oconee in 1805, Perry edited two Unionist papers before the Civil War and killed the editor of a pro-nullification paper in a duel in 1832. He owned a dozen slaves and was a lifelong Democrat, but as he declared in 1860, he "was unwilling to break up the Union on an uncertainty."[15] A longtime legislator, he was one of two South

Carolina delegates to the national convention at Charleston in 1860 who refused to leave their seats when the rest of the delegation bolted. When his state left the Union, however, he reluctantly went along, becoming a district attorney, an impressment commissioner, and finally a district judge during the war.

Officially relieved of his duties as provisional governor in December 1865, he went to Washington to claim his seat in the U. S. Senate but was refused admission. He remained active in Democratic politics, however, and was instrumental in their triumph in 1876. *Photo courtesy of Clemson University*

When the Union convention met in 1866, Gov. James L. Orr, a former Confederate colonel and senator, walked into the meeting hall arm in arm with a representative from Massachusetts. This demonstration of regional reconciliation infuriated many people, and probably did more harm than good.

Orr had served briefly as colonel of the 1st South Carolina Rifles, but resigned in early 1862 to return to his first love, politics, by accepting a seat in the Confederate Senate. Born in Anderson County, he had devoted most of his life to politics after attending the University of Virginia. He won a reputation as a moderate—rejecting outspoken extremists on such disparate issues as nullification, abolition, and nativism—while serving in the legislature and Congress. In 1857 he was elected speaker of the U. S. House of Representatives.

He opposed secession, but rather than promote an intrastate split, he served on the committee that wrote the secession ordinance. He also served as an envoy to Georgia to urge secession and was one of three commissioners sent to Washington to negotiate a transfer of Federal property in South Carolina. These actions, as well as his Confederate service and opposition to universal black suffrage, made him suspect to many Northerners. *Photo courtesy of University of South Carolina, Columbia*

JAMES L. ORR
carte de visite
Quinby and Company

Despite the misgivings of many Northerners, Pres. Andrew Johnson declared the rebellion at an end in April 1866 and began reducing the number of troops in the South. Within seven months the number of Federal soldiers in South Carolina had fallen to fewer than three thousand.

Among the units mustered out after Johnson's proclamation was the 29th Maine Infantry, a regiment whose history began with its enlistment as the 1st Maine Infantry. It was then reorganized as the 10th Maine Infantry in October 1861, and two years later it was designated as the 29th Maine Infantry. Sgt. Charles E. Jordan of Company C was one of only nineteen men who served from May 1861 to the final mustering out in June 1866; when he got his discharge, he was a seasoned and probably weary veteran.

A farmer from Portland, Maine, Jordan had landed with his company at Georgetown on June 15, 1865. After quelling a mutiny among blacks at a nearby plantation, they were transported by steamer up the Pee Dee River and posted at Marion, and then they moved to Florence. The Union troops, who soon traded their wool uniforms for linen suits and straw hats, were generally well behaved, but there were problems with drinking and theft. Jordan was reduced in rank from sergeant to private in September 1865, but his rank was restored four months later. He returned to the coast and mustered out at Hilton Head. *Photo courtesy of U.S.A.M.H.I.*

Charles E. Jordan
copy print

MARTIN W. GARY
copy print

Conservative Democrats began mobilizing for a counterattack after the passage of the Reconstruction Acts in March 1867 facilitated the imposition of a Republican government in South Carolina. One of the most outspoken leaders of the resurgent conservatives was the inflexibly racist Martin W. Gary. Ironically, his effective use of coercion led to both a Democratic electoral triumph in 1876 and his subsequent exclusion from public office. Defeated for a seat in the U. S. Senate and the governorship of his home state, Gary died a bitter man in 1881.

At the war's end, Gary, a native of Abbeville County who had graduated from Harvard after being expelled from South Carolina College, had been a brigadier general for less than a year. An attorney, planter, and legislator before the war, Gary originally commanded a company in Hampton's Legion and then became regimental commander in the summer of 1862. He led his troops at Second Bull Run, Antietam, Fredericksburg, Chickamauga, and Knoxville. Upon their return from Tennessee, Gary's infantry were mounted and joined Wade Hampton's cavalry division. They were the last Confederate troops to leave Richmond in April 1865; Gary then refused to surrender at Appomattox. Breaking free, he and a few troopers joined Jefferson Davis; the last Confederate cabinet meeting took place at the home of Gary's mother in Cokesbury, South Carolina. *Photo courtesy of University of South Carolina, Columbia*

298

JOHNSON HAGOOD
carte de visite
Quinby and Company

Resplendent in his uniform as colonel of the 1st South Carolina Infantry, Johnson Hagood confidently looked forward to his career as a Confederate officer. In 1876 he campaigned successfully for the office of comptroller general on Wade Hampton's ticket and then succeeded him as governor a few years later.

A Barnwell County native, Hagood graduated from the Citadel and was admitted to the bar. Gov. John H. Means appointed him as a deputy adjutant general of the militia in 1851; by 1860 he was a brigadier general. He fought at First Bull Run as a volunteer with Joseph B. Kershaw's 2nd South Carolina Infantry and then commanded his own regiment at Secessionville in June 1862, after which he was promoted to brigadier general. He won further distinction in the defense of Charleston before being ordered in May 1864 to Petersburg, where his troops arrived in time to block a Federal advance. They again fought well at Drewry's Bluff, and they took part in the battle at Cold Harbor in June 1864. During the siege of Petersburg, Hagood's brigade earned a reputation as hard fighters, especially after Hagood, unhorsed in a desperate assault, shot a Federal officer and mounted his horse to lead his men to safety. Hagood and his brigade were sent in December 1864 to North Carolina, where they surrendered at the end of the war. *Photo courtesy of University of South Carolina, Columbia*

ROBERT SMALLS
copy print

No black won a statewide campaign for public office after the conservatives regained control of South Carolina, but a few won local races. One of the most successful of these was Robert Smalls, whose pardon for charges of corruption leveled by his Democratic foes in 1877 allowed him to serve three more terms in the U. S. House of Representatives.

Smalls was a genuine war hero. On May 13, 1862, four black crewmen of the CSS *Planter* took possession of the little ship. Led by Smalls, a twenty-three-year-old slave from Beaufort, they took advantage of the early morning darkness to slip by sentries. They stopped to retrieve their families, who waited on another steamer and then Smalls navigated his prize out of the harbor and surrendered it to the Union fleet, informing them as well of the disposition of local Confederate forces. He divided a reward with his crew. He remained in Federal service as pilot and then as captain of the *Planter* along the South Carolina coast.

Smalls became involved in politics in 1864, serving as one of four black delegates from South Carolina to the National Union convention in 1864. He served in the constitutional convention of 1868 and in the legislature; in 1875 he began the first of five terms as a congressman. As a delegate to the constitutional convention in 1895, he remained a vocal opponent of the Democrats in South Carolina. *Photo courtesy of MOLLUS, Mass., U.S.A.M.H.I.*

JOHN T. GASTON
carte de visite

Although the dominance of former Confederates in state politics ended after the triumph of the faction led by Benjamin R. Tillman in 1890, a number of veterans remained active in state affairs. One example is John T. Gaston, who had this image of himself made during 1866 in Edgefield County after he had returned home from the war.

Mustered as a private in Company B of the Cavalry Battalion of the Hampton Legion in the summer of 1861 at Greeneville, Gaston in 1862 was consolidated, along with the rest of his battalion and other units, into the 2nd South Carolina Cavalry. They were sent home in the spring of 1864 to secure new horses, and he was allowed to visit his home. This was fortunate for him, because after he returned to service in North Carolina, he suffered from intermittent bouts of fever that required hospitalization, so he was not paroled until May 18, 1865, at Augusta, Georgia.

He was elected to the legislature from Aiken County in 1894. In 1895, shortly before he was elected Code Commissioner for South Carolina and resigned his seat as a legislator, he moved to Columbia with his wife, whom he had married in 1869. *Photo courtesy of University of South Carolina, Columbia*

Confederate veteran's organizations and auxiliary clubs became quite popular in postwar South Carolina, as in other Southern states, and seemed to become more numerous as the veterans grew older. Benjamin H. Teague had this interesting cabinet print of himself made when he became the commander of the Bernard E. Bee Camp of United Confederate Veterans in 1896, the second camp to be established in South Carolina. He later became the state commander of the United Confederate Veterans.

He had the earlier photograph taken in 1864, the year in which he enlisted, six months before his sixteenth birthday, as a private at Columbia in Company B of the Hampton Legion, then commanded by Brig. Gen. Martin W. Gary. He apparently was one of the South Carolinians present at Appomattox who refused to participate in the surrender of the Army of Northern Virginia. When Gary escaped from the encircling Federals with a few members of his brigade, Private Teague was among them. Teague's name was on the list of those paroled at Appomattox, but he was personally paroled at Augusta, Georgia, during June 1865. He may well have ridden with Gary while Gary was escorting Pres. Jefferson Davis through South Carolina and into Georgia. *Photo courtesy of Museum of the Confederacy, Richmond, Virginia*

BENJAMIN H. TEAGUE
cabinet print
C. D. Hardt, Aiken

WADE HAMPTON III
carte de visite
George S. Cook

Charleston hosted the United Confederate Veterans' Reunion in May 1899. More than thirty thousand people attended activities in the newly constructed Thomson Auditorium and viewed the reenactment of the bombardment of Fort Sumter staged on Colonial Lake. During the huge parade, Wade Hampton III led the veterans of the Army of Northern Virginia, capably handling a spirited horse despite the loss of his leg two decades earlier. It was a fitting climax to a dramatic career as a Confederate general, governor, and senator.

Descended from a well-known line of soldiers and planters, Hampton attended South Carolina College and managed thousands of slaves in his home state, Louisiana, and Mississippi. Although he was a moderate South Carolina legislator who opposed secession, in 1861 he equipped a legion at his own expense and was wounded while leading them at First Bull Run and Seven Pines. Promoted to command a cavalry brigade, he participated in the Antietam and Gettysburg campaigns, in which he suffered several wounds, as well as in a number of raids. When Stuart was killed in 1864, Maj. General Hampton assumed command of all cavalry in Virginia. In 1865 he led a division to South Carolina, where he was promoted to lieutenant general. He became governor in 1876, ending Republican rule, and then served in the U. S. Senate. *Photo courtesy of University of South Carolina, Columbia*

303

Appendix

Allen, Robert H.

Allen recovered from the wound suffered at Secessionville and in September 1862 took Michael Donohoe's place as the captain of Company C in the 3rd New Hampshire Infantry. While serving as officer of the day on Pinckney Island in April 1863, he shot himself in the left leg while using a small hammer to seat the percussion caps on his revolver. The ball was not removed until May, after which he had to use crutches, so he watched the assault at Battery Wagner on July 18. After a bout of cholera during the fall of 1863 and an attack of "bilious fever," he resigned due to poor health at Bermuda Hundred in June 1864. He operated a clothing store in Rockford, Illinois, until 1870 and then established a churn-making company. He died in 1904 at the age of seventy-six.

Anderson, Robert

Anderson became a brigadier general but retired in 1863. Breveted a major general in February 1865, he died in France in 1871. His remains were interred at West Point.

Atherton, Arlon S.

Atherton's wound left his right arm partially paralyzed, but he recovered enough to marry on Christmas Day, 1865, and to become an inspector with the state police, a three-term legislator, and a successful grocer in Wakefield, Massachusetts. He died in 1922 at the age of eighty.

Atkinson, William R.

Atkinson became an Episcopal minister. He operated the Charlotte Female Institute beginning in 1878, earned a Doctorate of Divinity from the University of South Carolina in 1890, and founded South Carolina College for Women at Columbia in September of that same year (his school later merged with Queen's College). He died in 1901.

Auld, Donald J.

Auld married Venetia Hammet in September 1866 and prospered as a grocer in Sumter. In 1886 he was serving as the "Grand Keeper of Records and Seal" for the Knights of Pythias in South Carolina. He died in 1900.

Baskin, William P.

Baskin became a planter in Bishopville. He died in 1876.

Beauregard, Pierre G. T.

Beauregard considered leaving the United States after the war, but he ultimately refused offers to command the armies of Egypt and Romania. Instead, he became president of two railroad companies and a supervisor of the Louisiana Lottery, for which he was bitterly criticized, and adjutant general of that state. He died in 1893.

Benbow, Henry L.

Benbow lost twenty-three slaves and declared bankruptcy in 1868, though he continued to farm a portion of the family plantation until his death. He remained in the legislature until late 1866 and then, ten years later, became a leader of the Red Shirts that restored Democratic rule in Clarendon County. Two years later, in 1878, he began the first of four consecutive terms in the state senate. Never married, he died in 1907 at the age of sixty-eight.

Blackwood, Gibbs

Blackwood was released from the prison camp at Elmira, New York, in July 1865. No further record of him has been found.

Bingham, Newton

Bingham's health had deteriorated greatly during his first two years of service, but he had continued with the army despite his infirmity, which increasingly appeared to be tuberculosis. He lived only three years after the close of the war, dying in November 1868 at the age of twenty-seven in Mishawaka, Indiana. He left behind no wife or children; only a widowed and partially paralyzed father who had been dependent on the financial support provided by his eight children.

Birchmeyer, Paul

Birchmeyer died of tuberculosis during 1882 at the age of thirty-seven in Syracuse, New York, where he worked as a mechanic.

Bland, M. Alberto

No further record of Bland has been found.

Boinest, John E.

After returning to Charleston, his hometown, Boinest worked as a bookkeeper. He died in 1896 at the age of fifty-one.

Bonham, Milledge L.

Bonham was elected to the South Carolina legislature once more after the war. In 1878 he became the first railroad commissioner of South Carolina, and he served as chairman of the railroad commission until his death in 1890.

Bornemann, Charles F.

No further record of Bornemann has been found.

Boswell, James P.

Boswell settled in Camden, where in 1868 he married a woman who was sixteen years younger than he. In 1870 he was the sheriff of Kershaw County. He died in 1926 at the age of ninety-three.

Bradley, George A.

Bradley settled in Connecticut. He worked as a mason, laborer, and welldigger, but deafness resulting from the saber wound in his head inflicted at Cedar Mountain made it difficult for him to support himself and his family (he had eight children from two marriages, the first in 1863, the second in 1890). He died at the age of seventy-seven in 1922.

Branch, John L.

Branch moved to Alabama and worked as a civil engineer until his death in 1894 at the age of sixty-eight.

Bratton, John

Bratton was a delegate to the South Carolina constitutional convention of 1865 and was elected as a Democrat to the state senate that same year. He also served a single term in the U. S. House of Representatives and was the state comptroller before his death in 1898 at the age of sixty-seven.

Brown, Pressley

Brown, a thirty-two-year-old clerk, enlisted as a lieutenant in Company A of the 15th South Carolina Infantry in August 1861; when his regiment was reorganized during the spring of 1862, he became captain of his company. He emerged unharmed from the many engagements in which his troops fought—Second Bull Run, Antietam, Fredericksburg, Chancellorsville, Gettysburg, Chickamauga, and Knoxville—until May 12, 1864, when he was seriously wounded at Spotsylvania. Released from the hospital in Columbia, South Carolina, he returned to duty and was captured at Halltown, Virginia, on August 26, 1864. Released from Fort Delaware in June 1865, he was listed by the 1870 census taker as a clerk living with his wife and four children in Columbia.

Burton, Aaron D.

Burton immigrated to Arkansas a year after the war ended and farmed there until his death in 1923 at the age of seventy-nine.

Butler, Matthew C.

Butler once noted that he returned home after the Civil War with one leg, a wife and three children, a debt of $15,000, and $1.75 in his pocket. He returned to the practice of law in South Carolina and also became president of a mining operation in New Mexico. An active Democrat, he was elected to the South Carolina legislature and the U. S. Senate. During the Spanish-American War he accepted a commission as a major general of volunteers, and afterward he became the vice-president of the Southern Historical Association. He died in 1909.

Calhoun, John C.

Calhoun apparently recovered from his wartime ailments because he lived until the age of seventy-five, dying in 1918. He invested in cotton, railroads, and other business ventures in postwar South Carolina.

Capers, Ellison

Capers returned to Anderson, whence he was chosen to be secretary of state by the South Carolina legislature in December 1865. He resigned this position in 1868 after he became an Episcopal minister. He was an assistant bishop of South Carolina beginning in 1893, served as chaplain general of the United Confederate Veterans, and in 1904 became the chancellor of the University of the South. He died in 1908, at the age of seventy.

Casson, William H.

Casson, a native of Pennsylvania who was forty-three years of age when the war began, mustered the Governor's Guards as Company A of the 2nd South Carolina Infantry at Columbia in April 1861. He commanded his company at First Bull Run, but he resigned in the spring of 1862. In the fall of 1864 he was enlisted into the 5th Battalion of South Carolina Reserves, which was assigned to guard the prisoners of war held at Florence. After the war he remained in Columbia, where he worked as a clerk for a railroad company in 1870.

Chesnut, James

Chesnut resumed the management of his family's plantations near Camden and remained active in South Carolina politics as an ally of Wade Hampton and Matthew C. Butler. He died at his home in Camden in 1885 at the age of seventy.

Chesnut, Mary Boykin

Chesnut began to write after the war to cope with boredom once more. The recovery of the family finances permitted the construction of a town-house in Camden, with a library where she produced several unpublished works of fiction and revised her wartime journals. Only one anecdote from them appeared in print before her death in 1886, but they have since been published in part or in toto several times since then.

Clemson, John Calhoun

Clemson was freed from the prison camp at Johnson's Island in June 1865 under the provisions of an order issued by Pres. Andrew Johnson. He was killed shortly after his thirtieth birthday in a train wreck on the Blue Ridge Railroad in 1871.

Clemson, Thomas G.

Paroled at Shreveport, Louisiana, Clemson returned to South Carolina, settling in Pendleton and managing the plantation of his late father-in-law, John C. Calhoun. At his death in 1888, he left his entire estate for the support of Clemson University, which bears his name.

Cobb, Norman E.

Cobb, a native of Vermont, reenlisted as a private on Morris Island during February 1864, even though he had suffered cruelly from malaria and lost teeth due to scurvy two years earlier. He mustered out at Goldsboro, North Carolina, in July 1865. He then settled in New Hampshire, where he worked as a blacksmith, married, and had three children. He died in Nashua, New Hampshire, at the age of fifty-four in 1887.

Cody, Walter

Cody, a machinist born in Ireland, was hospitalized at Hilton Head. A series of painful operations left his right leg several inches shorter than the other, and he suffered almost constant discomfort. He resigned from the army in November 1862 while he was still confined in a hospital at Boston. He later served for a year in the Veteran Reserve Corps, from which he was discharged in November 1864. He returned to Manchester, New Hampshire, where he married and had three children while working as a clothing merchant and a shoemaker. He died in 1904 at the age of sixty-five.

Copes, Frederick

Copes settled with his wife and son in Winnsboro, where in 1870 he was employed as a miller.

Cornelius, William H.

Cornelius fought at Secessionville and then went home on recruiting duty in July. He did not return to his company until January 1863, and he was discharged at Hilton Head two months later for a disability. He became a lieutenant in the Veteran Reserve Corps in October 1863, and remained with that organization until he succumbed to a disease at New Orleans in 1867.

Courtenay, William A.

Under the provisions of Pres. Andrew Johnson's general order, Courtenay took an oath of allegiance on June 16, 1865, at Johnson's Island in Ohio and was allowed to return home, which he reported was Old Store, South Carolina. He became active in the shipping business and was president of the Charleston Chamber of Commerce for three years in the 1870s. While serving as mayor of Charleston from 1879 to 1887, he was active in reopening the Citadel. He later moved to Newry, where he founded a cotton mill. He then retired to Columbia, where he died in 1908.

Coward, Asbury

Coward reopened the King's Mountain Military Academy after the Civil War and then was elected superintendent of education for South Carolina in 1882 and 1884. In 1890 he became commandant of the Citadel, a post he retained until 1909. He died in 1925.

Crawford, Andrew

Crawford returned to his hometown of Columbia, whence he was elected in 1880 to a single term in the legislature. He died in 1907.

Crawford, John A.

Crawford returned to Columbia, his hometown, where he died in 1910 at the age of seventy.

Crawford, Samuel W.

Although trained as a physician at the medical school of the University of Pennsylvania, Crawford commanded a brigade in the Shenandoah Valley during 1862 and at Antietam (where he was severely wounded). He then commanded a division at Gettysburg and was breveted a major general for his performances in the Wilderness and at Petersburg. He became a colonel in the postwar army, but he was retired as a brigadier general in 1873. He died in 1892 at the age of sixty-three.

Croft, Edward

Croft became an attorney and a trial judge at Greeneville; he died in 1892 while serving on the Board of Visitors for the Citadel, his alma mater.

Dahlgren, John A.

Dahlgren remained in the U. S. Navy until he died of heart disease in 1870.

Davis, Caleb

Davis was shot in the foot during a skirmish in the summer of 1863; he then was shot in the left arm on August 16, 1864, at Deep Bottom, Virginia. He soon thereafter left the army due to the expiration of his term, but he reenlisted in the 17th Massachusetts Infantry in September 1864, serving until the end of the war. He settled in Massachusetts after briefly residing in Michigan. He then moved to San Antonio, Texas, Portland, Oregon (where he married), and Kelso County, Washington. He supported himself and his daughter—his wife having died in 1890, less than two years after they were married—by working as a carpenter, bridge builder, and farmer. He died in 1910.

Davis, George H.

Davis married during November 1865 after returning home to Winchester, New Hampshire, where he farmed until his death in 1905 at the age of seventy-four.

Davis, Jefferson C.

Davis, one of the few Federal officers at Fort Sumter in April 1861 who was not a West Point graduate, was breveted a major general in the western theater, where he commanded troops at Pea Ridge, Corinth, Murfreesboro, Chickamauga, and Atlanta. He was recommended for a permanent promotion to major general, but his killing a fellow officer after an argument probably prevented his receiving a higher rank. He commanded a regiment in the postwar army, serving in Alaska and during the Modoc War before he retired. He died in 1879 at the age of fifty-one.

Dial, G. L.

No further record of Dial has been found.

Ditcher, Benjamin

No further record of Ditcher has been found.

Dodge, William L.

Dodge returned to Massachusetts and became a clerk in a sugar refinery in Boston, near where he had been born. He held an appointment in the Boston customs house from 1867 to 1890, but he lived in a number of Massachusetts and New Hampshire communities and apparently remained in the sugar refining business until his death in 1916 at Brookline, Massachusetts.

Donohoe, Michael T.

Donohoe—a native of Lowell, Massachusetts, whose parents were both Irish immigrants—enlisted as the captain of Company C, most of whom were of Irish descent, of the 3rd New Hampshire Infantry at Concord in August 1861. They were in the thick of the fighting at

Secessionville; Donohoe did well and the next month became the colonel of the 10th New Hampshire Infantry, composed entirely of Irish soldiers, at the age of twenty-three. He was breveted a brigadier general after being shot in the hip at Fort Harrison near Petersburg in September 1864. He remained in the army through the end of the war and then worked as a conductor and ticket agent for a number of railroads in New Hampshire and Massachusetts. He died in Boston in 1895 at the age of fifty-six.

Dorn, Elijah A.

Dorn returned to his farm in Edgefield County. By 1870 his children had increased in number from eight to an even dozen, the eldest of whom was twenty years of age and the youngest just one year. He died October 13, 1903, at the age of seventy-five.

Doubleday, Abner

Doubleday led a brigade at Second Bull Run, a division at Antietam and Fredericksburg, and a corps at Gettysburg. He had administrative duties for the rest of the war and then retired from the army in 1873. He wrote two books about his Civil War experiences before his death in 1893 at the age of seventy-four.

Drayton, Percival

Drayton was captain of the USS *Hartford* during the capture of Mobile. He then became chief of the Bureau of Navigation at Washington after the war. He died in August 1865; a torpedo boat was named in his honor.

Drayton, Thomas F.

Drayton farmed in Georgia and then moved to Philadelphia, where he had lived when his father was president of the Bank of the United States during the 1840s, to participate in a life insurance firm. He finally settled in Charlotte, North Carolina, as an insurance agent and as the president of the South Carolina Immigrant Society. He died in 1891.

DuBose, William P.

DuBose served as pastor of the Episcopal church in Winnsboro from 1865, when he was ordained, until 1868, and of a church in Abbeville from 1868 to 1871. He became a chaplain and a professor of ethics at the University of the South in 1871 and then resigned the chaplaincy to accept an endowed chair as dean of the theology department in 1880. An accomplished theologian and author, as well as teacher, he received an honorary degree from Columbia College of New York in 1875.

Dunbar, Charles F.

Dunbar resigned from the army on June 22, 1862, six days after Secessionville, complaining that an affliction had made it impossible for him to wear his belt for the previous three months. He succumbed to cancer at Hampton, New Hampshire, in 1889 at the age of sixty.

Dunovant, Robert G. M.

Dunovant lost a bitter campaign for reelection to the South Carolina Senate in 1865 and retired from politics to be a planter in Edgefield County until his death in 1898.

Dwight, William M.

Dwight returned to Winnsboro, where he worked as a dry-goods merchant to support four children, all but one of whom were born after he returned home from prison near the end of the war. He died in 1877.

Edgerly, J. Homer

Edgerly went to work in the navy yard at Charlestown, Massachusetts, where by 1871 he was a master painter and serving on the city council. He retired in the late 1880s and became a sign painter and then a building inspector for the city of Boston.

Elliott, Stephen, Jr.

Elliott returned to his home at Beaufort and was elected to the legislature, but he died at the age of thirty-four from the effects of his wounds less than a year after the war ended.

Emanuel, William P.

Emanuel was a prosperous Marlboro County farmer with a wife and eight children, one of whom was less than a year old, in 1870.

Emerson, George W.

Emerson was certainly the oldest enlisted man in Company F of the 3rd New Hampshire Infantry, if not in the regiment: he was forty-four years of age when he enrolled as a private in August 1861. During the summer of 1862 he was detailed to the Quartermaster Department as a carpenter. He remained with that outfit until February 1863. In March 1864 he was assigned to the machine shop on St. Helena Island, where he worked until he was mustered out at the end of his term of service in August 1864. No further record of him has been found.

Emmons, George W.

Emmons was detailed as commander of companies I and K in the 3rd New Hampshire Infantry during March and April 1862 and then was promoted to captain of his original company, in place of Pierce L. Wiggin, during the latter month. He resigned from the army in mid-September 1863. After the war he worked as a railroad conductor in Illinois and then settled in Boston, where he was a conductor for the Old Colony Railroad until his death in 1895.

Evans, Nathan G.

Evans became the principal of a high school at Midway, Alabama, where he died in 1868.

Evans, Thomas A.

Evans returned to Anderson, where he prospered as a physician just as his father had done. By 1870, however, the elder Evans was retired and living with his son, who also had to support a wife and two children, both of whom were born after the war ended.

Fair, Robert A.

No further record of Fair has been found.

Fellows, Enoch Q.

Fellows served as colonel of the 9th New Hampshire Infantry (commanding them at South Mountain and Antietam) until November 1862, when he left the service due to ill health and returned to Sandwich, New Hampshire, after a brief stay in the West. He worked for a bank and as a tax collector and, though increasingly deaf, was elected as a Republican to three terms in the legislature. By 1890 he was retired; a doctor examined him that year and reported that he was a "wreck." Fellows died in 1897 at the age of seventy-two.

Ferguson, Thomas B.

Ferguson moved in 1867 to Maryland, where he married the daughter of a former governor and established the Maryland State Fish Commission, on which he served for many years. He was appointed as an assistant commissioner of fish and fisheries for the federal government in 1878. He was the U. S. minister to Sweden and Norway beginning in 1894 and then settled in Washington, D.C. He died in 1922 at the age of eighty-one.

Fifield, Stephen S.

Fifield remained a nurse in the regimental hospital until he left the service at the end of his enlistment in August 1864 at Bermuda Hundred in Virginia. He returned to his hometown of Candia in New Hampshire, where he worked as a shoemaker and farm laborer. In 1872 he moved to Manchester and was employed in the mills and worked as a store clerk until he was forced to retire due to his ruined health, which he said began declining when his regiment had to sleep without tents in a cotton field during a rainstorm after their arrival at Hilton Head in 1861. He died in 1912 at the age of seventy-six.

Fish, Ira

Fish died of pneumonia at Poughkeepsie, New York, in March 1879, just four months after the birth of his first daughter (his fourth child). He was thirty-nine years of age.

Follin, Gustavus A.

No further record of Follin has been found.

Foster, John G.

Foster left South Carolina to command the garrison at Savannah in February 1865. He remained in the army until he died in 1874, at the age of fifty-one, while serving as a lieutenant colonel of engineers. He was recognized as an expert on underwater demolition due to a postwar publication that he wrote on the topic.

Gaillard, Alfred S.

Gaillard died in 1870 as a consequence of the wound he had received at Bentonville five years earlier.

Gaston, John T.

Gaston died in 1911.

Gibbes, Robert W.

Gibbes' home in Columbia, which contained his collection of fossils and minerals on which he had based a series of publications, was set afire by Union soldiers during the night of February 17, 1865, when much of the capital city was consumed by fire. When they entered and declared their intention to burn his house, he asked for time to get his specimens out, but they pocketed some of them and burned the remainder. The erstwhile doctor, author, politician, and newspaper proprietor died in 1866 at the age of fifty-seven.

Gibbes, Wade Hampton

Gibbes became a farmer and railroad contractor. He served as treasurer of Richland County from 1877 to 1883 and as postmaster at Columbia from 1885 to 1890. After leaving the post office, he invested in machinery and became the vice-president of a bank. He then became the president of a wine company. He died in 1903, at the age of sixty-six.

Gibbs, John S.

Gibbs was again in command of Battery D, 1st United States Artillery, when it was transferred to Virginia during April 1864. He resigned in May 1864; no further record of him has been found.

Gilfillin, James G.

No further record of Gilfillin has been found.

Gillmore, Quincy A.

Gillmore remained in the engineers, reaching the rank of colonel in 1883. During his postwar career in the army he served on many boards and commissions, including a term as president of the Mississippi River Commission, and wrote a number of books and treatises. He died in 1888 while still on active duty in New York.

Gist, William H.

Gist retired to his home in Union County, where he died in 1874 at the age of sixty-seven.

Greer, Henry J.

No further record of Greer has been found.

Greer, William R.

Imprisoned at Elmira, New York, Greer was freed in late June 1865 under the provisions of Pres. Andrew Johnson's general order. No further record of him has been found.

Hagood, Johnson

As the comptroller general and as the governor of South Carolina, Hagood supported sectional reconciliation; he was proud of the fact that he aided the Federal officer whom he had shot and unhorsed to obtain a pension. He also proudly served as chairman of the board of visitors for the Citadel from 1876 until his death in 1898 at the age of sixty-eight.

Halpine, Charles G.

Halpine returned to New York and became involved once more in journalism and politics. He was editor of the *Citizen*, a reform organ, and in 1866 was elected register of the county and city of New York. Published collections of the writings of Miles O'Reilly and other material sold well, but Halpine came to a tragic end. A frequent insomniac, he succumbed to an overdose of chloroform in August 1868 at the age of thirty-eight.

Hampton, Wade, III

Hampton served in the U. S. Senate until 1891. He subsequently served as the federal railroad commissioner for five years before his death in 1902 at the age of eighty-four.

Handerson, Henry C.

Handerson temporarily commanded Company G, 3rd New Hampshire Infantry, in April 1862 and then was shot through the arm at Secessionville. Recovering from his wound, he was sent home on recruiting duty, where he remained until early 1863, when he was promoted to captain and given command of Company K. Less than two weeks after the successful conclusion of the siege of Battery Wagner, he resigned, complaining of poor health. He was a postmaster at Keene, New Hampshire, until he committed suicide in 1874 at the age of forty-six. It was alleged that his death was the result of the lingering effects of a sunstroke suffered the year before he died.

Hartstene, Henry J.

No further record of Hartstene has been found.

Haskell, Alexander C.

Haskell married in September 1861, but his young bride died in June 1862. He was married again after the war, this time to the sister of Confederate general E. P. Alexander. Haskell served in the South Carolina legislature in 1865 and 1866. He then was elected judge of the district court at Abbeville. He soon resigned that position to accept an appointment as a professor of law at the University of South Carolina, his alma mater. In 1868 he resumed an active political and business career that included stints as an attorney, state supreme court justice, president of at least two railroad companies, and officer for several banks. He died in 1910 at the age of seventy-one.

Hatch, John P.

Hatch remained in the army, serving in the west as he had before the Civil War, until he retired in 1886 as colonel of the 2nd United States Cavalry. He then settled in New York City, in the state of his birth, and died there in 1901 at the age of seventy-nine.

Hayne, Isaac W.

Hayne remained in Charleston and served as attorney general of South Carolina until 1868. He died twelve years later at the age of seventy-one.

Haynsworth, Moses S.

Haynsworth became a farmer in Florence County and developed Idylwild Plantation. He died in 1928.

Hazen, William B.

A prolific author on the military and history, Hazen stayed in the army, serving on the frontier and as chief of the Signal Office and Weather Bureau, until his death in 1887.

Hester, Samuel J.

No further record of Hester has been found.

Hill, Alfred J.

Hill returned to Portsmouth, New Hampshire, and resumed work as a carpenter at the navy yard, where he had worked before accepting a pension in 1852. His injuries restricted his ability to provide for himself, and in 1886 the U. S. House of Representatives attempted to double his pension through a special appropriation, which Pres. Grover Cleveland vetoed. Hill died three years later.

Hill, Calvin

Pursuant to Pres. Andrew Johnson's general order, Hill was paroled at Point Lookout on June 27, 1865, and returned to his farm near Timmonsville in Darlington County. By 1870 he had a grown son to help him take care of the farm, as well as a daughter, age sixteen, and a son that was only six months of age.

Hill, Henry

Hill, a Methodist minister from Manchester, remained with the 3rd New Hampshire Infantry until August 1864, when his enlistment expired. He returned to Caledonia County, Vermont, where he had been married in 1844, and worked there as a Methodist minister. In 1871 he became the pastor of the first of two Methodist churches in which he served in Chicago. As his health declined, he was reassigned several times to other churches and finally was unable to minister at all due to persistent illness. He returned to Chicago, where he died in 1884.

Holland, Thomas J.

Holland remained in South Carolina and married in 1870. He died in 1893.

Hollis, Peter T.

Hollis was released from Johnson's Island in June 1865, at which time he reported that he was twenty-one years of age and that he resided in Garnet Hill. He represented Chester County in the South Carolina legislature from 1894 until 1902 and then applied from Richburg, South Carolina, for a pension in 1919.

Holstead, Charles H.

After mustering out at Louisville, Kentucky, in July 1865, Holstead returned to his father's farm and then married and moved to Tecumseh, Nebraska, in 1869. He settled briefly on a nearby farm before moving into the town and opening a livery stable, which he operated for twenty-five years before retiring. He fathered ten children and survived most of them; he did not die until March 1941 at the age of ninety-eight.

Hopkins, Henry F.

Hopkins resigned from the 3rd New Hampshire Infantry due to chronic "climatic sickness" in April 1863, a few days after lying sick on a transport in Folly Inlet while the Federal ironclads challenged Fort Sumter. After several futile attempts to reenlist, he joined the 1st New Hampshire Cavalry in April 1865 and served for a month. After the war, he worked as an attorney in Illinois, New Hampshire, and Massachusetts, successively, and he became clerk of the Police Court in Lawrence, Massachusetts, in 1874. He died at the age of seventy-two in 1899.

Howard, Oliver O.

Howard served as the commissioner of the Freedmen's Bureau during its stormy existence. He then founded Howard University in the District of Columbia and was its president from 1869 to 1874.

Continuing in the army, he commanded a number of departments in the West and the Division of the East, and he also was superintendent of West Point before he retired in 1894. He received the Medal of Honor for heroism at Fair Oaks, where he lost his right arm, in 1893. After an active career as a reformer, he died in 1909.

Huger, Benjamin

Huger became the president of an iron company in New York City in the spring of 1866 and then retired to a farm in Virginia three years later. He returned to Charleston shortly before his death in December 1877.

Hunt, Josiah F.

Hunt was paroled in October at Richmond. He was ordered to Annapolis, Maryland, to serve in the parolee battalion, but he was soon discharged for ill health. A small man wracked by a nagging cough, he died at home in Rockingham County, New Hampshire, on February 10, 1864, at the age of twenty-four. A doctor who attended him said he succumbed to tuberculosis.

Ingalls, Gustavus W.

Ingalls had returned to New Hampshire from Augusta, Georgia, to take charge of the 3rd New Hampshire Infantry Band, which also served as the post band at Hilton Head. He went home on leave in July 1862, after the abolition of regimental bands, and was mustered out with his musicians the following month, but he returned to South Carolina with recruits in April 1863 for the 2nd Brigade Band, which served through the end of the war. He afterward settled in Worcester, Massachusetts, where he manufactured organ reed boards.

Jefferies, Goodman

Jefferies was released from Fort Delaware under Pres. Andrew Johnson's general order on June 17, 1865. He later served in the South Carolina legislature.

Jennings, John W.

John W. Jennings returned home to Abbeville County, where he married in 1866. He later served in the legislature. He died in 1898.

Jordan, Charles E.

No further record of Jordan has been found.

Jordan, William P.

Jordan returned to Maine, where he resumed his work as a tailor, despite the injury to his hand, and remarried, though he had no more children. He died in 1905 at the age of seventy-five.

Keith, Thomas D.

No further record of Keith has been found.

Kershaw, Joseph B.

Released from Fort Warren in July 1865, Kershaw resumed the practice of law in Camden and was elected to the state senate, in which he served as president. In 1877 he was elected to the Fifth Circuit Court of South Carolina, and he served as judge for sixteen years until poor health forced his retirement. He died in 1895 while serving as postmaster of Camden.

Kilpatrick, Judson

Kilpatrick resigned his military commissions in 1866 to accept an appointment from Pres. Andrew Johnson as U. S. minister to Chile, where he served for two years. He remained active in politics but failed to win a congressional seat in 1880; Pres. Grover Cleveland consoled him with another appointment as minister to Chile in 1881. Kilpatrick died in Chile that same year.

Klinck, Gustavus W.

Klinck returned to Charleston and became a successful wholesale grocer, like his father, after the Civil War. He died in 1916 at the age of seventy-two.

Langdon, Loomis L.

In February 1864 Langdon led Battery M of the 1st United States Artillery to Florida, where they fought that month at Olustee, losing six crewmen and three 12-pounder Napoleons before retreating to Jacksonville. Langdon won a brevet to major for that action. In April, he led his battery to Virginia; after hard fighting in the Bermuda Hundred and Petersburg campaigns it was sent in November to New York City, whence it returned again to Virginia. On April 9, 1865, at Appomattox, Langdon suffered the indignity of having a gun and sixteen officers and men captured. He ended the war, however, with a brevet as a lieutenant colonel. He remained in the army and was sent to various hot spots in Texas, Louisiana, Florida, Alabama, and even South Carolina during Reconstruction. He retired as a colonel but in 1894 was breveted a brigadier general. He died in New York City in 1910 at the age of eighty.

Langley, John F.

Langley later accepted an appointment as a captain in the 12th New Hampshire Infantry. He was wounded at Gettysburg but remained with the 12th New Hampshire and was promoted to major in February 1864. After his discharge, he settled in Boston. In 1890 he was a clerk in the post office there, but he retired and by the next year, when he was sixty-two years of age, he was living with his daughter in Amherst, New Hampshire.

Lee, Stephen D.

Lee moved to Mississippi, where he was elected to the state senate and the state constitutional convention, and became the first president of Mississippi State University. In 1904 he was elected commander-in-chief of the United Confederate Veterans, serving until his death four years later at the age of seventy-five.

Lloyd, Edward W.

Lloyd, who was operated on for "hydrocile" in August 1863 and left his command on sick leave again on June 25, 1864, retired to the Invalid Corps in August 1864. He settled after the war at Florence in Darlington County, where he resumed the manufacturing of carriages.

Logan, John A.

Logan left the army in 1865, after winning the Medal of Honor, and returned to politics as a Republican, serving as a representative and as a senator for a number of terms. He died in 1886, two years after failing to win the vice-presidency on the Republican ticket.

Logan, Thomas M.

Logan married in May 1865. He then managed a coal mine in Chesterfield County, Virginia. He moved to Richmond to practice law and then began investing in railroads. He parlayed a tiny initial investment into a conglomerate that was officially christened the Southern Railway in 1894. He died a wealthy man, and a staunch Democrat to the last, in 1914.

Lord, Charles P.

Lord was crippled by malaria and rheumatism contracted while directing the construction of a road through the swamps at Hilton Head and by a hernia he suffered when a drunken soldier kicked him in the groin. He worked as a clerk and was a census taker in 1870 before applying for a pension. He explained in his application that "In order to keep about at all I am absolutely compelled to become a sort of movable drug store."[1] He died in 1906 at the age of seventy-five.

Lord, Nathaniel W.

No further record of Lord has been found.

Lucas, John J.

Lucas moved to Society Hill in Darlington County, where he was reported by the 1870 census taker as a planter with four children, three of whom were born after the end of the war. He became noted as a winemaker and served as president of the Darlington Agricultural and Mechanical Fair Company.

MacBeth, Alexander

MacBeth returned to Charleston, where in 1870 he was working as a merchant to support a crowded household that included a wife and child, his sister and retired father, and six black or mulatto servants. MacBeth later settled in Greeneville, where he died in 1933 at the age of ninety-eight.

McGowan, Samuel

McGowan served as a delegate to the 1865 constitutional convention and was elected to Congress that fall, but he was refused a seat. He served in the legislature; then in 1879 he was elected to the South Carolina Supreme Court, on which he sat as an associate justice for fourteen years. He died in 1897.

McIntosh, David G.

McIntosh remained in Richmond, where he married the sister of Confederate general John Pegram, until 1866 and then briefly resumed his law practice in Darlington. In 1868 he moved to Maryland, where he established a law partnership that became one of the most highly respected in the state. He wrote a number of works on the Civil War and compiled a chapter on Confederate artillery for the landmark work on Civil War photography edited by Francis T. Miller, *The Photographic History of the Civil War*. McIntosh died in 1916 at the age of eighty.

McIntosh, Edward

McIntosh appears in the 1870 census for Darlington County as a prosperous planter. His mother and three grown siblings lived with him.

Maxwell, William H.

Maxwell was one of the few veterans who enlisted in the 3rd New Hampshire Infantry; he had served as a corporal in the 10th United States Infantry on the western frontier from 1855 to 1860. He was thirty years of age when he enlisted as a lieutenant in Company H at Concord in August 1861. In June 1862 he temporarily commanded Company E as skirmishers at Secessionville and then was detailed to command Company D, to which he was permanently assigned the next September and promoted to captain, leading it in the assault on Battery Wagner on July 18, 1863. He was shot in the left hip on June 16, 1864, at Hatcher's Run in Virginia, and so he was assigned to conscript duty at New York. He resigned from the military in December 1864 and settled in Manchester, New Hampshire, where he worked as an overseer in a carding mill to support himself and an invalid daughter, with whom he was left when his wife, whom he married in May 1861, suddenly died. Later he worked for the city as a disburser of relief funds for the poor. He died in 1903.

Maynadier, William M.

Maynadier remained in the army and achieved the rank of major before his retirement.

Mew, John R.

After being released from Fort Delaware in June 1865, Mew worked for the Charleston and Savannah Railroad. He then settled down as a planter near Ridgeland. He died in 1916 at the age of seventy-six.

Miles, William P.

Miles remained in Virginia for fifteen years. He was nominated for the presidency of Johns Hopkins University and failed to get that position, but in 1880 he became the president of the newly reorganized University of South Carolina. After two years he resigned to take charge of his father-in-law's planting operations in Louisiana and became one of the wealthiest planters in that state, managing thirteen plantations that produced twenty million pounds of sugar each year. He died in 1899.

Millett, Henry R.

Millett returned to Maine and married; the couple had one child, a son. The elder Millett worked as a route agent for the post office and as a "canvasser" until his retirement. He died in 1914 at the age of seventy-eight.

Mitchell, Julian

No further record of Mitchell has been found.

Mooney, John M.

Discharged from Haddington Hospital at Washington in April 1865, Mooney returned to Sullivan County in Pennsylvania, where he worked as a farmer and as a teamster.

Moore, James Nott

No further record of Moore has been found.

Moore, Samuel P.

Moore remained in Richmond, where he served on the city school board and on the executive board of the Virginia Agricultural Society. He died in May 1889 and was buried with a small Confederate flag on his chest.

Mower, Joseph A.

Mower received a number of brevets, including one for fighting along the Salkehatchie River, after the war. He died in 1870 while serving as colonel of the 25th United States Infantry, a regiment of black troops.

Nottage, Thomas, Jr.

Nottage, a bootmaker from Quincy, Massachusetts, was discharged for disabilities due to malaria and kidney stones at Hilton Head in September 1862. His captain admitted that "altho always willing his services are ever uncertain."[2] He returned to Nashua, New Hampshire, but was unable to work steadily because of his ruined health. He and

his wife had two children before he died in January 1879 at the age of forty-eight.

O'Brien, John T.

No further record of O'Brien has been found.

Ogier, Thomas L.

Ogier returned to private practice in Charleston, where he died in 1900 at the age of ninety.

Orr, James L.

After leaving office as governor, Orr joined the Republican Party and served as a state circuit court judge until his appointment in 1872 as the U. S. minister to Russia, where he suddenly died of pneumonia the next year.

Parker, Arthur M., Jr.

No further record of Parker has been found.

Parker, John M.

Parker operated a general store in Cheshire County, New Hampshire. He died in 1920 at the age of eighty-four.

Patrick, John W.

Other than a notation on his picture that Patrick was alive in 1883, no further record of him has been found.

Perry, Benjamin F.

Perry remained active in local politics until his death in 1886 at the age of eighty-one.

Pickens, Francis W.

Pickens' term as governor was hectic and undistinguished. Interestingly, his beautiful and influential wife, Lucy Petway Holcombe Pickens, proved to be more popular than he; a South Carolina regiment was named in her honor

(Holcombe Legion), and her picture adorned several denominations of Confederate currency and bonds. After the war, he served as a delegate to the constitutional convention of 1865, though he never received a personal pardon from Pres. Andrew Johnson. He then retired to his plantation at Edgefield, where he died in 1869 at the age of sixty-three. Allegedly, he was deeply in debt, but his popular widow entertained lavishly for thirty years after his death.

Preston, John S.

After surrendering with Joseph E. Johnston and returning to South Carolina, Preston, who had lost a son in Confederate service, immigrated to England. In 1867 he returned to the United States and settled in Columbia, where he won a well-deserved reputation as a diehard opponent of sectional reconciliation. He died in 1881 at the age of seventy-two.

Ramsay, Andrew H.

Ramsay remained in Edgefield, where he was serving as clerk of court in 1870.

Ramsay, George D., Jr.

Ramsay remained in the army and served in arsenals in the North until December 1870, when he was assigned to the Charleston arsenal. He left that post in 1873 and returned to duty in northern arsenals until June 1878, when he was declared insane and confined in the Hospital for the Insane in Washington. The physician for the Indianapolis Arsenal, from which Ramsay had been committed, wrote that he had deteriorated rapidly in just two months, was violent toward himself and his family (especially at night), and should be carefully watched or put in restraints. Ramsay, covered with abscesses and in great pain, died less than a month after he was admitted.

Raysor, Thomas E.

Raysor was freed from Fort Delaware on June 17, 1865, under the provisions of Pres. Andrew Johnson's general order. He became a teacher and was active in efforts to reopen his alma mater, the Citadel.

Rhett, Alfred M.

Imprisoned at Fort Delaware, Rhett was released in July 1865 under a general order issued by Pres. Andrew Johnson. Rhett died in Charleston in 1889 at the age of sixty.

Rhett, Robert Barnwell

Rhett wrote a history of the Confederacy, which was never published, and assisted his son in publishing ventures. He died in Louisiana, at the home of his son-in-law, Alfred Roman, in 1876 at the age of seventy-five.

Richards, Gregg G.

Other than a notation on his picture that Richards was alive in 1869, no further record of him has been found.

Rion, James H.

Rion served as a delegate to the constitutional convention of 1865 and then reestablished his lucrative law practice in Winnsboro. He sat on the board of directors of a number of corporations that were involved in banking and railroads, and he became a trustee for the University of South Carolina. He remained active in Democratic politics until his death in 1886 at the age of fifty-eight.

Ripley, Roswell S.

Ripley returned briefly to South Carolina and then went to France and to England, where he engaged in manufacturing until his operations failed. He once more returned to Charleston and later moved to New York City before his death in 1887.

Saxton, Rufus, Jr.

Saxton remained an assistant commissioner of the Freedmen's Bureau until he was mustered out of volunteer service in 1866 and returned to the

Quartermaster's Department of the army as a major. He retired in 1888 as a colonel and assistant quartermaster general. He received the Medal of Honor in 1893 for repulsing Confederate general Richard S. Ewell's attack on Harper's Ferry, Virginia, in 1862. Saxton died in 1908 at the age of eighty-three.

Seymour, Truman

Seymour remained in the army, retiring in 1876 as a major in the 5th United States Artillery. He then settled in Italy, where he died in 1891 at the age of sixty-seven.

Shelton, Malcolm A.

Shelton, a native of Connecticut, stayed with the Governor's Guards and retained his rank of lieutenant after they were mustered as Company A of the 2nd South Carolina Infantry. In March 1862 he took William H. Casson's place as captain of the company and then resigned in May 1863 after the regiment suffered heavy casualties in the operations of the Army of Northern Virginia (almost one third of those engaged in the Seven Days, and 37 percent of those who fought at Antietam). He was thirty-five years of age at the time. The next February he was conscripted into the 8th South Carolina Reserves at Georgetown, South Carolina, but took a leave of absence. After the war he settled in Columbia.

Sheppard, Benjamin T.

No further record of Sheppard has been found.

Sheppard, John L.

No further record of Sheppard has been found.

Sherman, William T.

Sherman succeeded Ulysses S. Grant as commander-in-chief of the army when the latter became president in 1869. He retired in 1884 and spent the last seven years of his life on the lecture circuit. He died in New York City in 1891.

Silk, Thomas

Silk was promoted to corporal in July 1865, but he was then reduced in rank during October. No further record of him has been found.

Simkins, William S.

Simkins returned to Monticello, Florida, where he was allegedly instrumental in organizing the local Ku Klux Klan. He studied law, passed the bar in 1870, and practiced in Florida for three years. He then immigrated with his brother to Texas where, after a successful career as an attorney and as a founding member of the state bar association, he became a professor of law at the University of Texas in 1899. During his academic career at that institution he wrote a number of legal textbooks and became renowned for his oratory, which reflected his classical education.

Simonton, Charles H.

Simonton was sent to Old Capitol Prison, then to Fort Delaware, whence he was released in the summer of 1865. He had served in the legislature from 1858 to 1861; when he returned to that body in 1865, he was chosen to be Speaker of the House. After the Democrats regained control of South Carolina in 1876, Simonton was elected to the first of five consecutive terms as a state representative.

Slocum, Henry W.

Slocum resigned from the army in September 1865 and subsequently served three terms in Congress. He died in 1894.

Smalls, Robert

Smalls' career nearly derailed in 1877, after the Democrats resumed control of South Carolina, when he was convicted for allegedly accepting a bribe. He received a pardon from the governor, but he relinquished his rank as a major general in the militia and lost the congressional race in 1880. Seven years later he completed a final term in Congress; in 1889 he began an almost unbroken tenure of twenty-four years as collector of the port at Beaufort. He died in 1915 at the age of seventy-five.

Snowden, William H.

Snowden returned to his hometown of Charleston, where he became a wholesale grocer with operations in Macon, Georgia, as well. He died in 1906.

Stevens, Albert H.

Stevens was captured on Pinckney Island in August 1862, but he still reenlisted as a veteran volunteer on Morris Island in January 1864. He was shot through the pelvis in the fight along the Weldon Railroad on August 16, 1864. He was unable to return to duty so he mustered out of the army in his hometown of Manchester, New Hampshire, in July 1865 at the age of twenty-two. His wound never closed; pieces of bone and other matter were often discharged, which made it hard for him to find employment or a boarding house that would admit him. He never married, though he apparently lived for at least ten years after the war ended.

Stone, Albert N.

Stone moved to Jasper County, Texas, with his parents and three brothers in 1866. He married in 1870; though he and his wife never had children of their own, they raised a number of nieces and nephews after their parents died. He served as tax collector and sheriff for Jasper County from 1880 to 1900; after a sojourn in Leesville, Louisiana, he returned to Jasper County, where he died in 1931 at the age of ninety.

Stoney, William E.

Stoney returned to his plantation near Charleston and then went west and worked as a civil engineer. He returned to South Carolina in 1876 and worked for his old commander, Johnson Hagood, and for John Bratton, who succeeded Hagood in the South Carolina comptroller general's office. After Bratton retired, Stoney served three terms as comptroller general. He was the auditor for the South Carolina Railroad Company at his death in 1896 at the age of fifty-eight.

Stribling, Warren W.

Stribling died in 1872.

Taylor, James H.

Taylor returned to Darlington County and applied for a pension in April 1919.

Teague, Benjamin H.

Teague worked as a dentist in Aiken after the war and in 1894 became lieutenant colonel of the 1st Regiment, South Carolina State Troops. He was still living in 1920 when he applied for a pension.

Thomas, Charles E.

Thomas served one term as a legislator for Fairfield from 1880 to 1882 and was instrumental in reopening the Citadel in the latter year. He died in 1887.

Thomas, Edward

Thomas, like all of the other surviving members of the Citadel class of 1865, received his diploma with the class of 1886, the first to graduate after his alma mater reopened in 1882. He worked for a railroad company and settled in Hope, Arkansas, where he died in 1895 at the age of fifty-two.

Thomas, John P.

Thomas became a building contractor and then was elected to the South Carolina legislature in 1866. He remained active in state politics until 1873, when he moved to North Carolina and founded the Carolina Military Institute in Charlotte. He left there in 1882 to become the superintendent of the Citadel for three years. Elected to the legislature again in 1886, he served a single term. He then became an editor and sold insurance. In October 1897 he was appointed state historian and completed the task of compiling muster rolls of all South Carolinians who fought in the Civil War, an effort begun by Joseph B. Kershaw. Thomas died in 1912.

Todd, Hilliard

Todd settled in Conway, in Horry County, where he became a farmer and married shortly after the war ended. He died in 1902.

Tradewell, Alester G.

No further record of Tradewell has been found.

Trapier, James H.

Trapier survived the end of the war by only a few months, dying at the home of a friend in December 1865 at the age of fifty.

Waddell, William L.

Waddell settled in Ohio, where he died in 1903 at the age of sixty-six.

Wadsworth, David, Jr.

Wadsworth was promoted to lieutenant in November 1862, after fighting at Secessionville and Pocotaligo. He then became the captain of Company F in the 3rd New Hampshire Infantry in April 1864. Wounded at Drewry's Bluff in Virginia in May 1864, he resigned from the army four months later because of disabilities from "climatic diseases."[3] He settled in Nashua, New Hampshire, where his first wife, whom he had married in 1860, died in 1866. After remarrying, he moved in 1876 to Manchester, where he worked as a jailer. He died in 1926 at the age of eighty-eight.

Wiggin, Pierce L.

Wiggin resigned in April 1862 from the 3rd New Hampshire Infantry and later accepted a commission as a captain in the 1st New Hampshire Cavalry, which was assigned to picket duty in Virginia during the last year of the war. He settled in Beaufort, South Carolina, where he married in 1869 and had a son while working as solicitor of the local state circuit court. He later served as judge for the court from 1877 until his death two years later.

Wilkie, Octavius

Wilkie, who remained in Charleston with the commissary department despite the protests of Capt. Edward W. Lloyd, probably left with the rest of the Confederate garrison in February 1865. He was paroled at Greensboro, North Carolina, in May. He then worked as a bank clerk and lived with three of his sisters at Charleston by 1870.

Williams, Henry H.

No further record of Williams has been found.

Wilson, Harrison

Wilson settled in Shelby County, Ohio, where he married and had nine children. He served as a judge of the state circuit court and then in 1912, after his retirement, relocated to Ventura County, California. He died in 1929 at the age of eighty-eight.

Woodberry, S. B.

Woodberry settled in Barnwell County, where by 1870 he worked as a superintendent in a "steam mill" to support his wife and their two children. He also boarded workers from the mill.

Yeadon, Richard

Financially ruined and saddened by the loss of a nephew, whom he had adopted as his son, during the war, Yeadon nevertheless remained active in public life until his death in 1870 at the age of sixty-seven.

Notes

Chapter 1

1. A. Lawrence Kocher and Howard Dearstyne, *Shadows in Silver* (New York: Charles Scribner's Sons, 1954), 13 (first quote); Frederic E. Ray, "The Photographers of the War," in William C. Davis, ed., *Shadows of the Storm*, vol. 1, *The Image of War, 1861–1865*, (Garden City, N.Y.: Doubleday and Company, 1981), 413 (second quote).

2. Francis T. Miller, ed., *The Photographic History of the Civil War* (New York: Review of Reviews Company, 1911), 1:24.

3. Miller, *Photographic History of the Civil War*, 3:170.

4. *Jowitt's Illustrated Charleston City Directory and Business Register, 1869–70* (Charleston, S.C.: Walker, Evans and Cogswell, 1869), 173.

5. Brent H. Holcomb, ed., *Record of Deaths in Columbia, South Carolina and Elsewhere as Recorded by John Glass 1859–1877* (Columbia, S.C.: Privately printed, 1986), 163–64.

6. William C. Davis, "Introduction," in William C. Davis, ed., *The South Beseiged*, vol. 5, *The Image of War, 1861–1865* (Garden City, N.Y.: Doubleday and Company, 1983), 12.

7. "Mr. Cooley of Beaufort and Mr. Moore of Concord," in William C. Davis, ed., *The Guns of '62*, vol. 2, *The Image of War, 1861–1865* (Garden City, N.Y.: Doubleday and Company, 1982), 86.

8. Rowena Reed, "The Siege of Charleston," in William C. Davis, ed., *Fighting for Time*, vol. 4 , *The Image of War, 1861–1865* (Garden City, N.Y.: Doubleday and Company, 1983), 210.

9. John M. Bigham asserts it is Company F of the 3rd South Carolina Artillery Battalion, which served at Charleston until its evacuation in February 1865. John M. Bigham, "Palmetto Soldiers," *Military Images* 11 (May–June 1990): 6.

10. Jennings C. Wise, *The Long Arm of Lee: The History of the Artillery of the Army of Northern Virginia* (New York: Oxford University Press, 1959), 269, 297, 370, 419–20, 685, 899.

11. W. A. Swanberg, "The Guns at Fort Sumter," in *Shadows of the Storm*, William C. Davis and Bell I. Wiley, eds., 97–99. Swanberg credits F. K. Houston for the seven-star flag image and the partnership of James M. Osborn and F. E. Durbec for the facade and Hampton pictures.

12. Daniel Eldredge, *The Third New Hampshire and All About It* (Boston: E. B. Stillings and Company, 1893), 174.

13. Johnson Hagood, *Memoirs of the War of Secession* (Columbia, S.C.: State Company, 1910), 174–75.

Chapter 2

1. Quoted in Charles E. Cauthen, *South Carolina Goes to War, 1860–1865* (Chapel Hill: University of North Carolina Press, 1950), 134.

2. Ibid., 27.

3. Ibid., 69.

4. Abner Doubleday, *Reminiscences of Forts Moultrie and Sumter* (New York: Harper and Brothers, 1876), 56.

5. Ibid., 56.

6. Alfred Roman, *The Military Operations of General Beauregard in the War Between the States, 1861 to 1865* (New York: Harper and Brothers, 1884), 1:24.

7. Doubleday, *Reminiscences*, 151.

8. Laura A. White, *Robert Barnwell Rhett: Father of Secession* (Gloucester, Mass.: Peter Smith, 1965), 181.

9. Arney R. Childs, ed., *The Private Journal of Henry William Ravenel, 1859–1887* (Columbia: University of South Carolina Press, 1947), 163.

10. Quoted in Steven A. Channing, *Crisis of Fear: Secession in South Carolina* (New York: W. W. Norton and Company, 1970), 269.

11. U.S. National Archives, "Compiled Service Records of Confederate Soldiers Who Served in Organizations from South Carolina," John L. Branch, Record Group 109, National Archives, Washington, D.C. (Hereafter cited as U.S. National Archives, "Compiled Service Records.")

12. Ibid., Benjamin T. Gibbes; John P. Thomas, *The History of the South Carolina Military Academy* (Charleston: Walker, Evans and Cogswell, 1893), 275.

13. Channing, *Crisis of Fear*, 190.

14. Roman, *Operations of Beauregard*, 1:37; James Chester, "Inside Sumter in '61," in *Battles and Leaders of the Civil War*, Robert U. Johnson and Clarence C. Buel, eds. (New York: Thomas Yoseloff, 1956), 1:56.

15. Doubleday, *Reminiscences*, 154.

16. Childs, *Ravenel Journal*, 150.

17. Roy Meredith, *Storm Over Sumter: The Opening Engagement of the Civil War* (New York: Simon and Schuster, 1957), 204.

Chapter 3

1. Douglas S. Freeman, *Lee's Lieutenants: A Study in Command* (New York: Charles Scribner's Sons, 1944), 1:82.
2. Ibid., 192.
3. Ibid., 242.
4. Ibid., 520.
5. Clement A. Evans, *Confederate Military History* (Atlanta: Confederate Publishing Company, 1899), vol. 5, *South Carolina*, by Ellison Capers, 124.
6. Freeman, *Lee's Lieutenants*, 2:116–17.
7. Ibid., 363.
8. Ibid., 374.
9. Ezra J. Warner, *Generals in Gray: Lives of the Confederate Commanders* (Baton Rouge: Louisiana State University Press, 1959), 235.

Chapter 4

1. Daniel Ammen, "Du Pont and the Port Royal Expedition," in *Battles and Leaders*, Johnson and Buel, eds., 1:689.
2. Robert E. Lee to Wife, February 8, 1862, in *The Wartime Papers of Robert E. Lee*, Clifford Dowdey and Louis H. Manarin, eds. (New York: Bramhall House, 1961), 111.

3. Robert E. Lee to Judah P. Benjamin, December 20, 1861, in *Wartime Papers*, Dowdey and Manarin, 92–93.

4. Robert Carse, *Department of the South: Hilton Head Island in the Civil War* (Columbia, S.C.: State Printing Company, 1961), 65.

5. J. Thomas Scharf, *History of the Confederate States Navy* (Albany, N.Y.: Joseph McDonough, 1894), 647.

6. Don C. Seitz, *The James Gordon Bennetts, Father and Son* (Indianapolis: Bobbs-Merrill, 1928), 180–82. Seitz argues that this vessel is not the *Rebecca* but the *Henrietta*, but other sources agree that it is indeed the former.

7. *Recollections and Reminiscences 1861–1865 through World War I* (Columbia: South Carolina Chapter, United Daughters of the Confederacy, 1991), 2:282.

8. Hagood, *Memoirs*, 53.

9. U.S. Veterans Administration, "Pension Records of Volunteer Union Soldiers," Horatio C. Moore, Record Group 15, National Archives, Washington, D.C. (Hereafter cited as Veterans Administration "Pension Records.").

10. Samuel Jones, *The Siege of Charleston and the Operations on the South Atlantic Coast in the War among the States* (New York: Neale Publishing Company, 1911), 108.

11. Veterans Administration "Pension Records," John Knox.

Chapter 5

1. John Johnson, *The Defense of Charleston Harbor: Including Fort Sumter and the Adjacent Islands, 1863–1865* (Charleston, S.C.: Walker, Evans and Cogswell, 1890), 8.

2. "Fort Sumter—Career of Colonel Rhett," *Confederate Veteran* 1 (November 1893): 338; Quincy A. Gillmore, "The Army before Charleston in 1863," in *Battles and Leaders*, Johnson and Buel, eds. 4:61–62.

3. Luis F. Emilio, *History of the 54th Regiment of Massachusetts Volunteer Infantry, 1863–1865* (Boston: Boston Book Company, 1894), 77, 80.

4. U.S. National Archives, "Compiled Service Records," John Ward Hopkins.

5. Earl Schenck Miers, ed., *When the World Ended: The Diary of Emma LeConte* (New York: Oxford University Press, 1957), 114–15.

Chapter 6

1. Jay Monaghan, "Civil War Slang and Humor," *Civil War History* 3 (June 1957): 133.

2. R. Lockwood Tower, *A Carolinian Goes to War: The Civil War Narrative of Arthur Middleton Manigault* (Columbia: University of South Carolina Press, 1983), 192–93, 200, 201.

3. Ibid., 224.

4. Ibid., 237.

5. James R. Davis to Wife, May 2, 1864, and May 20, 1864, Darlington County Historical Society Records, Darlington County Historical Society, Darlington, S.C.

Chapter 7

1. Jacob D. Cox, *The March to the Sea, Franklin, and Nashville* (New York: Charles Scribner's Sons, 1898), 176n.

2. Burke Davis, *Sherman's March* (New York: Random House, 1980), 139.

3. Cox, *March to the Sea,* 172.

4. George W. Nichols, *The Story of the Great March* (New York: Harper and Brothers, 1865), 127.

5. Cox, *March to the Sea,* 176.

6. Davis, *Sherman's March,* 183.

7. Nichols, *Story of the Great March,* 153.

8. Cox, *March to the Sea,* 175.

9. Henry W. Slocum, "Sherman's March from Savannah to Bentonville," in *Battles and Leaders,* Johnson and Buel, eds., 2:686.

10. Cauthen, *South Carolina Goes to War,* 224.

11. Arthur P. Ford, *Life in the Confederate Army* (New York: Neale Publishing Company, 1905), 43–44.

12. Hagood, *Memoirs,* 347.

13. B. Davis, *Sherman's March,* 226.

14. Ezra J. Warner, *Generals in Blue: Lives of the Union Commanders* (Baton Rouge: Louisiana State University Press, 1964), 267.

15. John G. Barrett, *Sherman's March through the Carolinas* (Chapel Hill: University of North Carolina Press, 1956), 72.

Chapter 8

1. Francis B. Simkins and Robert H. Woody, *South Carolina during Reconstruction* (Chapel Hill: University of North Carolina Press, 1932), 4; George C. Rogers, Jr., *Charleston in the Age of the Pinckneys* (Norman: University of Oklahoma Press, 1969), 169.

2. John B. Edmunds, Jr., *Francis W. Pickens and the Politics of Destruction* (Chapel Hill: University of North Carolina Press, 1986), 176.

3. Ernest M. Lander, *A History of South Carolina, 1865–1960,* 2d ed. (Columbia: University of South Carolina Press, 1970), 15.

4. Simkins and Woody, *South Carolina during Reconstruction,* 500; Lander, *History of South Carolina,* 19.

5. Manly W. Wellman, *Giant in Gray: A Biography of Wade Hampton of South Carolina* (New York: Charles Scribner's Sons, 1949), 265.

6. John T. Trowbridge, *The Desolate South, 1865–1866,* ed. Gordon Carroll (New York: Duell, Sloan and Pearce, 1956), 275.

7. Ibid., 305.

8. Miers, *When the World Ended,* 61, 62.

9. Meredith, *Storm Over Sumter,* 8–9.

10. Simkins and Woody, *South Carolina during Reconstruction,* 18; Wellman, *Giant in Gray,* 195.

11. John M. Gould, *History of the First–Tenth–Twenty-Ninth Maine Regiment* (Portland, Maine.: Stephen Berry, 1871), 583.

12. Simkins and Woody, *South Carolina during Reconstruction,* 228.

13. Martin Abbott, *The Freedmen's Bureau in South Carolina, 1865–1872* (Chapel Hill: University of North Carolina Press, 1967), 9.

14. Rupert S. Holland, *Letters and Diary of Laura M. Towne* (Cambridge, Mass.: Riverside Press, 1912; reprint, New York: Negro Universities Press, 1969), 172.

15. Lillian A. Kibler, *Benjamin F. Perry, South Carolina Unionist* (Chapel Hill: University of North Carolina Press, 1946), 329.

Appendix

1. Veterans Administration "Pension Records," Charles P. Lord.

2. Veterans Administration "Pension Records," Thomas Nottage, Jr.

3. U.S. Adjutant General, "Service Records of Volunteer Union Soldiers," David Wadsworth, Jr., Record Group 94, National Archives, Washington, D.C.

Bibliography

General Sources

Baker, Gary R. *Cadets in Gray: The Story of the Cadets of the South Carolina Military Academy and the Cadet Rangers in the Civil War.* Columbia, S.C.: Palmetto Bookworks, 1989.

Bigham, John H. "Palmetto Soldiers." *Military Images* 11. (May–June 1990): 6–21.

Boatner, Mark M., III. *The Civil War Dictionary.* New York: David McKay Company, 1959.

Cardozo, Jacob N. *Reminiscences of Charleston.* Charleston, S.C.: J. Walker, 1866.

Carse, Robert. *Blockade: The Civil War at Sea.* New York: Rinehart and Company, 1958.

———. *Department of the South: Hilton Head Island in the Civil War.* Columbia, S.C.: State Printing Company, 1961.

Cauthen, Charles E. *South Carolina Goes to War, 1860–1865.* Chapel Hill: University of North Carolina Press, 1950.

Channing, Steven A. *Crisis of Fear: Secession in South Carolina.* New York: W. W. Norton and Company, 1970.

Chester, James. "Inside Sumter in '61." In *Battles and Leaders of the Civil War,* Robert U. Johnson and Clarence C. Buel, eds. Vol. 1. New York: Thomas Yoseloff, 1956.

Cisco, Walter B. *States Rights Gist: A South Carolina General of the Civil War.* Columbia, S.C.: White Mane Publishing Company, 1991.

Clark, Mrs. S. J. "Sketch of Colonel Harry L. Benbow." In *Recollections and Reminiscences 1861–1865 through World War I.* Vol. 1. Columbia: South Carolina Division, United Daughters of the Confederacy, 1992.

Courtenay, William A. "The Coast Defense of South Carolina, 1861–1865." *Southern Historical Society Papers* 26 (1898): 62–87.

Crute, Joseph H., Jr. *Units of the Confederate States Army.* Midlothian, Va.: Derwent Books, 1987.

Cullum, George W. *Biographical Register of the Officers and Graduates of the United States Military Academy.* Boston: Houghton Mifflin, 1891.

Darlington County Historical Society Records. Darlington County Historical Society, Darlington, S.C.

Davis, William C., ed. *The Image of War, 1861–1865.* 6 vols. New York: Doubleday and Company, 1984.

Dowdey, Clifford, and Louis H. Manarin, eds. *The Wartime Papers of Robert E. Lee.* New York: Bramhall House, 1961.

Dyer, Frederick H. *A Compendium of the War of the Rebellion.* 3 vols. New York: Thomas Yoseloff, 1959.

Edmunds, John B., Jr. *Francis W. Pickens and the Politics of Destruction.* Chapel Hill: University of North Carolina Press, 1986.

Eldredge, Daniel. *The Third New Hampshire and All About It.* Boston: E. B. Stillings and Company, 1893.

Evans, Clement A., ed. *Confederate Military History.* Atlanta: Confederate Publishing Company, 1899. Vol. 5, *South Carolina,* by Ellison Capers.

Ford, Arthur P. *Life in the Confederate Army.* New York: Neale Publishing Company, 1905.

"Fort Sumter—Career of Colonel Rhett." *Confederate Veteran* 1 (November 1893): 338.

Freeman, Douglas S. *Lee's Lieutenants: A Study in Command.* 3 vols. New York: Charles Scribner's Sons, 1944.

Glatthaar, Joseph T. *Forged in Battle: The Civil War Alliance of Black Soldiers and White Officers.* New York: Free Press, 1990.

Gragg, Rod. *Confederate Goliath: The Battle of Fort Fisher.* New York: Harper Collins, 1991.

Hagood, Johnson. *Memoirs of the War of Secession.* Columbia, S.C.: State Company, 1910.

Hattaway, Herman. *General Stephen D. Lee.* Jackson: University Press of Mississippi, 1976.

Hemphill, J. C. *Men of Mark in South Carolina.* Vol. 1. Washington, D.C.: Men of Mark Publishing Company, 1907.

Horan, James D. *Timothy O'Sullivan: America's Forgotten Photographer.* Garden City, N.Y.: Doubleday, 1966.

Johnson, Allen, ed. *Dictionary of American Biography.* 11 vols. New York: Charles Scribner's Sons, 1957.

Johnson, John. *The Defense of Charleston Harbor: Including Fort Sumter and the Adjacent Islands, 1863–1865.* Charleston, S.C.: Walker, Evans and Cogswell, 1890.

Jones, Samuel. *The Siege of Charleston and the Operations on the South Atlantic Coast in the War among the States.* New York: Neale Publishing Company, 1911.

Jones, Virgil C. *The Blockaders.* Vol. 1, *The Civil War at Sea.* New York: Holt, Rinehart and Winston, 1960.

———. *The River War.* Vol. 2, *The Civil War at Sea.* New York: Holt, Rinehart and Winston, 1961.

———. *The Final Effort.* Vol. 3, *The Civil War at Sea.* New York: Holt, Rinehart and Winston, 1962.

Lee, Stephen D. "The First Step in the War." In *Battles and Leaders of the Civil War,* Robert U. Johnson and Clarence C. Buel, eds. Vol. 4. New York: Thomas Yoseloff, 1956.

"Lieutenant General S. D. Lee." *Confederate Veteran* 2 (March 1894): 70.

McIlwaine, H. R. "Samuel Preston Moore, Surgeon General, C.S.A." *Confederate Veteran* 33 (November 1925): 406–07.

May, John A., and Joan R. Faunt. *South Carolina Secedes.* Columbia: University of South Carolina Press, 1960.

Miers, Earl Schenck, ed. *When the World Ended: The Diary of Emma LeConte.* New York: Oxford University Press, 1957.

Miller, Francis T., ed. *The Photographic History of the Civil War.* 10 vols. New York: Review of Reviews Company, 1912.

Morrill, Lily L. *A Builder of the New South: Notes on the Career of Thomas M. Logan.* Boston: Christopher Publishing House, 1940.

Muhlenfeld, Elisabeth. *Mary Boykin Chesnut: A Biography.* Baton Rouge: Louisiana State University Press, 1981.

The National Cyclopaedia of American Biography. 63 vols. to date. New York: James T. White and Company, 1898.

Rhett, R. Barnwell. "Fort Sumter and the Siege of Charleston—Corrected Sketch." *Confederate Veteran* 1 (December 1893): 372.

Rhoades, Jeffrey L. *Scapegoat General: The Story of Major General Benjamin Huger, C.S.A.* Hamden, Conn.: Archon Books, 1985.

Ripley, Warren, ed. *Siege Train: The Journal of a Confederate Artilleryman in the Defense of Charleston.* Columbia: University of South Carolina Press, 1986.

Robertson, A. I. "Ellison Capers, General and Bishop." *Confederate Veteran* 7 (June 1899): 260–61.

Roman, Alfred. *The Military Operations of General Beauregard in the War Between the States, 1861 to 1865.* 2 vols. New York: Harper and Brothers, 1884.

Ross, Fitzgerald. *Cities and Camps of the Confederate States.* Ed. Richard B. Harwell. Urbana: University of Illinois Press, 1958.

Simkins, Francis B., and Robert H. Woody. *South Carolina during Reconstruction.* Chapel Hill: University of North Carolina Press, 1932.

"South Carolina. Confederate Pension Records." South Carolina State Archives, Columbia, S.C.

Still, William N., Jr. *Iron Afloat: The Story of the Confederate Armorclads.* Nashville, Tenn.: Vanderbilt University Press, 1971.

Swanberg, W. A. *First Blood: The Story of Fort Sumter.* New York: Charles Scribner's Sons, 1957.

Thomas, John P. *The History of the South Carolina Military Academy.* Charleston, S.C.: Walker, Evans and Cogswell, 1893.

U.S. Adjutant General. "Service Records of Volunteer Union Soldiers." Record Group 94. National Archives, Washington, D.C.

U.S. Bureau of the Census. *Eighth Census of the United States, 1860.* Schedule 1 (Free Population), South Carolina. Record Group 29. National Archives, Washington, D.C.

U.S. Bureau of the Census. *Ninth Census of the United States, 1870.* Schedule 1 (Population), South Carolina. Record Group 29. National Archives, Washington, D.C.

U.S. Department of War. "Returns from Regular Army Artillery Regiments, June 1821–January 1901." Record Group 107. National Archives, Washington, D.C.

U.S. National Archives. "Compiled Service Records of Confederate Soldiers Who Served in Organizations from South Carolina." Record Group 109. National Archives, Washington, D.C.

U.S. Veterans Administration. "Pension Records of Volunteer Union Soldiers." Record Group 15. National Archives, Washington, D.C.

Walker, C. Irvine. "South Carolinians in the Civil War." Records of the Confederate Historian of South Carolina. South Carolina State Archives, Columbia, S.C.

The War of the Rebellion: A Compilation of the Official Records of the Union and Confederate Armies. 130 volumes. Washington, D.C: Government Printing Office, 1880–1902.

Warner, Ezra J. *Generals in Blue: Lives of the Union Commanders*. Baton Rouge: Louisiana State University Press, 1964.

———. *Generals in Gray: Lives of the Confederate Commanders*. Baton Rouge: Louisiana State University Press, 1959.

Wellman, Manly W. *Giant in Gray: A Biography of Wade Hampton of South Carolina*. New York: Charles Scribner's Sons, 1949.

Wise, Jennings C. *The Long Arm of Lee: The History of the Artillery of the Army of Northern Virginia*. New York: Oxford University Press, 1959.

Westwood, Howard C. "Captive Black Union Soldiers in Charleston—What to Do?" *Civil War History* 28 (March 1982): 28–44.

Chapter 1

Bond, Natalie Jenkins, and Osmun L. Coward. *The South Carolinians: Colonel Asbury Coward's Memoirs*. New York: Vantage Press, 1968.

Davis, Keith F. *George N. Barnard*. Kansas City, Mo.: Hallmark Cards, 1990.

Dickson, Frank A. *Journeys into the Past: The Anderson Region's Heritage*. Anderson, S.C.: Privately printed, 1975.

Edwards, Conley L., III. "The Photographer of the Confederacy." *Civil War Times Illustrated* (June 1974): 27–33.

Edwards, Gary. *International Guide to Nineteenth-Century Photographers and Their Works*. Boston: G. K. Hall, 1988.

Holcomb, Brent H., ed. *Record of Deaths in Columbia, South Carolina and Elsewhere as Recorded by John Glass 1859–1877*. Columbia, S.C.: Privately printed, 1986.

Johnson, William S. *Nineteenth Century Photography: An Annotated Bibliography, 1839–1879*. Boston: G. K. Hall, 1990.

Jowitt's Illustrated Charleston City Directory and Business Register, 1869–70. Charleston, S.C.: Walker, Evans and Cogswell, 1869.

Kocher, A. Lawrence, and Howard Dearstyne. *Shadows in Silver*. New York: Charles Scribner's Sons, 1954.

Levkoff, Alice F. *Charleston Come Hell or High Water*. Columbia, S.C.: R. L. Bryan Company, 1975.

Peach, Thomas J., III. "George Smith Cook: South Carolina's Premier Civil War Photojournalist." M.A. thesis, University of South Carolina, Columbia, 1982.

Salley, Marion. "Sixty-Seven Years of Married Life." *Confederate Veteran* 32 (July 1924): 259.

Sandweiss, Martha A., ed. *Photography in Nineteenth Century America*. New York: Henry N. Abrams, 1991.

Stutler, Boyd P., ed. "Notes and Queries." *Civil War History* 7 (December 1961): 450–59.

U.S. Bureau of the Census. *Population of the United States in 1860, Compiled from the Official Returns of the United States Census*. Washington, D.C.: Government Printing Office, 1864.

Welling, William. *Photography in America: The Formative Years, 1839–1900*. New York: Thomas Y. Crowell, 1978.

Chapter 2

Biographical Directory of the South Carolina House of Representatives. Columbia: University of South Carolina Press, 1974.

Burton, E. Milby. *The Siege of Charleston, 1861–1865*. Columbia: University of South Carolina Press, 1970.

Burton, Orville V. *In My Father's House are Many Mansions*. Chapel Hill: University of North Carolina Press, 1985.

Childs, Arney R., ed. *The Private Journal of Henry William Ravenel, 1859–1887*. Columbia: University of South Carolina Press, 1947.

Doubleday, Abner. "From Moultrie to Sumter." In *Battles and Leaders of the Civil War*, Robert U. Johnson and Clarence C. Buel, eds. Vol. 1. New York: Thomas Yoseloff, 1956.

———. *Reminiscences of Forts Moultrie and Sumter*. New York: Harper and Brothers, 1876.

Hagood, Johnson. "Captain William E. Stoney." *Confederate Veteran* 4 (November 1896): 383.

Johnson, John. "The Confederate Defense of Fort Sumter." In *Battles and Leaders of the Civil War*, Robert U. Johnson and Clarence C. Buel, eds. Vol. 4. New York: Thomas Yoseloff, 1956.

———. *The Defense of Charleston Harbor: Including Fort Sumter and the Adjacent Islands, 1863–1865*. Charleston, S.C.: Walker, Evans and Cogswell, 1890.

Meredith, Roy. *Storm Over Sumter: The Opening Engagement of the Civil War*. New York: Simon and Schuster, 1957.

Moore, Albert B. *Conscription and Conflict in the Confederacy*. New York: Macmillan, 1924.

Register of Officers of the Confederate States Navy, 1861–1865. Washington: Government Printing Office, 1931.

Rhett, Claudine. "Frank H. Harleston—A Hero of Fort Sumter." *Southern Historical Society Publications* 10 (1882): 307–20.

White, Laura A. *Robert Barnwell Rhett: Father of Secession*. Gloucester, Mass.: Peter Smith, 1965.

Chapter 3

Brown, B. F. "Gallant South Carolina Brigade." *Confederate Veteran* 33 (April 1925): 128.

———. "McGowan's South Carolina Brigade in the Battle of Gettysburg." *Confederate Veteran* 31 (February 1923): 51–52.

Butler, Matthew C. "The Cavalry Fight at Trevilian Station." In *Battles and Leaders of the Civil War*, Robert U. Johnson and Clarence C. Buel, eds. Vol. 4. New York: Thomas Yoseloff, 1956.

Caldwell, J. F. J. *The History of a Brigade of South Carolinians.* Philadelphia: King and Baird, 1866; reprint, Marietta, Ga.: Continental Book Company, 1951.

De Leon, T. C. "Remarkable Record of the Haskells of South Carolina." *Southern Historical Society Papers* 36 (1907): 151–54.

Doyle, J. H. "When Richmond was Evacuated." *Confederate Veteran* 39 (June 1931): 205–06.

Eliot, Ellsworth, Jr. *West Point in the Confederacy.* New York: G. A. Baker and Company, 1941.

Elmore, Albert R. "Incidents of Service with the Charleston Light Dragoons." *Confederate Veteran* 24 (December 1916): 538–43.

Govan, Gilbert E., and James W. Livingood, eds. *The Haskell Memoirs: John Cheves Haskell.* New York: George P. Putnam's Sons, 1960.

Hill, Daniel H. "The Battle of South Mountain, or Boonsboro." In *Battles and Leaders of the Civil War,* Robert U. Johnson and Clarence C. Buel, eds. Vol. 2. New York: Thomas Yoseloff, 1956.

Johnston, David E. "Concerning the Battle of Sharpsburg." *Confederate Veteran* 6 (January 1898): 27–29.

Kershaw, Joseph B. "Kershaw's Brigade at Gettysburg." In *Battles and Leaders of the Civil War,* Robert U. Johnson and Clarence C. Buel, eds. Vol. 3. New York: Thomas Yoseloff, 1956.

———. "Richard Kirkland: The Humane Hero of Fredericksburg." *Southern Historical Society Papers* 8 (1880): 186–88.

Krick, Robert K. "Maxcy Gregg: Political Extremist and Confederate General." *Civil War History* 19 (December 1973): 293–313.

"Last Colonel of Artillery, A.N.V." *Confederate Veteran* 25 (May 1917): 224–26.

"Life of Colonel Edward Croft: Brief Sketch of His Career as a Soldier of the Confederate War." In *Recollections and Reminiscences 1861–1865 through World War I.* Vol. 3. Columbia: South Carolina Division, United Daughters of the Confederacy, 1992.

McIntosh, David G. "McIntosh's Battery at Sharpsburg." *Confederate Veteran* 20 (May 1912): 204.

McMaster, F. W. "The Battle of the Crater, July 30, 1864." *Southern Historical Society Papers* 10 (1882): 119–30.

Robertson, Mrs. A. I. "Last Flag of Truce at Appomattox." *Confederate Veteran* 7 (September 1899): 398.

Smith, Gustavus W. "Two Days of Battle at Seven Pines." In *Battles and Leaders of the Civil War,* Robert U. Johnson and Clarence C. Buel, eds. Vol. 2. New York: Thomas Yoseloff, 1956.

Trescot, William H. *Memorial of the Life of J. Johnston Pettigrew.* Charleston, S.C.: John Russell, 1870.

Ware, Lowry. *Old Abbeville.* Columbia, S.C.: SCMAR, 1992.

Wilson, Clyde N. *Carolina Cavalier: The Life and Mind of James Johnston Pettigrew.* Athens: University of Georgia Press, 1990.

Chapter 4

Ammen, Daniel. "Du Pont and the Port Royal Expedition." In *Battles and Leaders of the Civil War,* Robert U. Johnson and Clarence C. Buel, eds. Vol. 1. New York: Thomas Yoseloff, 1956.

Beauregard, P. G. T. "The Defense of Charleston." In *Battles and Leaders of the Civil War,* Robert U. Johnson and Clarence C. Buel, eds. Vol. 4. New York: Thomas Yoseloff, 1956.

Burton, E. Milby. *The Siege of Charleston, 1861–1865.* Columbia: University of South Carolina Press, 1970.

Cardozo, Jacob N. *Reminiscences of Charleston.* Charleston, S.C.: J. Walker, 1866.

Cleveland, Mather. *New Hampshire Fights the Civil War.* New London, N.H.: Privately printed, 1969.

Cochran, Hamilton. *Blockade Runners of the Confederacy.* Indianapolis: Bobbs-Merrill Company, 1958.

Coulter, E. Merton. "Robert Gould Shaw and the Burning of Darien, Georgia." *Civil War History* 5 (December 1959): 363–73.

Davis, Burke. *Gray Fox: Robert E. Lee and the Civil War.* New York: Rinehart, 1956.

"Extracts from the Diary of Lieutenant-Colonel John G. Pressley." *Southern Historical Society Papers* 14 (1886): 39.

Jervey, Theodore. "Charleston during the Civil War." In *Annual Report of the American Historical Association, 1913.* Vol. 1. Washington, D.C.: Government Printing Office, 1913.

Jones, Samuel. *The Siege of Charleston and the Operations on the South Atlantic Coast in the War among the States.* New York: Neale Publishing Company, 1911.

Lord, Charles P. Papers. William Perkins Library, Duke University, Durham, N.C.

Merrill, James M. *The Rebel Shore: The Story of Union Sea Power in the Civil War.* Boston: Little, Brown and Company, 1957.

Recollections and Reminiscences 1861–1865 through World War I. Vol. 2. Columbia: South Carolina Chapter, United Daughters of the Confederacy, 1991.

Scharf, J. Thomas. *History of the Confederate States Navy.* Albany, N.Y.: Joseph McDonough, 1894.

"Scrapbook of Newspaper Clippings Pertaining to Preparation of Confederate Rolls, 1897–1900." Records of the Confederate Historian of South Carolina. South Carolina State Archives, Columbia.

Seitz, Don C. *The James Gordon Bennetts, Father and Son.* Indianapolis: Bobbs-Merrill, 1928.

Soley, James R. "Minor Operations of the South Atlantic Squadron Under Du Pont." In *Battles and Leaders of the Civil War,* Robert U. Johnson and Clarence C. Buel, eds. Vol. 4. New York: Thomas Yoseloff, 1956.

Wise, Stephen R. *Lifeline of the Confederacy: Blockade Running during the Civil War.* Columbia: University of South Carolina Press, 1988.

Chapter 5

Courtenay, William A. "Heroes of Honey Hill." *Southern Historical Society Papers* 26 (Richmond, 1898): 232–41.

Emilio, Luis F. *History of the 54th Regiment of Massachusetts Volunteer Infantry, 1863–1865.* Boston: Boston Book Company, 1894.

George, W. W. "In a Federal Prison." *Southern Historical Society Papers* 29 (1901): 229–39.

Gillmore, Quincy A. "The Army before Charleston in 1863." In *Battles and Leaders of the Civil War,* Robert U. Johnson and Clarence C. Buel, eds. Vol. 4. New York: Thomas Yoseloff, 1956.

Hesseltine, William B. *Civil War Prisons.* New York: Frederick Ungar, 1930.

Perry, Milton F. *Infernal Machines: The Story of Confederate Submarine and Mine Warfare.* Baton Rouge: Louisiana State University Press, 1965.

Ravenel, Samuel W. "The Boy Brigade of South Carolina." *Confederate Veteran* 29 (October 1921): 415–16.

Rhett, Claudine. "How the 'Patapsco' Went Down in Charleston Harbor." *Confederate Veteran* 5 (August 1897): 422–23.

Smith, Daniel E. H. *A Charlestonian's Recollections, 1846–1913.* Charleston, S.C.: Carolina Art Association, 1950.

———, Alice R. H. Smith, and Arney R. Childs. *Mason Smith Family Letters, 1860–1868.* Columbia, S.C.: University of South Carolina Press, 1950.

Stryker, William S. "The 'Swamp Angel.'" In *Battles and Leaders of the Civil War,* Robert U. Johnson and Clarence C. Buel, eds. Vol. 4. New York: Thomas Yoseloff, 1956.

Woods, W. D. "Sketch of Col. Alonzo T. Dargan." In *Treasured Reminiscences.* Columbia, S.C.: The State Company, 1911.

Chapter 6

Bleckley, Mrs. B. B., Sr. "The 4th South Carolina Volunteers." *Confederate Veteran* 39 (June 1931): 220–22.

Luker, Ralph E. "The Crucible of Civil War and Reconstruction in the Experience of William Porcher DuBose." *South Carolina Historical Magazine* 83 (January 1982): 50–71.

Monaghan, Jay. "Civil War Slang and Humor." *Civil War History* 3 (June 1957): 125–34.

"Sketch of Capt. A. J. Hoole." In *Treasured Reminiscences.* Columbia: State Company, 1911.

Tower, R. Lockwood. *A Carolinian Goes to War: The Civil War Narrative of Arthur Middleton Manigault.* Columbia: University of South Carolina Press, 1983.

Walker, C. Irvine. *Rolls and Historical Sketch of the Tenth Regiment, South Carolina Volunteers.* Charleston, S.C.: Walker, Evans and Cogswell, 1881.

Chapter 7

Barrett, John G. *Sherman's March through the Carolinas.* Chapel Hill: University of North Carolina Press, 1956.

Black, Robert C., III. *The Railroads of the Confederacy.* Chapel Hill: University of North Carolina Press, 1952.

Brodie, R. L. "Dr. Thomas Lewis Ogier." *Confederate Veteran* 8 (June 1900): 280–81.

Cox, Jacob D. *The March to the Sea, Franklin, and Nashville.* New York: Charles Scribner's Sons, 1898.

Davis, Burke. *Sherman's March.* New York: Random House, 1980.

Dwight, Rowena E. (Mrs. Richard Y.) "A War Experience without a Yankee." In *Recollections and Reminiscences 1861–1865 through World War I.* Vol. 1. Columbia: South Carolina Division, United Daughters of the Confederacy, 1990.

Gibson, John M. *Those 163 Days: A Southern Account of Sherman's March from Atlanta to Raleigh.* New York: Coward-McCann, 1961.

Jones, Katharine M., ed. *When Sherman Came: Southern Women and the "Great March."* Indianapolis: Bobbs-Merrill Company, 1964.

Marvin, Edwin E. *The Fifth Regiment Connecticut Volunteers.* Hartford, Conn.: Wiley, Waterman and Eaton, 1889.

Nichols, George W. *The Story of the Great March.* New York: Harper and Brothers, 1865.

Reid, Whitelaw. *Ohio in the War: Her Statesmen, Her Generals, and Soldiers.* 2 vols. Cincinnati: Moore, Wilstach and Baldwin, 1868.

Robertson, Mrs. A. I. "Gen. M. C. Butler as a Confederate." *Confederate Veteran* 8 (March 1900): 110–11.

Sanders, Robert W. "More about the Battle of Bentonville, N.C." *Confederate Veteran* 37 (December 1929): 460–61.

Slocum, Henry W. "Sherman's March from Savannah to Bentonville." In *Battles and Leaders of the Civil War,* Robert U. Johnson and Clarence C. Buel, eds. Vol. 2. New York: Thomas Yoseloff, 1956.

Chapter 8

Abbott, Martin. *The Freedmen's Bureau in South Carolina, 1865-1872.* Chapel Hill: University of North Carolina Press, 1967.

Ballard, Michael. *A Long Shadow: Jefferson Davis and the Final Days of the Confederacy.* Jackson: University Press of Mississippi, 1986.

Davis, Burke. *The Long Surrender.* New York: Random House, 1985.

Gillette, William. *Retreat From Reconstruction, 1869–1879.* Baton Rouge: Louisiana State University Press, 1979.

Gould, John M. *History of the First–Tenth–Twenty-Ninth Maine Regiment.* Portland, Maine: Stephen Berry, 1871.

Higginson, Thomas W. *Army Life in a Black Regiment.* Boston: Fields and Osgood, 1870; reprint, Williamstown, Mass.: Corner House Publishers, 1970.

Holland, Rupert S. *Letters and Diary of Laura M. Towne.* Cambridge, Mass.: Riverside Press, 1912; reprint, New York: Negro Universities Press, 1969.

Kibler, Lillian A. *Benjamin F. Perry, South Carolina Unionist.* Chapel Hill: University of North Carolina Press, 1946.

Lamson, Peggy. *The Glorious Failure: Black Congressman Robert Brown Elliott and the Reconstruction in South Carolina.* New York: W. W. Norton and Company, 1973.

Lander, Ernest M. *A History of South Carolina, 1865–1960.* 2d ed. Columbia: University of South Carolina Press, 1970.

Meredith, Roy. *Storm Over Sumter: The Opening Engagement of the Civil War.* New York: Simon and Schuster, 1957.

Perman, Michael. *Reunion without Compromise: The South and Reconstruction, 1865–1868.* Cambridge: Cambridge University Press, 1973.

Rogers, George C., Jr. *Charleston in the Age of the Pinckneys.* Norman: University of Oklahoma Press, 1969.

Simkins, Francis B., and Robert H. Woody. *South Carolina during Reconstruction.* Chapel Hill: University of North Carolina Press, 1932.

Taylor, Susie King. *Reminiscences of My Life in Camp.* New York: Arno Press, 1968.

Trowbridge, John T. *The Desolate South, 1865–1866.* Ed. Gordon Carroll. New York: Duell, Sloan and Pearce, 1956.

Appendix

Bailey, N. Louise et al. *Biographical Directory of the South Carolina Senate, 1776–1985.* 3 vols. Columbia: University of South Carolina Press, 1986.

"Capt. B. H. Teague." *Confederate Veteran* 2 (May 1894): 154.

"Capt. William Dunovant." *Confederate Veteran* 10 (September 1902): 422.

Chapman, John A. *History of Edgefield County.* Newberry, S.C.: Elbert H. Aull, 1897.

Elmore, A. R. "Testimony about Burning of Columbia." *Confederate Veteran* 20 (March 1912): 117.

Index

335